The
Canadian Style

A Guide to Writing and Editing

Revised and Expanded

Published by Dundurn Press Limited in co-operation with
Public Works and Government Services Canada
Translation Bureau

Toronto • Oxford
1997

Designer: Ron & Ron Design & Photography
Printer: Marquis Imprimeur

National Library of Canada Cataloguing in Publication Data

Main entry under title:

The Canadian style

Rev. ed.
Includes bibliographical references and index.
ISBN 1-55002-276-8

1. Authorship — Handbooks, manuals, etc. 2. Editing.
I. Canada. Public Works and Government Services Canada.

PN 147.C36 1997   808'.02   C96-932516-9

 Conseil des Arts du Canada Canada Council for the Arts   Canada

ONTARIO ARTS COUNCIL
CONSEIL DES ARTS DE L'ONTARIO

We acknowledge the support of the **Canada Council for the Arts** and the **Ontario Arts Council** for our publishing program. We also acknowledge the financial support of the **Government of Canada** through the **Book Publishing Industry Development Program** and **The Association for the Export of Canadian Books**, and the Government of Ontario through the **Ontario Book Publishers Tax Credit** program, and the **Ontario Media Development Corporation's Ontario Book Initiative.**

Care has been taken to trace the ownership of copyright material used in this book. The author and the publisher welcome any information enabling them to rectify any references or credit in subsequent editions.

J. Kirk Howard, President

Printed and bound in Canada.
Printed on recycled paper.
www.dundurn.com

Dundurn Press	Gazelle Book Services Limited	Dundurn Press
8 Market Street Suite 200	White Cross Mills	2250 Military Road
Toronto, Ontario, Canada	Hightown, Lancaster, England	Tonawanda NY
M5E 1M6	LA1 4X5	U.S.A. 14150

Table of Contents

Chapter Three

Spelling

Chapter Four

Capitalization

Chapter Five

Numerical expressions

Chapter Six

Italics

Chapter Seven

Punctuation

The period

The question mark

The exclamation mark

Chapter Eight

Quotations and quotation marks

Chapter Nine

Reference matter

1

2

3

4

5

6

7

8

9

Chapter Ten

Letters and memorandums

Letters

Chapter Eleven

Reports and minutes

Chapter Twelve

Usage

Chapter Thirteen

Plain language

Chapter Fourteen

Elimination of stereotyping in written communications

Elimination of sexual stereotyping

Elimination of racial and ethnic stereotyping

Fair and representative depiction of people with disabilities

Chapter Fifteen

Geographical names

Geographical names: types and composition

Chapter Sixteen

Revision and proofreading

Appendix

French typographical rules

Preface

The Translation Bureau, a special operating agency of the Department of Public Works and Government Services of Canada, is pleased to present the second edition of the Canadian government's English-language editorial style guide, *The Canadian Style*.

Internationally recognized for the quality of its language services and its writing and editing tools, the Translation Bureau co-operates actively with other institutions in promoting correct, uniform style and usage in communications. *The Canadian Style* is one of the Bureau's principal means of ensuring that this co-operation produces tangible results. The guide also makes a major contribution to the fulfilment of the Department's role of providing high-quality services and products for other federal government organizations and for Canadian society at large.

Public servants will find in this second edition standards, recommendations and information that will enable them to ensure quality, consistency and clarity in their writing.

At the same time this work, embracing as it does many aspects of editorial style, should serve as an invaluable tool to all Canadians seeking a set of standards and guidelines for solving the everyday problems of writing and editing.

Diana Monnet

Chief Executive Officer
Translation Bureau

Foreword to the Second Edition

Ten years have passed since the first edition of *The Canadian Style* saw the light of day. The guide has enjoyed great success, becoming a standard reference work not only for federal organizations but also for Canadians in many walks of life. A number of provincial ministries of education include *The Canadian Style* in their lists of books recommended for use in schools, colleges and universities.

Over the same period, new trends in society and government have brought about significant changes in written communications. Efforts to eliminate sexual and ethnic stereotyping have gathered steam and have in recent years been coupled with new requirements regarding the depiction of Aboriginal peoples and persons with disabilities. The microcomputer is now an indispensable tool for people in many occupations, particularly those required to write for a living. The principles of plain language have been adopted in both government and industry. As a result, this new edition contains a significantly expanded chapter on the elimination of stereotyping, a new section on electronic mail, and a new chapter on techniques for writing clearly and concisely.

The interest sparked by the first edition prompted readers to submit their writing problems to us in the hope that the second edition might provide solutions they had not found elsewhere. Accordingly, the chapters on abbreviations, capitalization, reference matter, reports and memorandums, usage and geographical names have been enlarged. The same is true of the appendix on proofreader's marks, which has become a fullfledged chapter on revision and proofreading.

Many readers have asked us to include some basic guidelines for the presentation of French text in an English document. A new appendix gives the basic rules of French typography, with specific reference to abbreviations, word division, capitalization, numerical expressions and punctuation.

We established the order of chapters in the second edition with the aim of providing the reader with typographical and format information first (chapters 1–11) and then broadening the scope of our recommendations to encompass issues of style and usage, revision, and the political and social aspects of writing (chapters 12–16).

The purpose of the guide has not changed: to provide solutions, in a readily accessible format, to problems regularly encountered by both professional and occasional writers. The recommendations are based on national and international standards, the opinions of authorities on editorial style, and a survey of current policy and practice in government communications.

We hope that readers find in this second edition the information required to ensure quality in written communications, both within the federal public service and outside.

Malcolm Williams
Translation Bureau

Vitalijs Bucens
Translation Bureau

Project Co-ordinator
Writer-Editor

Senior Editor

Acknowledgments

The following people made substantive contributions to this edition: Gene Bodzin, of the Canadian Mortgage and Housing Corporation; Carol Card, Chantal Cormier and Charles Skeete, of the Translation Bureau; and Michèle Devlin and Maria Kazamias, of Concordia University.

Several other writing specialists reviewed the first draft and made invaluable suggestions: Jane Buckley, Louis Majeau, Sheila Protti, Tom Vradenburg, Judith Whitehead and Kathleen Wright, all members of the Freelance Writers' Association of Canada; Martin McCormack, of Transport Canada; and Robert Taylor, of Public Works and Government Services Canada. We thank all these people for their expert advice and for the time and energy they put into the daunting task of revising several hundred manuscript pages.

M.W.

Over to You . . .

Even revised editions can be improved upon. Your comments and suggestions would therefore be most appreciated. They should be sent to

The Canadian Style
Client Services
Translation Bureau
Ottawa, Ontario K1A 0S5

Internet: http://www.pwgsc.gc.ca/termium

If, in order to back up a statement or justify a preference, you mention a reference not included in this guide, please send us the title and date of the publication being cited and, where possible, a photocopy of the pages containing the relevant information.

Thank you for your assistance.

Chapter One

Abbreviations

1

Abbreviations

1.01 Introduction

The use of abbreviations has gained greater acceptance as an increasing number of new products and organizations are identified by shorter and more easily recognizable word forms.

In addition to abbreviations in the strict sense (including the short forms of common nouns, Latin expressions and titles), this chapter contains information and recommendations regarding acronyms, initialisms, and symbols such as those for metric units, which are uniform in many languages.

1.02 General guidelines and observations

Many abbreviations will not be understood unless the term is written in full at first mention, with the abbreviation given in parentheses. Follow these general rules:

- In general, abbreviate words only when the short form will be immediately recognized by the reader, and ensure that the same abbreviation is used elsewhere in your text to represent the word or words involved.

- Some standard abbreviations such as *i.e., AD, IQ, ESP, CBC* and *MP* do not have to be spelled out because they are well known and in many cases occur as dictionary entries.

- Many commonly used words that are actually abbreviations are now rarely regarded as such, including *ad, fridge, phone, exam, memo, photo* and *math*. Most such words should be avoided in formal writing, although *cello* and *bus* are exceptions to this rule.

- Unless you are confident that the reader will know exactly what the abbreviation stands for, write the term in full at first mention, with the abbreviation following in parentheses:

    Several government departments were amalgamated to form Public Works and Government Services Canada (PWGSC).

- Common abbreviations often in the news need not be spelled out if the full term is rarely used or is difficult to pronounce:

DNA	deoxyribonucleic acid
HIV	human immunodeficiency virus
3M	Minnesota Mining and Manufacturing Company
RCMP	Royal Canadian Mounted Police

• If in doubt about the correct abbreviation, use the long form.

1.03 Periods

In recent years there has been a trend toward the omission of periods in abbreviations. This is particularly true of scientific and technical writing, but the practice has been spreading in general writing as well.

(a) Do **not** use periods with the following:

- chemical symbols and mathematical abbreviations: H_2O, *NaCl, cos, log, tan*;
- SI symbols and units: *cm, kg, L* (see 1.23);
- abbreviations for points of the compass, except with street addresses (*winds NNW* **but** *King St. E.*);
- the military rank abbreviations used in the Department of National Defence (see 1.07);
- short forms of words: *lab, flu, vet, stereo, typo*; abbreviations or acronyms consisting exclusively of upper-case letters or ending in an upper-case letter (except those for personal names, legal references and most place names), e.g. *NAFTA, PhD, YMCA, UN, GST, MiG, CTV.*

(b) Use periods

- with geographical abbreviations, e.g. *B.C., P.E.I.*, but **not** for the two-character symbols recommended by Canada Post (see 1.09).
- with most lower-case abbreviations, including *a.m., p.m. , e.g., i.e.* (*mph* is one of the few exceptions).
- at the end of abbreviations for single words: *Mr., Jr., Ltd., misc., pp., Nos.*
- after each abbreviated word of a multiword term or phrase, where the abbreviation of each word consists of more than single initials, e.g. *Rev. ed., Rt. Rev.* (space required after each element in the abbreviation).
- after initials in a person's name:

  Thelonius S. Monk   H. E. Hughes

(space required between each period and the following initial or name)

Note

If a sentence ends in an abbreviation taking a period, only one period is used.

For further information on spacing, see 7.02.

1.04 Plurals

1

Add an *s*, but not an apostrophe, to form the plural of most abbreviations:

ADMs	PCBs	CAs
CRs	FTEs	GICs
MPs	747s	BMWs

Use an apostrophe and *s* to form the plural of numerical names of aircraft ending in a single letter:

727-100C's	747B's	727-100's

In cases where the resulting form would be ambiguous, add an apostrophe before the *s:*

c.o.d.'s	Q's and A's	SIN's

Add an apostrophe and *s* to form the plural of abbreviations containing more than one period, and an *s* without an apostrophe, to form the plural of abbreviations with only one period. In the latter case, the *s* precedes the period:

G.M.'s	Gens.	pts.

The plurals of *Mr.* and *Mrs.* are irregular:

Mr., Messrs.	Mrs., Mmes.

The plural forms of the abbreviations for certain bibliographic references are different:

l. (line)	ll. (lines)
p. (page)	pp. (pages)
f. (and the one following)	ff. (and those following)
c., ch. (chapter)	c., ch. (chapters)
MS (manuscript)	MSS (manuscripts)

but

s. (section)	ss. (sections)
subs. (subsection)	subss. (subsections)

Note that SI/metric symbols maintain the same form for both singular and plural and are written without periods, except at the end of a sentence:

1 cm	5 cm
75 kg	The boxer weighed only 75 kg.

1.05 Capital letters and hyphens

In general, an abbreviation is capitalized or hyphenated if the unabbreviated word or words are so treated:

Lt.-Gov.	Lieutenant-Governor
MLA	Member of the Legislative Assembly
UBC	University of British Columbia

When an abbreviation is formed from letters most or all of which are part of a single word, it is capitalized, even though the full term is not:

ACTH	adrenocorticotrophic hormone
DNA	deoxyribonucleic acid
ESP	extrasensory perception
TV	television

See 1.16 for rules governing the capitalization of acronyms and initialisms.

1.06 Titles used with personal names

Use the following abbreviations for non-military titles preceding or following personal names:

Mr.	Dr.
Mrs.	Hon.
Ms.	Rt. Hon.
Messrs.	Msgr.
Mmes.	St.
Esq.	Prof.
Jr.	Rev.
Sr.	

Use *Ms.* when referring to a woman unless a preference for *Mrs.* has been indicated. Although not an abbreviation, *Ms.* is written with a period, by analogy with *Mr.* and *Mrs.* Note that *Miss* is not an abbreviation and does not take a period.

Do **not** use *Mr., Mrs., Ms., Dr.* or *Esq.* with any other abbreviated title or with an abbreviation denoting an academic degree or honour:

Dr. Roberta Bondar **or** Roberta Bondar, MD
not
Ms. **or** Dr. Roberta Bondar, MD

Mr. Paul Kelly **or** Paul Kelly, Esq.
not
Mr. Paul Kelly, Esq.

Do **not** use the abbreviation *Dr.* and *Rev. Dr.* before the names of individuals who hold only honorary doctorates.

Saint is written out for names of persons revered as holy, but may be abbreviated in informal contexts and in lists and tables:

Saint Francis of Assisi	Saint Theresa
Saint Peter	Saint Catherine

St. and *SS.* (plural) are the abbreviations used.

Abbreviate professional and official titles only when they are used with surnames preceded by first names or initials:

Gen. Lewis MacKenzie **but** General MacKenzie

Dr. Irene Taguchi **but** Doctor Taguchi
Prof. A. N. Chomsky **but** Professor Chomsky

Note that there are spaces between each period and the following initial or name.

Even when used to address someone in correspondence, *Rt. Hon, Hon.* and *Rev.* must be preceded by *the*:

The Rt. Hon. Jean Chrétien, Prime Minister of Canada
The Hon. Diane Marleau, Minister of Public Works and Government
    Services
The Rev. John Smith

Note

The honorary title "the Honourable" is used before the names of members of the Canadian Privy Council, lieutenant-governors and certain other officials. The title "the Right Honourable" applies for life to the governor general, prime minister and chief justice of Canada. See Department of Canadian Heritage, *Precedence of Canadian Dignitaries and Officials*.

Do **not** abbreviate *Mayor, Vice-President, Professor* and *Father* when used with personal names.

1.07 Military abbreviations

In the following table, the middle column gives the abbreviations used by the Department of National Defence (DND) and the right-hand column those used in non-DND writing:

Army and Air Force

Officers

General	Gen	Gen.
Lieutenant-General	LGen	Lt.-Gen.
Major-General	MGen	Maj.-Gen.
Brigadier-General	BGen	Brig.-Gen.
Colonel	Col	Col.
Lieutenant-Colonel	LCol	Lt.-Col.
Major	Maj	Maj.
Captain	Capt	Capt.
Lieutenant	Lt	Lieut.
Second Lieutenant	2Lt	2nd Lieut.
Officer Cadet	OCdt	(not abbreviated)

Other ranks

Chief Warrant Officer	CWO	(not abbreviated)
Master Warrant Officer	MWO	(not abbreviated)
Warrant Officer	WO	(not abbreviated)
Sergeant	Sgt	Sgt.
Master Corporal	MCpl	(not abbreviated)
Corporal	Cpl	Cpl.
Private	Pte	Pte.

Navy

Admiral	Adm	(not abbreviated)
Vice-Admiral	VAdm	(not abbreviated)
Rear-Admiral	RAdm	(not abbreviated)
Commodore	Cmdre	(not abbreviated)
Captain	Capt	Capt.
Commander	Cdr	Cmdr.
Lieutenant-Commander	LCdr	Lt.-Cmdr.
Lieutenant	Lt	Lieut.
Sub-Lieutenant	SLt	Sub-Lieut.
Commissioned Officer	Comm Offr	(not abbreviated)
Acting Sub-Lieutenant	A/SLt	(not abbreviated)
Midshipman	MD	(not abbreviated)
Naval Cadet	Nav Cdt	(not abbreviated)
Chief Petty Officer, 1st Class	CPO 1	(not abbreviated)
Chief Petty Officer, 2nd Class	CPO 2	(not abbreviated)
Petty Officer, 1st Class	PO 1	(not abbreviated)
Petty Officer, 2nd Class	PO 2	(not abbreviated)
Leading Seaman	LS	L.S.
Able Seaman	AB	A.B.
Ordinary Seaman	OS	O.S.

In non-DND writing, the plurals of these abbreviated titles are formed by adding *s* to the principal element:

Gens.	Maj.-Gens.	Cols.

Note that at the Department of National Defence, *Ret* is the abbreviation for *Retired.*

1.08 University degrees, professional designations, military decorations, honours, awards and memberships

Give these and other distinctions in abbreviated form after the name of the bearer:

Marta Borowska, MA, BLS	The Rev. Edwin O'Malley, SJ
The Hon. John Smith, BCom, LLD	T. S. Wong, PhD, FRSC

Unless all honours have to be indicated for information or protocol purposes, no more than two abbreviations need follow a person's name—as, for example, in correspondence. Select the two highest honours of different types and list them in the following order of precedence: first, distinctions conferred directly by the Crown (*VC, QC,* etc.); second, university degrees; and third, letters denoting membership in societies and other distinctions. Note that no periods are used.

1.09 Geographical names

The names of provinces, territories and districts may be abbreviated when they follow the name of a city, town, village or geographical feature:

Wawa, Ont.	Mount Robson, B.C.

It is not necessary to use the provincial abbreviation after the names of well-known cities such as Vancouver, Winnipeg, Toronto, Ottawa and Fredericton. However, since the same name is often shared by several places in Canada and other parts of the English-speaking world (e.g. Perth, Windsor, Hamilton), add the appropriate abbreviation in cases where doubt could arise.

The following abbreviations are used officially for the names of provinces and territories in Canada. The right-hand column lists the two-character symbols recommended by Canada Post for use with mailing addresses. For other purposes, use the traditional provincial abbreviations:

	Traditional	**Canada Post**
Alberta	Alta.	AB
British Columbia	B.C.	BC
Manitoba	Man.	MB
New Brunswick	N.B.	NB
Newfoundland	Nfld.	NF
Northwest Territories	N.W.T.	NT
Nova Scotia	N.S.	NS
Ontario	Ont.	ON
Prince Edward Island	P.E.I.	PE
Quebec	Que.	QC
Saskatchewan	Sask.	SK
Yukon Territory	Y.T.	YT

Note

A territory to be known as **Nunavut** was established under the *Statutes of Canada,* Bill C-132, assented to on June 10, 1993. The Act is to come into force on or before April 1, 1999. Nunavut is to consist of the eastern part of the present-day Northwest Territories.

Do **not** abbreviate words such as *County, Fort, Mount, North, Point, Island, Port* and *Saint* used as part of a proper noun, unless the official name for the location shows the abbreviated form:

Port Radium	St. John's, Nfld.
Fort Garry	Saint John, N.B.
Sable Island	Point Pelee

For further information on the official form of geographical names, see Chapter 15.

1.10 Addresses: streets and buildings; points of the compass

• Streets and buildings

Words such as *Street, Avenue, Place, Road, Square, Boulevard, Terrace, Drive, Court* and *Building* are spelled out in general writing but may be abbreviated in footnotes, endnotes, sidenotes, tables and addresses. If the word forms part of a longer name, do **not** abbreviate it under any circumstances:

He worked at the Journal Building.
Get off at Queen Street Station.

• Points of the compass

Abbreviate compass directions as follows:

N	NE
S	SW
E	NNW
W	ESE

In general writing, the abbreviations *NE, NW, SE* and *SW* may be used to denote town and city divisions, but the words *north, south, east* and *west* should always be spelled out:

NW Toronto
Ottawa east

In street addresses, abbreviated compass directions are **not** followed by a period:

75 BOOTH ST N

Do **not** abbreviate words such as *East, West, Southeast, Northwest* when they appear before a street name:

150 East 52nd Street
111 Southeast Central Park Avenue

For further information on abbreviations in addresses, see Canada Post Corporation, *The Canadian Addressing Standard Handbook.*

1.11 Latitude and longitude

Do **not** abbreviate the words *latitude* and *longitude* when used alone or in ordinary prose:

What is the latitude of the Tropic of Cancer?
The wreck was found at 36°7′25″ north latitude and 15°24′00″ west longitude.

In technical work and when lists of co-ordinates are given, use the abbreviations *lat.* and *long.*:

lat. 42°15′30″ N	long. 89°17′45″ W
lat. 18°40′16″ S	long. 20°19′22″ E

1.12 Parts of a book or document

Capitalize, but do **not** abbreviate, parts of a document when followed by a number or letter, e.g. *Part 4, Table 14, Appendix C.*

Smaller subdivisions such as *paragraph, line, page* and *verse* are also written in full but are not capitalized except in main headings. See 4.30 for further treatment of these points.

In footnotes, endnotes, bibliographies and indexes, words referring to parts of a publication should, in the interest of conciseness, be abbreviated:

abr.	abridged	fwd.	foreword
	abridgment	jour.	journal
bk., bks.	book(s)	mag.	magazine
bull.	bulletin	pt., pts.	part(s)
c., ch.	chapter(s)	ser.	series
ed., eds.	edition(s)	supp.	supplement
	editor(s)	vol., vols.	volume(s)
fig.	figure		

1.13 Latin terms

Beware of confusing and misusing the following abbreviations:

e.g.	for example
I.e.	that is, specifically, namely
etc.	and so on
et al.	and others
c., ca.	about, approximately
q.v.	see this word (*in cross-references*)

Note that the following Latin terms are not abbreviations and are never followed by a period unless they are placed at the end of a sentence:

ad	ex	idem	per	*sic*
ad hoc	finis	*infra*	pro	*supra*
et	in	par	re	via

1.14 Scientific and technical terms

There is a vast array of technical and scientific abbreviations such as those for mathematical ratios and operations, physical quantities and constants or statistical formulas and notations. Most unabridged dictionaries list such abbreviations. People working in specific disciplines should consult the appropriate manuals in their field.[1]

In biology, the Latin name for a genus is not abbreviated if used alone. When used with the species name, it is abbreviated as of the second reference. The species name is not abbreviated:

Clematis (genus)
Clematis virginiana (full scientific name at first reference)
C. virginiana (second and subsequent references)

In symbols for chemical elements, compounds and formulas, use subscript, not superscript, numerals, e.g. H_2SO_4, SO_2.

---

1. For a comprehensive list of such abbreviations, see *ABBR: Abbreviations for Scientific and Engineering Terms.*

1.15 Corporate names

The following is a list of terms often abbreviated in the names of companies or business corporations. The abbreviated forms may be freely used in footnotes, tables or bibliographic references. Avoid using *Assoc., Bros., Co.* and *Corp.* within the body of your text. *Inc.* and *Ltd.*, however, may be used unless it is necessary to preserve the company's full legal title:

Association	Assoc.	Corporation	Corp.
Brothers	Bros.	Manufacturing	Mfg.
Limited	Ltd.	Manufacturers	Mfrs.
Company	Co.	Incorporated	Inc.
Company	Cie. (*Compagnie*)		

1.16 Acronyms and initialisms

- An acronym is a pronounceable word formed from the first letters of a series of other words, such as *NAFTA, NATO* or *GATT*. An initialism is formed from the initial letters of a series of words and may not be pronounceable as a word. Examples are *GST, RCMP, OECD* and *IDRC*. The distinction is a fine one and is often overlooked in practice. Do **not** use periods or spacing between the letters of an acronym or initialism.

- In general, acronyms are not preceded by the definite article:

  The members of NATO rejected the idea.
  NAFTA may be expanded to Chile and other South American countries.
  CIDA provides grants, loans and lines of credit.

- Usage varies with respect to initialisms. Those representing the names of organizations generally take the definite article, while those representing a substance, method or condition do not:

  The CLRB is reviewing the case.
  The unit has provided training in CPR for some time.

- The correct form of the indefinite article (*a* or *an*) to use before acronyms and initialisms is determined by the consonant or vowel sound of the initial syllable, letter or number. The following examples illustrate correct English usage. Note that ease of pronunciation is the key:

a 3M product	a QFL convention
a UFO sighting	a NAFTA-related issue
an IMF loan	an NHL referee
an ACTRA award	an FM station

- Use upper-case letters for acronyms or initialisms in their entirety, even if some of the component words or their parts are not normally capitalized—unless the organization concerned prefers lower case:

CAA	Canadian Automobile Association
OSSTF	Ontario Secondary School Teachers' Federation
FORTRAN	formula translation
CISTI	Canada Institute for Scientific and Technical Information

1

Exceptions

Acronyms (**not** initialisms) of company names formed by using more than the initial letters of the words they represent. Usually, only the first letter of the acronym is capitalized:

Alcan	Aluminum Company of Canada
Inco	International Nickel Company
Nabisco	National Biscuit Company
Nortel	Northern Telecom Ltd.
Stelco	Steel Company of Canada Ltd.

- Initialisms are always fully capitalized:

    BBS, VIP, TSE, CNCP Telecommunications, HRDC[2]

- Common-noun acronyms treated as fullfledged words, such as *radar, laser, scuba* and *snafu*, are written entirely in lower case without periods.

- When using acronyms or initialisms such as *SIN* (social insurance number), *PIN* (personal identification number) or *ISBN* (International Standard Book Number) do **not** repeat the word *number* (e.g. "SIN number"). Either write the expression out in full or use the abbreviated form on its own.

1.17 Number and percentage symbols

When abbreviating the words *number* or *numbers* within the body of a text, use *No.* or *Nos.* but **not** the symbol #, which is generally reserved for tabular and statistical material:

    Nos. 56–86 are missing.

Use the percent sign (%) in economic, financial, statistical or other documents where figures are abundant. In material of a general nature containing isolated references to percentages, the term is usually written out, except when used adjectivally:

    15 percent   a 15% bond (*no space between numeral and %*)

1.18 Ampersand

The ampersand (&) is properly used only when it forms part of a corporate name:

    The publisher was Ginn & Co.
    The case is being defended by Collins, Smith, White & Jones.

Do **not** use the ampersand in federal department legal or applied titles:

    The Department of Public Works and Government Services
    The Department of Indian Affairs and Northern Development

---

2. For a comprehensive list of the official acronyms and initialisms of Canadian government organizations, consult the Treasury Board's *Federal Identity Program Manual*, "Titles of Federal Organizations."

not

The Department of Public Works & Government Services
The Department of Indian Affairs & Northern Development

1.19 Monetary units

When it is necessary to distinguish dollar amounts in one currency from those in another, use the appropriate symbol with the figure in question:

The loan will be repaid in eighty instalments of C$650
(**or** CAN$650) each.
Please enclose a cheque in the amount of US$100.

See 5.11 and 5.26 for further information on monetary units.

1.20 Months and days

Always spell out the names of the months in the body of your text and in footnotes. They may be abbreviated in tabular matter, citations and references, forms and sidenotes. *May,* however, should **not** be abbreviated and *June* and *July* are shortened only in military writing.

The names of the days of the week are **not** abbreviated, except in tables.

1.21 Time of day and elapsed time

Present exact time as follows:

11 a.m. **or** 11:00 a.m.   1 p.m. **or** 1:00 p.m.
3:30 p.m.

For elapsed time, use colons, periods and no spaces:

2:30:21.65 (hours, minutes, seconds, tenths, hundredths)

See 5.12 and 5.13 for additional information.

1.22 Time zones

Time zones are abbreviated when used with a specific time. Note that capitals are used, without periods. Otherwise they are written out in full:

4:30 p.m. EST   7:15 a.m. MST
Pacific standard time   daylight saving time

1.23 The International System of Units (SI)

The International System of Units (SI), which has replaced other metric systems and is now used in Canada and many other countries, is a decimal-based system that includes units for physical quantities.

There are seven base units in SI:

Table 1

Quantity	Unit name	Symbol
length	metre	m
mass	kilogram	kg
time	second	s
electric current	ampere	A
thermodynamic temperature	kelvin	K
amount of substance	mole	mol
luminous intensity	candela	cd

In addition, a number of derived units are used. Like the kelvin and the ampere, almost all of them are named after scientists associated with a scientific discovery. Thus, when the symbol is used, its initial letter is capitalized. When written in full, however, the unit name is in lower case, e.g. *H* for *henry* and *F* for *farad*.

Exception

Celsius takes an initial capital whether written in full or as a symbol.

The table below gives a complete list of derived units:

Table 2

Name	Symbol	Quantity
coulomb	C	quantity of electricity, electric charge
degree Celsius	°C	Celsius temperature*
farad	F	capacitance
gray	Gy	absorbed dose of ionizing radiation
henry	H	inductance
hertz	Hz	frequency
joule	J	energy, work, quantity of heat
lumen	lm	luminous flux
lux	lx	illuminance
newton	N	force
ohm	Ω	electric resistance
pascal	Pa	pressure, stress
radian	rad	plane angle
siemens	S	electric conductance
sievert	Sv	dose equivalent of ionizing radiation
steradian	sr	solid angle
tesla	T	magnetic flux density
volt	V	electric potential, potential difference, electromotive force
watt	W	power, radiant flux
weber	Wb	magnetic flux

* The Celsius temperature scale (previously called Centigrade, but renamed in 1948 to avoid confusion with "centigrad," associated with the centesimal system of angular measurement), is the commonly used scale, except for certain scientific and technological purposes where the thermodynamic temperature scale is preferred. Note the use of upper-case *C* for *Celsius*.

Multiples and submultiples of base units and derived units are expressed by adding one of the prefixes from the following table directly to the unit name:

Table 3

Factor	Prefix	Symbol	Factor	Prefix	Symbol
10^{24}	yotta	Y	10^{-1}	deci	d
10^{21}	zetta	Z	10^{-2}	centi	c
10^{18}	exa	E	10^{-3}	milli	m
10^{15}	peta	P	10^{-6}	micro	μ
10^{12}	tera	T	10^{-9}	nano	n
10^{9}	giga	G	10^{-12}	pico	p
10^{6}	mega	M	10^{-15}	femto	f
10^{3}	kilo	k	10^{-18}	atto	a
10^{2}	hecto	h	10^{-21}	zepto	z
10^{1}	deca	da	10^{-24}	yocto	y

- The prefix and unit names are always spelled as one word:

  centimetre   decagram
  hectolitre   kilopascal

- When symbols are used, the prefix symbol and unit symbols are run together:

  5 cm   4 dag
  7 hL   13 kPa

- When a symbol consists entirely of letters, leave a full space between the quantity and the symbol:

  45 kg **not** 45kg

- When the symbol includes a non-letter character as well as a letter, leave no space:

  32°C **not** 32° C **or** 32 °C

- For the sake of clarity, a hyphen may be inserted between a numeral and a symbol used adjectivally (see also 2.10):

  35-mm film   60-W bulb

- Unit symbols and prefixes should always be in lower case, even when the rest of the text is in upper case:

  SIBERIA DRIFTS 5 cm CLOSER TO ALASKA

Exceptions

The symbol *L* for *litre* (to distinguish it from the numeral *1*) and, as mentioned above, those symbols derived from the names of scientists.

- SI usage prescribes that both numerals and unit names be written in full or that both be abbreviated:

  two metres **or** 2 m

Current usage, however, accepts the use of numerals with spelled-out unit names to facilitate comprehension:

> He ran the 100 metres in 10 seconds.

In scientific and technical writing, the preferred form is numerals with unit symbols:

> The specific latent heat of fusion of sulphur is 38.1 K/kg.

When no specific figure is stated, write the unit name in full:

> The means of transportation chosen depends on how many kilometres an employee has to travel to work.

- Area and volume in the metric system are expressed by means of superscript numerals:

  5 cm^3 20 m^2

Do **not** use abbreviations such as *cc* or *cu. cm* for *cubic centimetre (cm³)*, *kilo* for *kilogram (kg)*, *amp* for *ampere (A)* or *kph* for *kilometres per hour (km/h)*.

Because of their practical importance, the following additional units are approved for use with SI, although they do not, strictly speaking, form part of it:

Table 4

Quantity	Unit name	Symbol
time	minute	min
	hour	h
	day	d
	year	a
plane angle	degree	°
	minute	′
	second	″
	revolution	r
area	hectare	ha
volume	litre	L
mass	metric ton, tonne	t
linear density	tex	tex

Note that there is no standard symbol for *week* or *month*. These units should therefore always be spelled out in technical writing.

When a unit symbol is combined with a symbol for time, or with a derived unit implying a division, an oblique (/) separates the two:

80 km/h	**not**	80 kmh **or** 80 kph
1800 r/min	**not**	1800 rpm
50 A/m	**not**	50 Am
200 J/kg	**not**	200 Jkg

More detailed information on the International System of Units (SI) can be found in the National Standard of Canada, *Canadian Metric Practice Guide* (CAN/CSA–Z234.1-89).

1.24 The imperial system

Abbreviations for imperial weights and measures take the same form for singular and plural. Area and volume in this system are usually expressed by means of the abbreviations *sq.* and *cu.* rather than a superscript numeral. Leave a space between *sq.* or *cu.* and the abbreviation that follows it:

1 ft. (foot)	4 oz. (ounces)
38 yd. (yards)	1 mi. (mile)
55 mph (miles per hour)	4 gal. (gallons)
100 sq. ft.	20 cu. yd.
17 in. (inches)	

1.25 Business terms, expressions and symbols

Terms are often abbreviated for the purpose of conserving space in routine business correspondence. The following are common abbreviations used in tables and on business forms:

acct.	account	bal.	balance
Assn.	Association	bldg.	building
CEO	chief executive officer	dis.	discount
cont.	continued	dtd.	dated
ea.	each	fwd.	forward
FY	fiscal year	G.M.	general manager
gr.	gross	hdlg.	handling
ins.	insurance	max.	maximum
Ltd.	Limited	n.d.	no date
min.	minimum	pd.	paid
oz.	ounce(s)	recd.	received
qty.	quantity	treas.	treasury, treasurer
sec.	secretary	V.P.	vice-president
whsle.	wholesale		

The following is a list of symbols for terms used in business correspondence and in tabular and statistical material:

at	@	number (before a figure)	#
and	&	pounds (after a figure)	#
percent	%	feet	'
dollar(s)	$	inches; ditto	"
cent(s)	¢	paragraph	¶
degree(s)	°	section	§
equals	=	by; multiplied by	x

Note that a space is usually required before and after the symbols @, =, &
and *x*:

> Yearwood & Boyce   2 shirts @ $19.95 each

Exception

No extra space is required for upper-case abbreviations or in e-mail
addresses:

> R&D at AT&T   sales@wordlink.ca

Note also that no space is required between figures and the symbols
%, ¢, °, #, ', ":

> 10% deficit reduction   nearly 75¢ a pound
> 43# per bag   159' x 259' deck

Do **not** leave any space after the symbols $, #, ¶, § when they precede a
figure:

> less than $278   as mentioned in ¶21
> package #3412   Refer to §1.28.

Chapter Two

Hyphenation: compounding and word division

2

Hyphenation: Compounding and Word Division

2.01 Introduction

A compound term is a combination of two or more words that, to varying
degrees, have become unified in form and meaning through frequent use
together. In many cases only one syllable in the compound is stressed. The
trend over the years has been for the English compound to begin as two
separate words, then be hyphenated and finally, if there is no structural
impediment to union, become a single word written without a space or
hyphen. Whatever its form, the compound frequently serves to avoid
circumlocution and create a more concise style.

The existence of three different forms for compounds leads to considerable
instability and variation in their presentation, and hyphenation has become
one of the most controversial points of editorial style. Dictionaries vary
widely in the forms they choose for specific compounds: "hot-line" in the
Gage Canadian Dictionary, "hot line" in the *Canadian Dictionary of the
English Language* and "hotline" in *The Concise Oxford Dictionary,* for
example.

All authorities agree that the matter of hyphenation is one where the
exercise of individual judgment is required, and the rules that follow are
not intended to preclude its use. Where various authorities disagree, it is
desirable to err on the side of caution and recommend use of the hyphen
for the sake of clarity.

Bear in mind the distinction between a compound term used before a noun
(attributively) and one in some other position (predicatively). As a general
rule, terms that take a hyphen when preceding a noun do not take one in
other positions, but there are enough exceptions to warrant their being
noted, and this is done below.

Although they do not form true compounds, prefixes and suffixes are
treated in this chapter because they pose similar problems with respect to
hyphenation.

Consult the *Gage Canadian Dictionary* for the form of frequently used
compounds (including those based on prefixes and suffixes), and then
follow the rules below for those not found in Gage.

For information on hyphens with place names in French, see Chapter 15.

2.02 Compound nouns and nouns in compounds

(a) Hyphenate two nouns representing different but equally important functions, i.e. where the hyphen denotes the relationship "both A and B":

soldier-statesman	comedy-ballet
city-state	dinner-dance
tractor-trailer	writer-editor

(b) Hyphenate nouns normally written as two words, when they have a modifier and when ambiguity would otherwise result:

colour filter **but** red colour-filter
letter writers **but** public letter-writers

Similarly, compound nouns normally written as a single word must be separated into their component parts and then joined to their modifier by a hyphen when the modifier applies only to the first component:

ironworker **but** structural-iron worker
housekeeper **but** lodging-house keeper

(c) Hyphenate compound units of measurement made by combining single units that stand in a mathematical relationship to each other:

car-miles	light-year
kilowatt-hours	person-day

(d) Hyphenate compounds that include a finite verb:

a has-been	a stay-at-home
a sing-along	a stick-in-the-mud
a Johnny-come-lately	a ne'er-do-well

(e) Hyphenate nouns of family relationship formed with *great* and *in-law:*

mother-in-law	great-grandfather

but

foster father	half sister
stepson	godmother

2.03 Nouns with adjectives and participles

(a) Hyphenate noun-plus-adjective compounds (in that order), whether used attributively or predicatively:

duty-free goods	The goods were duty-free.
tax-exempt bonds	The bonds are tax-exempt.

(b) Hyphenate noun-plus-participle compounds regardless of the position:

snow-capped mountains	The mountains are snow-capped.
a time-consuming activity	This activity is time-consuming.

Exceptions

There are a number of them, including *handmade* and *handwritten.*

(c) Do **not** hyphenate noun-plus-gerund compounds (present participle used as a noun); they may be written as one or as separate words:

decision making	housekeeping
power sharing	shipbuilding
problem solving	sightseeing
deficit spending	cabinetmaking

Exceptions

foot-dragging, gut-wrenching

See 2.04(e) for such compounds used adjectivally.

2.04 Compound adjectives; adjectives and participles in compounds

(a) Hyphenate adjective-plus-noun and participle-plus-noun compounds modifying another noun, when ambiguity might otherwise result:

cold-storage vaults	large-scale development
crude-oil exporting countries	special-interest groups

When the compound is used predicatively, retain the hyphen only when the expression remains adjectival:

The development was large-scale.
His position is full-time.

but

Development proceeded on a large scale.
He works full time.

(b) Hyphenate compound adjectives made up of two adjectives that describe a colour without the suffix *ish,* whether they are placed before or after the noun. Hyphenate compounds with the suffix only when they precede the noun:

It was covered with blue-green algae.
It was blue-green.
The leaves were bluish green.
The tree had bluish-green leaves.

Do **not** hyphenate adjectives indicating a specific shade (even if they precede the noun):

dark green paint
a bright red dress
strawberry blond hair

(c) Hyphenate adjective-plus-participle compounds, whether used before the noun or after it:

an odd-sounding name
The name was rather odd-sounding.
a smooth-talking salesman
The visitor was smooth-talking.

(d) Hyphenate compounds made up of an adjective plus a noun to which the ending *ed* has been added, in any position in the sentence:

able-bodied   many-sided
strong-willed   short-handed

(e) Hyphenate two-word compound adjectives consisting of a noun plus a gerund when they precede the noun:

the decision-making process   a profit-sharing plan
a problem-solving approach   a tape-recording session

See also 2.03(c).

(f) Hyphenate compound adjectives whose final constituent is an adverb of direction or place (*in, out, down, up,* etc.) when they precede the noun:

a drive-by shooting   a built-up area
all-out competition   the trickle-down theory

(g) Hyphenate compound adjectives made up of a preposition and a noun:

on a per-gram basis   in-service courses
out-of-province benefits   after-tax income

(h) Hyphenate a compound adjective one of whose constituents is a finite verb:

a would-be writer   a pay-as-you-go approach

(i) Hyphenate phrases of more than two words, at least one of which is an adverb or preposition, used as attributive adjectives:

the cost-of-living index
a long-drawn-out affair
a subject-by-subject analysis
a work-to-rule campaign
an up-to-date approach
on-the-job training

(j) Do **not** hyphenate French or foreign words used as adjectives or in italics, proper nouns used as adjectives, or words in quotation marks:

a Privy Council decision
a New York State chartered bank
a *pure laine* Quebecker

2

a *dolce far niente* attitude
a priori reasoning
a "zero tolerance" approach

Note that this rule does not apply to French or foreign words no longer considered as such:

avant-garde filmmaking
a laissez-faire approach

(k) Do **not** hyphenate chemical terms used as adjectives:

a sodium chloride solution   a calcium nitrate deposit

(l) Hyphenate compound proper adjectives that form a true compound, but do **not** hyphenate those in which a proper adjective is combined with a simple modifier:

Anglo-Saxon period	Latin American governments
Sino-Russian border	Middle Eastern affairs
Austro-Hungarian Empire	North American interests
Greco-Roman art	Central Asian republics

2.05 Verbs

(a) Compound verbs may be either hyphenated or written solid. The only safe rule is to check your dictionary:

freeze-dry	mass-produce
age-harden	spoon-feed
bad-mouth	extra-bill

but

waterproof	downgrade
sidetrack	proofread

(b) If the infinitive form of the verb (e.g. *to air-condition*) is hyphenated, retain the hyphen in all other forms, except as illustrated in (c):

The theatre was air-conditioned.
You need an air-conditioning expert.
Please double-space the letter.

(c) Hyphenate gerunds formed from hyphenated compound verbs only if they are followed by a noun object:

Dry cleaning is the simplest way to clean a sweater.

but

Dry-cleaning the sweater should remove the stain.

Air conditioning is sometimes needed in summer.

but

Consider the cost in deciding whether air-conditioning the building is feasible.

2.06 Adverbs in compounds

(a) Adverb-plus-participle compounds are among the most troublesome. Do **not** hyphenate those in which the adverb ends in *ly*:

richly embroidered   fully employed

In other cases, hyphenate before the noun:

far-reaching events   ill-educated person
ever-changing tides   well-fed cattle

Do **not** hyphenate when the compound follows the noun or pronoun and contains a past participle:

She is well known.
This applicant is ill suited for the job.

When the compound follows the noun or pronoun and contains a present participle, do **not** hyphenate if the participle has a verbal function, but hyphenate if it is adjectival in nature:

The narrative is fast-moving. (*adjectival*)

but

The narrative is fast moving toward a climax. (*verbal*)

(b) Do **not** hyphenate compounds consisting of an adverb or adverbial phrase plus an adjective (in that order) unless there is a danger of misreading:

equally productive means
a reasonably tall tree
an all too complacent attitude

2.07 Prefixes

(a) Hyphenate a prefix joined to a proper noun or adjective:

mid-July   sub-Arctic
neo-Christian   trans-Siberian
pro-Canadian   un-American

Exceptions

transatlantic and *transpacific.*

(b) Hyphenate expressions beginning with the prefixes *ex* (when it means "former"), *self, quasi* and *all,* when used to form adjectives or nouns, and those beginning with *quasi* when used to form adjectives:

all-inclusive   quasi-judicial

all-powerful	quasi-stellar
ex-wife	self-assured
ex-premier Getty	self-control

However, when *self* is the base word to which a suffix is added, do **not** hyphenate:

selfish	selfhood
selfsame	selfless

(c) Most words beginning with the following prefixes are written as one word: *after, ante, anti, bi, co, counter, de, down, extra, infra, inter, intra, iso, macro, micro, multi, over, photo, poly, post, pre, pro, pseudo, re, retro, semi, stereo, sub, super, trans, tri, ultra, un, under* and *up:*

afterthought	isometric	retroactive
antecedent	macrocosm	semiquaver
antiballistic	microscope	stereophonic
bimonthly	multistage	subspecies
covalent	overestimate	supernatural
counterclockwise	photovoltaic	transcontinental
decertify	polyurethane	triennial
downturn	postnatal	ultrasound
extrasensory	preposition	unassuming
infrastructure	proconsul	underrate
interstellar	pseudonym	upswing
intramural	readapt	upwind

However, there are many exceptions. Check the *Gage Canadian Dictionary* when in doubt, and see below and 2.07(a) for specific types of exception.

Use a hyphen when the word following the prefix begins with the same vowel as the one with which the prefix ends and when the compound's appearance would be confusing without the hyphen:

pre-eminent	re-educate
co-opt	semi-invalid
co-author	de-icing

In certain cases, use the hyphen to preserve a difference in meaning between the hyphenated and the solid compound:

re-cover (cover again)	re-solve (solve again)
recover (get better, get back)	resolve (settle)
re-create (create again)	re-sign (sign again)
recreate (take recreation)	resign (quit a job)

(d) Write SI/metric unit compounds as one word:

centimetre	kilokelvins
gigagram	milliampere

(e) Hyphenate chemical terms preceded by an italicized prefix:

> *cis*-dimethylethylene
>
> *β*-lactose

2.08 *Any, every, no* and *some*

The words *any, every, no* and *some* form solid compounds when combined with *body, thing* and *where:*

anybody	everybody	nobody	somebody
anything	everything	nothing	something
anywhere	everywhere	nowhere	somewhere

However, when *one* is the second element, write *no* as a separate, unhyphenated word in all situations and write *any* and *every* as separate, unhyphenated words if *one* is followed by a prepositional phrase beginning with *of:*

> No one came.
>
> Any one of us can do it.
>
> Each and every one of you must take the responsibility.

but

> Someone must tell the Minister.
>
> Everyone is in agreement.
>
> Anyone can participate.

2.09 Suffixes

(a) like

Write the following compounds as one word, except where this would result in a double *l* and where the compound is a temporary one coined for a specific purpose or text:

businesslike	ladylike
childlike	lifelike

but

nut-like	petal-like

(b) wide

Since usage depends on the degree of familiarity of the compound, no general rule can be stated. Note the following:

worldwide	storewide

but

industry-wide	province-wide

(c) Hyphenate compounds made up of a numerical expression plus *odd* or *strong:*

sixty-odd	thirty-strong

(d) Write compounds with *fold* and *score* as one word, except when the numerical expression itself already has a hyphen:

> twofold sixtyfold
> threescore fourscore
>
> **but**
>
> twenty-two-fold

2.10 Numerals and units of measurement

(a) Hyphenate compound cardinal and ordinal numerals from *twenty-one (twenty-first)* to *ninety-nine (ninety-ninth)* when written out:

> There are twenty-nine members on the committee.

(b) Hyphenate a compound adjective in which one element is a cardinal or ordinal numeral and the other a noun:

> a five-kilometre trek a two-car family
> a first-class coach a third-rate play
> a $4-million project a 60-W bulb

Do **not** hyphenate before a symbol that is not a letter, and do **not** hyphenate a modifier in which the numeral, written in full, is itself a compound:

> a 100°C thermometer
> a two hundred and fifty hectare farm

In cases such as the second example, use the abbreviated form (*a 250-ha farm*) if at all possible.

See 5.05 for further information.

(c) Do **not** hyphenate a possessive noun preceded by a numerical expression:

> one week's pay 40 hours' work
> three weeks' vacation 10 months' leave

(d) Hyphenate expressions of time of day as follows when writing out numerals:

> eight-thirty four-twenty
> eight thirty-five four twenty-six

2.11 Fractions

Hyphenate fractions used as modifiers and written in full, unless the numerator or denominator already contains a hyphen:

> a one-third share
> twenty-fiftieths calcium
>
> **but**
>
> one thirty-second
> twenty-nine fiftieths calcium (*In this case numerals are preferable.*)

Exception

> *one and a half months*

Usage is divided on whether fractions used as nouns should be hyphenated. We recommend that the hyphen **not** be used in such cases:

> Four fifths of the load was wheat, and one fifth barley.

2.12 The suspended compound

Hyphenate as follows when an element common to successive compound adjectives is omitted:

> first- and second-class fares
> high- and low-pressure turbine
> interest- or revenue-producing schemes
> short- and long-term plans
> two-, four- and six-metre widths

2.13 Points of the compass

Write as one word compass directions consisting of two points, but use a hyphen after the first point in those compounds consisting of three points:

> northeast north-northeast
> southwest south-southwest

2.14 Titles of office

- Hyphenate compounds with the endings *elect* and *designate:*

> president-elect minister-designate

- Hyphenate most titles beginning with the prefix *vice* or with *then* and the names of certain military and administrative positions in which a noun is followed by another noun, an adjective or a prepositional phrase:

> vice-president Commander-in-Chief
> vice-chairman secretary-general
> aide-de-camp Lieutenant-Governor
> then-Prime Minister sergeant-at-arms

There are, however, many common exceptions to this rule, e.g.:

> Governor General Solicitor General
> Governor in Council Receiver General for Canada
> Judge Advocate General Viceroy

Note that in Canadian usage the hyphen is used in compounds designating military ranks such as *Lieutenant-General, Vice-Admiral* and *Rear-Admiral,* whereas the American practice is to omit the hyphen. Similarly, the official title of the second-highest-ranking official of the United States is *Vice President.*

2.15 Numerals and single letters

Hyphenate numerals or single letters and the words they modify:

e-mail	T-shirt
S-hook	U-turn
1,2-dimethylbutylene	2,4-D

Do **not** hyphenate a compound adjective when the second element is a letter or figure:

Class II railroad	Grade A milk

2.16 Plurals of compound terms

(a) In forming the plurals of compound terms, pluralize the significant word. If both words are of equal significance, pluralize both. Pluralize the last one if no one word is significant in itself:

attorneys general	men drivers
brigadier-generals	women writers
trade unions	assistant chiefs of staff
judge advocates	courts-martial
orders-in-council	poets laureate

(b) When a noun is hyphenated with a preposition, the plural is formed on the noun:

fillers-in	hangers-on
passers-by	makers-up

(c) When neither word of a compound is a noun, the plural is formed on the last word:

also-rans	go-betweens
run-ins	higher-ups

(d) Add *s* to nouns ending in *ful*:

teaspoonfuls	cupfuls
handfuls	sackfuls

2.17 Word division

In order to ensure clear, unambiguous presentation, avoid dividing words at the end of a line as much as possible. If word division is necessary, text comprehension and readability should be your guides. The accepted practice is summarized below:[1]

(a) Usually, words may be divided between syllables (the *Gage Canadian Dictionary* shows syllabication clearly for all its entries), but not all syllable breaks are acceptable as end-of-line breaks, as rules (b) to (m) explain.

---

1. See also P. Kirby, "English Word Division," *Termiglobe*, VII, 4 (November 1984): 24.

(b) Two-letter syllables should **not** be carried over to the next line (*fully*, not *ful-ly*; *stricken*, not *strick-en*). Similarly, final syllables in which a liquid *l* is the only pronounced vowel sound should **not** be carried over (*pos-sible*, not *possi-ble*; *prin-ciples*, not *princi-ples*).

(c) Do **not** divide words of one syllable or words in which the second "syllable" contains only a silent *e* (*aimed, helped, vexed,* etc.).

(d) One-letter word divisions are **not** permissible. Do **not** divide words such *as again, item, enough* and *even.*

(e) Avoid awkward divisions that would result from attempting to divide words such as *every, only, eighteen* and *people.*

(f) Divide between a prefix and a following letter (*pre-fix, re-location*).

(g) Divide a word between the root and the suffix (*care-less, convert-ible, world-wide*).

(h) When a consonant is doubled, divide it for purposes of word division (*equip-ping, rub-ber*).

(i) Avoid misleading breaks that might cause the reader to confuse one word with another, as in *read-just* and *reap-pear*. Similarly, such words as *women* and *often* should be left unbroken.

(j) Divide compounds only at the hyphen, if possible (*court-martial,* **not** *court-mar-tial*). A compound written as one word should be divided between its elements (*hot-house, sail-boat*).

(k) Most words ending in *ing* may be divided at that syllable. When the final consonant is doubled before *ing,* however, the second consonant is carried over (*bid-ding, control-ling*).When the verb has an *l* preceded by a consonant, carry over the letter preceding the *l* (*han-dling, dwin-dling, tin-kling*).

(l) Do **not** divide abbreviations, contractions and numbers (*UNDP, won't, 235 006 114.37*). Abbreviations or symbols used with numerals should not be separated from the numerals (*16 kg, 0°C, s. 4, 11:55 a.m.*).

(m) Do **not** divide the last word on a page.

Chapter Three

Spelling

3

Spelling

3.01 Introduction

Spelling poses a major problem in English because it is not phonetic and because the rules that can be formulated nearly always have significant exceptions. In addition, there are hundreds of words that have variant spellings in different parts of the English-speaking world, the principal cleavage being between the United Kingdom and the United States. Partly as a result of our historical links with Britain and our proximity to the United States, Canadian spelling has tended to waver between the forms used in these two countries, so that, to this day, there is no clearly established Canadian standard.

While a list of words that have variant spellings in British and American practice would run into the hundreds and still not be exhaustive, the great majority of them fall into a few well-defined classes, as listed below. The British variants are given in the left-hand column, the American in the right-hand column:

* verbs ending in *ise/ize* and their derived forms:

civilise, civilisation	civilize, civilization
organise, organisation	organize, organization
specialise, specialisation	specialize, specialization

* nouns ending in *our/or*:

colour, honour, favour	color, honor, favor

* nouns ending in *re/er*:

centre, fibre, theatre	center, fiber, theater

* verbs with single *l*/double *l* and their derivatives:

instil	instill
fulfil, fulfilment	fulfill, fulfillment
enrol, enrolment	enroll, enrollment

* nouns in *ce/se*:[1]

defence, offence, pretence	defense, offense, pretense

---

1. British spelling also makes a distinction between certain noun and verb forms that is not maintained in American spelling. Thus, British *licence* (noun), *license* (verb) and *practice* (noun), *practise* (verb); American *license* and *practice* for both forms.

51

- double *l*/single *l* in the past tense of verbs:

  counselled, labelled,   counseled, labeled,
  travelled   traveled

- treatment of the digraphs *ae* and *oe* in words derived from Greek and Latin:

  anaemia, encyclopaedia   anemia, encyclopedia
  diarrhoea, oecumenical   diarrhea, ecumenical

The recommended spelling authority is the *Gage Canadian Dictionary*, since it reflects the usage of most federal government departments and agencies more closely than do the *Webster's* or *Oxford* dictionaries, is based on research into Canadian usage, and contains specifically Canadian terms. When it lists two spellings for a word in the same entry, choose the one entered first. When two spellings are given separate entries, choose the primary spelling, which is the one followed by the definition (the variant simply refers the reader to the primary spelling entry). For scientific and technical words not in *Gage*, check *Webster's Third New International Dictionary*.

In light of these recommendations, use the following variant spellings: endings in *ize, ization, our, re*, single *l* (as in *instil*) and *ce*; single *l* in words such as *enrolment*; *ll* in *travelled*, etc.; and *e* for digraphs (exceptions: *aesthetic* and *onomatopoeic*).

Note

Respect the official spelling of names of U.S. institutions, e.g. Department of Defen*s*e, Cent*er* for Disease Control.

The rules and lists of words given in this chapter are intended to supplement, not replace the use of the *Gage Canadian Dictionary*. The important point with respect to spelling is to be consistent in your written work unless a good reason exists for using variant or archaic spellings.

3.02 Spell-checking

Spell-checking functions are now included in word-processing programs for use with computers. They can help you eliminate, at the proofreading stage, most of the spelling and typographical errors in a document. Especially useful are the "search" feature, which can instantly locate a specific combination of letters, and the "search-and-replace" feature, which can find all instances of a misspelled word or variant spelling and replace them with the correct or preferred form.

Spell-checking programs do have the following drawbacks:

- They cannot detect omissions of words.

- They do not flag correctly spelled words that are incorrect in the specific context. Thus the sentence

  Ewe bake two manly arrows.

would be approved by a spell-checker for a sentence that should read

> You make too many errors.

- Unless they are part of a larger grammar-checking utility, they do not identify words that are grammatically wrong. Thus the sentence

> He **do** not understand**s**.

would not be flagged.

- They may not respect the spelling preferences of your organization or your clients. In this case, you can usually modify the content of the spell-checker dictionary.

- The search-and-replace feature can result in misspellings that have to be reversed manually. For example, you may have decided to use the spelling *honour* instead of *honor*, the variant listed in American spell-checker dictionaries. Instructing the spell-checker to make a universal change will affect even correctly spelled words such as *honorarium, honorific* and *honorary* as well as words placed in quotes or followed by [*sic*]. To avoid the error, give the command

> <space>honor<space>

instead of just

> honor

A variation of this command is required to cover specific occurrences such as *honor* followed by a period.

3.03 Frequently misspelled words

The following is a list of words that are often misspelled. The letters that are usually the object of the errors–through inversion, omission, doubling, addition or substitution–are in boldface:

ab**h**or	ab**y**smal	acc**omm**odate
ac**q**uaintance	ag**g**ressive	all right
an**om**alous	ap**p**ellant	arc**t**ic
argu**m**ent	at**t**orney	awk**w**ard
bat**t**alion	calend**a**r	can**i**ster
Cari**bb**ean	cartila**g**e	cens**u**s
Chile (*the country*)	chlorophy**ll**	coherent, coherence
Colombia (*the country*)	com**m**itment	compar**a**tive
conco**m**itant	connec**t**ion	conse**n**sus
consist**e**nt, consistency	coroll**a**ry	cor**r**espondence
crystal**l**ographic	Dene (*no accents in English*)	descend
desi**cc**ate	de**v**elop	diar**rh**ea
di**ph**theria	di**s**appoint	discern**i**ble
domain (**not** domaine)	dysentery	ec**st**asy
embar**r**ass	exag**g**erate	excerpt

exhilarate	existent, existence	exonerate
exorbitant (not exhorbitant)		Filipino
focus	foreseen	gauge
genealogy	grammar	guerrilla
harass	hemorrhage	hereditary
histogram	honorary	hypocrisy
hypothesis	independent, independence	indispensable
infinitesimal	inoculate	inscribe
insistent, insistence	Inuit	Inuk
iridescent	irrelevant	laboratory
liaison	lightning	liquefy
marshal	measure	medicine
memento	Métis	minuscule
Mississippi	misspell	moccasin
Morocco	naphtha	negotiation
nickel	occasional	occurrence
ophthalmology	paraffin	parallel
pastime	perinatal	permissible
Philippines	polyethylene	polystyrene
polyurethane	possession	precede
preferential	privilege	proceed
pronunciation	ptomaine	quadriplegia
rarefy	recede	recommendation
reminiscent	resistant, resistance	responsible
rheumatism	rhythm	sacrilegious
separate	siege	soybean
spatial	stochastic	supersede
tariff	tendency	thorough
threshold	until	weird
withhold	written	

3.04 SI/metric units

Preferred spellings of terms have been established in National Standard of Canada CAN/CSA-Z234.1-89 for a number of SI/metric units and prefixes: *deca* (not *deka*), *gram* (not *gramme*), *litre* (not *liter*) and *tonne* or *metric ton* (not *metric tonne*).

In two cases the final vowel of a unit prefix is omitted: *megohm* and *kilohm*. In other cases where the unit name begins with a vowel, both vowels are retained.

Note that *meter* is the spelling for a measuring device, while *metre* is the unit of length.

Note also that the singular and plural of the following unit names are identical: *hertz, lux* and *siemens*.

3.05 Homonyms and similar-sounding words

Many words are misspelled because they are confused with similar-sounding and similarly spelled words which, in fact, have a different meaning. In the following list of word pairs (and one group of three), information is given in parentheses to indicate which spelling should be used in a particular context:

3

affect (influence)
effect (*verb*: bring about, result in; *noun*: consequence, impact)

allusion (reference)
illusion (misleading appearance)

all ready (prepared)
already (previously)

ascent (climb)
assent (agreement)

bloc (group of persons, companies or nations)
block (group of things; obstruct; solid piece, etc.)

born (of birth)
borne (carried)

breach (gap; violation)
breech (lower part)

broach (pointed tool or rod; begin to talk about)
brooch (type of jewellery)

canvas (cloth)
canvass (solicit)

capital (city; very significant)
capitol (government building in U.S.A.)

carat (unit of mass for precious stones)
caret (proofreader's mark)
karat (unit used to specify proportion of gold in alloy)

cast (actors; verb meanings)
caste (exclusive social class)

censor (check the morality or acceptability of; person who does this)
censure (criticize, blame; criticism)

chord (music; geometry; engineering)
cord (other uses)

complement (complete; that which completes)
compliment (praise)

councillor (member of a council)
counsellor (adviser; lawyer)

dependant (noun)
dependent (adjective)

discreet (prudent, tactful)
discrete (distinct, separate)

dyeing (colouring)
dying (approaching death)

elicit (draw forth)
illicit (unlawful)

envelop (verb)
envelope (noun)

faze (disturb)
phase (stage, period)

flair (talent)
flare (flame, light)

forbear (hold back)
forebear (ancestor)

foreword (preface)
forward (ahead)

hoard (save up)
horde (crowd)

immanent (inherent)
imminent (about to occur)

inequity (unfairness)
iniquity (sin)

its (belonging to it)
it's (it is)

loath (adjective)
loathe (verb)

loose (set free; untight, etc.)
lose (mislay; forfeit)

mantel (shelf above fireplace)
mantle (cloak, etc.)

mucous (adjective)
mucus (noun)

ordinance (law)
ordnance (military weapons)

pedal (operate levers with feet; activation device)
peddle (sell, hawk)

personal (individual; private)
personnel (staff)

phosphorous (adjective)
phosphorus (noun)

principal (chief, main, leading; school administrator)
principle (rule)

prophecy (noun)
prophesy (verb)

sceptic (one who doubts)
septic (involving putrefaction, sepsis)

stationary (fixed, motionless)
stationery (writing materials)

therefor (for this purpose or thing)
therefore (for that reason, consequently)

troop (soldiers)
troupe (actors, performers)

waive (give up, forego)
wave (move up and down, etc.)

3.06 Words with *ei* and *ie*

The jingle "*i* before *e* except after *c* or when sounded as *a* as in *neighbour* and *weigh*" covers the rule.

Exceptions

either	heifer	neither
foreign	height	seize
forfeit	leisure	sovereign
weird		

3.07 Verbs ending in *sede, ceed* and *cede*

Supersede is the only verb ending in *sede. Exceed, proceed* and *succeed* are the only common verbs ending in *ceed*. Verbs ending in *cede* include the following:

accede	concede	recede
antecede	intercede	secede
cede	precede	

3.08 *Able/ible* and *ative/itive* endings

There is no basic rule for these endings. However, if there is a corresponding word ending in *ation*, the ending is usually *able* or *ative*; if the corresponding word ends in *sion* or *tion* not preceded by *a*, the ending is usually *ible* or *itive*:

affirmation	affirmative
duration	durable
information	informative
competition	competitive
division	divisible
reproduction	reproducible

3.09 Final consonants doubled before a suffix

Double the final consonant before *y* or before a suffix beginning with a vowel in a word of one syllable that ends in a single consonant preceded by a single vowel:

bed	bedded	log	logged
dip	dipped	mad	madden
fat	fatty	rot	rotted
fit	fitted	scrub	scrubbing
flit	flitting	sit	sitting
gum	gummy	stop	stopping

Exceptions

Do **not** double the final consonant in a word of one syllable if the vowel sound is long:

boat	boating
light	lighten
stoop	stooped
read	reading

Note that the preferred plural spelling of the noun *bus* is *buses*.

The final consonant is doubled in words of more than one syllable ending in a single consonant preceded by a single vowel, if the accent is on the last syllable and the suffix begins with a vowel:

acquit	acquittal
commit	committal
occur	occurrence
rebel	rebellion
regret	regretted
transmit	transmitted

Note that there is no doubling of the consonant in *targeted* and *benefited.*

3.10 Words ending in *n*

When the suffix *ness* is added to a word ending in *n*, a double *n* is formed:

even	evenness	keen	keenness
green	greenness	sudden	suddenness

3.11 Combinations with *all*

The final *l* is usually dropped when *all* is used as a prefix:

all together	altogether
all ready	already

(see 3.05 for distinctions in meaning)

but

all right

58

3.12 Words ending in a silent *e*

The final *e* is usually dropped before a suffix beginning with a vowel:

debate	debatable	make	makable
desire	desirable	move	movable
dine	dining	rate	ratable
excite	excitable	sale	salable
like	likable	size	sizable
love	lovable	subdue	subduing

but

age	ageing
mile	mileage

However, when *e* follows *c* or *g* it is retained before the vowels *a* and *o* to preserve the soft sound of these consonants:

change	changeable	**but**	changing
courage	courageous		
gauge	gaugeable	**but**	gauging
knowledge	knowledgeable		
notice	noticeable	**but**	noticing
peace	peaceable		
trace	traceable	**but**	tracing

Note that the *e* is retained even before *i* in some cases in order to distinguish a word from a similarly spelled one or to preserve a particular pronunciation:

dyeing	singeing
shoeing	toeing

but

routing

Words ending in a silent *e* generally retain the *e* before a suffix beginning with a consonant:

complete	completeness
hope	hopeless
waste	wasteful
whole	wholesome

Exceptions

due	duly
subtle	subtly
true	truly
whole	wholly

Abridgment, acknowledgment and *judgment* can be spelled with or without the *e*, but the preferred spelling is as given.

3.13 Words ending in *c*

In words ending in a *c* that has the sound of *k*, add *k* before *e, i* or *y*:

picnic	picnicking
panic	panicky
Quebec	Quebecker
traffic	trafficking

3.14 Verbs ending in *ie*

In verbs ending in *ie*, change *ie* to *y* before *ing*:

die	dying
lie	lying
tie	tying
vie	vying

3.15 Words ending in *y*

In words ending in *y* preceded by a consonant, change the *y* to *i* before a suffix, unless the suffix itself begins with *i*:

heavy	heaviest
lively	livelihood
salary	salaried
necessary	necessarily

but

copyist	flying
denying	trying

Note the distinction between *dryer* (something or someone that dries) and *drier* (the comparative of *dry*).

Words ending in *y* preceded by a vowel generally retain the *y* before a suffix:

annoy	annoyance	annoying
pay	payable	paying

3.16 Words ending in *ise* and *ize*

The following are the only common words ending in *ise*:

advertise	compromise	exercise	premise
advise	demise	franchise	reprise
apprise	despise	guise	revise
arise	devise	improvise	supervise
chastise	disguise	incise	surmise
circumcise	enterprise	merchandise	surprise
comprise	excise	mortise	televise

To this list should be added all words with *wise* as a suffix.

Note that the suffix *ise* cannot be replaced with *ize* in this group.

Use the suffix *ize* for most other words, including *civilize, criticize, italicize, itemize, memorize* and *organize*.

3.17 Plural forms of nouns

Note the following singular and plural forms:

addendum	addenda
alumna	alumnae
alumnus	alumni
analysis	analyses
antenna	antennae (*feelers*)
	or
	antennas (*aerials*)
appendix	appendixes (**or** appendices)
bacterium	bacteria
basis	bases
bureau	bureaus
bus	buses
census	censuses
crisis	crises
criterion	criteria
ellipsis	ellipses
erratum	errata
focus	focuses (**not** focusses, *which is the preferred verb form*)
formula	formulas (**or** formulae)
gas	gases (**not** gasses, *which is the verb form*)
hypothesis	hypotheses
index	indexes (*of a book*)
	or
	indices (*in mathematics, statistics*)
matrix	matrices
medium	mediums **or** media (*check dictionary for plural form to use in a given context*)
memorandum	memorandums (**or** memoranda)
nucleus	nuclei
parenthesis	parentheses
phenomenon	phenomena
plateau	plateaus
surplus	surpluses
symposium	symposiums (**or** symposia)

Many other English words form their plurals irregularly, including some of those ending in *y, o, f* and *fe*.

Chapter Four

Capitalization

4

Capitalization

4.01 Introduction

Capital letters have three basic uses, of which nearly all others may be regarded as particular cases: (1) to give emphasis, as in official titles and initial words: (2) to distinguish proper nouns and adjectives from common ones; and (3) to highlight words in headings and captions.

In English the first letter of certain words is capitalized to give emphasis and to clarify sentence structure and meaning for the reader. This chapter gives rules to define which words require capitals, but editorial practice varies considerably on this subject, depending on the desired degree of formality, the intended readership and the organization's house style.

In order to ensure consistency in your own style, follow the rules below, which apply to most general types of writing, and consult the *Gage Canadian Dictionary*, which gives the upper-case use of many words. Capitalization in specialized documents should be based on professional style guides.

4.02 Initial words

(a) Capitalize the first word of a sentence or sentence equivalent:

> There are no other constraints.
> Come.
> What a pity!
> Why?
> Exit
> All rights reserved

(b) Capitalize the first word of a direct quotation that is itself a complete sentence:

> The candidates said, "We are in favour of a free vote on the death penalty."

Do **not** use the upper case if the quotation is merely a sentence fragment or is worked into the structure of the sentence:

> The candidates said that they were "in favour of a free vote on the death penalty."

In quotations where historical, legal, documentary or scientific accuracy is crucial, reproduce upper-case letters as faithfully as possible.

For more detailed information on quotations, see Chapter 8.

(c) Capitalize the first word of a complete sentence enclosed in parentheses when it stands alone, but **not** when it is enclosed within another sentence:

> The speaker concluded by citing facts and figures to support her contention. (Details may be found on p. 37.)

> **but**

> The increasing scarcity of the species is attributable to overfishing (statistics will be found in the appendix), to acid rain and to other factors outlined in the report.

(d) Capitalize the first word of a direct question within a sentence:

> The question to be asked in every case is this: Does the writer express himself or herself clearly?

Consistently capitalize (or lower-case) parallel sentence fragments used as questions:

> Will farmers be taxed under this plan? Lumberjacks? Trappers?

> Will farmers be taxed under this plan? lumberjacks? trappers?

Do **not** capitalize words that normally introduce questions (*who, why, when, how*) when they stand alone as a verb complement:

> He knew he had to meet the deadline. The question was how.

(e) Capitalize the first word after a colon if it begins a direct question (see 4.02(d) above) or a formal statement, introduces a distinct idea, or is followed by more than one sentence:

> There are several possibilities: For example, the Director General might resign.

> The jury finds as follows: The defendant is guilty as charged on all counts.

> Our position is clear: We will not permit new landfill sites in our region.

> In conclusion, I answer the question asked at the outset: Revenues will be greater this year than in the past three years. However, they will not match expenditures.

See Chapter 7 for further information on use of the colon.

(f) The word following a question mark or exclamation mark may or may not be capitalized, depending on how closely the material it introduces is considered to be related to what precedes:

> What a piece of work is man! how noble in reason! how infinite in faculty!

> Progress where? or, even more fundamentally, progress for whom?

What factors contributed to the decline of Rome? Did the barbarian invasions play a significant part?

(g) Capitalize the first words of truisms and mottoes run into text:

His watchword was Learn to write well, or not to write at all.

Her motto in life is Do unto others . . . before they do unto you.

(h) The personal pronoun *I* and the vocative *O* are always capitalized in English; *oh* is capitalized only when it begins a sentence or stands alone.

(i) The first word of a line of poetry is traditionally capitalized, but some modern poets do not follow this practice. It is therefore best to check the original and respect the poet's preference.

4.03 Personal names

(a) Capitalize proper nouns and epithets that accompany or replace them:

John Diefenbaker   Peter the Great
Margaret Thatcher   the Sun King

(b) When *O'* forms part of a proper noun, it and the first letter after the apostrophe are capitalized:

O'Brien   O'Malley

(c) When the particle *Mc* or *Mac* forms part of a name, the letter *M* is capitalized. Capitalization and spacing of the letters that follow may differ and individual preferences should be respected:

McDonald **or** MacDonald **or** Mac Donald **or** Macdonald

(d) Individual preferences regarding the capitalization and spacing of articles and particles in French or foreign names should also be respected when they can be ascertained.[1] The following are correct forms:

Walter de la Mare   Ethel Vandenberg
John Dos Passos   Cornelius Van Horne
Pierre de Savoye   Paul DeVillers

(e) In the case of historical figures, treatment in English may differ from that in the original language, and no real standard appears to exist. Consistency in treating a particular name (such as *Leonardo da Vinci, Luca della Robbia* or *Vincent van Gogh*) is all that can be aimed for. In some cases, the most familiar form of the name omits the particle entirely:

Beethoven (Ludwig van Beethoven)
Torquemada (Tomás de Torquemada)

---

1. *Anglo-American Cataloguing Rules* is an excellent source of such information.

(f) Capitalize a nickname (a word or phrase used as part of, or instead of, a personal name):

> the Chief
> the Rocket
> the Iron Lady

Similarly, capitalize names of fictitious or anonymous persons, and names used as personifications:

> Johnny Canuck
> Paul Bunyan
> the Caped Crusader
> John Bull

4.04 Words derived from proper nouns

As a general rule, capitalize an adjective derived from a proper noun or a name used adjectivally:

> Canadian whisky   Franciscan friar
> Digby chicken   Newtonian physics

Proper adjectives are associated with the person or place from whose name they are derived. When this association is remote, the adjective becomes common and in most cases no longer takes a capital, as illustrated below:

> bohemian lifestyle   manila envelope
> chinaware   platonic relationship

Verbs derived from proper nouns are also capitalized unless their association with the proper noun is remote:

> Anglicize   Russianize

but

> italicize   vulcanize

Check proper noun derivatives carefully, however. Usage in this regard is not standardized.

4.05 Governments and government bodies

(a) Capitalize the titles of international, national, provincial, state, regional and local governments; the titles of government departments and agencies and their organizational subdivisions; the names of boards, committees and royal commissions; and *the Crown* when it means the supreme governing authority:

> the United Nations
> the Government of Canada
> the Parliament of Canada
> the House of Commons

the Senate of Canada
the Public Service Commission
the Department of Citizenship and Immigration
the Public Affairs Section
the Federal Cultural Policy Review Committee
the Royal Commission on National Development in the Arts, Letters and Sciences

Note that both the legal title and the applied title of a federal department are capitalized:

Department of the Environment   Environment Canada

(b) It is in the use of short forms that the greatest uncertainty arises. Short forms are normally written in lower case when used in a non-specific sense, when preceded by a possessive, demonstrative or other type of adjective, and when used adjectivally or in an adjectival form:

We have formed a committee to study the matter.
Our section held its monthly meeting yesterday.
This division has 60 employees.
The Canadian (federal, provincial, present) government has issued a policy statement.
An interpretation of the departmental rules and regulations is required.
The question of parliamentary procedure was raised.
Unfortunately division practice proscribes such an approach.
The decision was based on government (governmental) policy.

However, when short forms of government bodies stand for the full title and are intended to carry its full force, they are usually capitalized. This style is almost always used in in-house documents:

The Government has adjourned for the summer.
The Minister's message was circulated throughout the Department.

If the short title is a specific term which the organization shares with no other body within the government concerned, that title retains the upper case when used adjectivally:

the question of Senate reform
some House committees

(c) The word *Government* is capitalized when it refers to the political apparatus of a party in power. It is lower-cased when it refers in a general way to the offices and agencies that carry out the functions of governing:

The Liberal Government introduced this measure.
It is government policy not to discuss matters before the courts.

(d) Do **not** capitalize the plural forms of *government, department, division,* etc., even when the full titles of the bodies concerned are given:

> Representatives from the departments of Finance, National Defence and Natural Resources were present.

4.06 Institutions

(a) Capitalize the official names of organized churches (religious denominations, sects, orders) and their adherents, universities, school boards, schools, courts of law, clubs, corporations, unions, alliances, associations, political parties, etc.:

> the Carleton School Board   the Rotary Club
> Lisgar Collegiate Institute   Canadian Airlines International
> the Supreme Court of Canada   the Canadian Medical Association
> the Quebec Superior Court   the New Democratic Party
> the International Court of Justice   the University of Manitoba
> the Opposition (official)   the First Baptist Church

The official capitalization is that used by the institution itself.

(b) The names of administrative subdivisions of these institutions are also capitalized:

> the Department of Political Science
> the Toronto Synod

(c) A generic noun used as a short form of a title is often capitalized, especially in corporate writing:

> the Institute
> the Board
> the Party

(d) Capitalize short forms that use only the specifying element:

This afternoon, Concordia and Western will play in the final.

(e) Do **not** capitalize generic short forms used in a non-specific sense, preceded by a possessive, demonstrative or other type of adjective, or used adjectivally or in an adjectival form:

> The university is our town's major employer.
> Our family attended a Baptist church regularly.
> She tries to attend all board meetings.
> Only strict adherence to the party line was tolerated.
> Every board of education in the province has adjourned for the season.

(f) But, if the short form refers to a specific, unique institution, it retains the upper case when used as a noun or adjectivally:

> The Scouts held a rally over the weekend.
> A city-wide Red Cross blood drive replenished the hospital's supply.

(g) Documents intended for an internal readership often capitalize terms that would be lower-cased in writings of a general nature:

> He worked for the Company for almost forty years.
> The document was forwarded to the Regional Office.

(h) In second and subsequent references, short forms may be treated generically and lower-cased:

> He was invited to address the Second Annual Conference on Biotechnology but declined because the conference was not sufficiently broad in scope.

> She applied for a grant under the External Scholars Program, but only graduate students were eligible under the program.

(i) Do **not** capitalize the plural of common nouns, even when the full titles of the bodies concerned are given:

> He held degrees from the universities of Saskatchewan and Toronto.

> Candidates for the Liberal and Progressive Conservative parties attended the rally.

4.07 Political parties and movements

- Adjectives and nouns referring to the ideas, actions, documents and members of specific political parties, movements and groups are capitalized. Capitalization often helps distinguish these terms from the same words used descriptively:

> a Liberal policy paper (*of the Liberal government or party*)
> New Democrats
> a Progressive Conservative government (*refers to the Progressive Conservative Party*)

> **but**

> the liberal arts
> a conservative on moral issues

- Capitalize the word *party* when it is preceded by the official name of a political party, unless it is used as a generic term:

> He was a member of the Social Democratic Party.
> A new agrarian party was founded at the rally.

- General terms describing political movements and their adherents are lower-cased unless they are derived from proper nouns:

fascism	Marxist
democracy	Thatcherite

4.08 Titles of office or rank

(a) Capitalize civil, military, religious and professional titles and titles of nobility when they precede and form part of a personal name:

Queen Elizabeth II	Professor Layton
Pope John Paul II	General de Chastelain
Lord Carrington	President Clinton
Prime Minister Chrétien	Archbishop Gervais
Finance Minister Paul Martin	

(b) Capitalize all titles following and placed in apposition to a personal name, except those denoting professions:

Clare Smith, Director of Public Affairs
Ron Irwin, Minister of Indian Affairs and Northern Development

but

Jane Tanaka, professor of physics

(c) Capitalize a title referring to a specific person and used as a substitute for that person's name, even if it is a short form:

the President of the Treasury Board
the Chief, Public Affairs Section
the Leader of the Opposition

According to the Assistant Deputy Minister, this is a unique agreement.
They discussed the matter with the Colonel.
The Archbishop made no further comment.

(d) Do **not** capitalize spelled-out titles in the plural or titles preceded by an indefinite article:

the lieutenant-governors of Quebec and Ontario
a member of Parliament

but

the Member for Winnipeg North Centre

(e) Capitalize abbreviated titles in the plural:

We met Profs. Sami and Nicolet.

(f) Do **not** capitalize titles modified by a possessive or other type or adjective, or by an indefinite article:

They discussed it with their colonel.
They discussed it with the former ambassador.
They discussed it with the Canadian prime minister.
They discussed it with a member of Parliament.

(g) Capitalize titles only when they refer to a specific person; do **not** capitalize a term that refers to a role rather than a person:

> As prime minister [*that is, while occupying a certain position*], Lester Pearson introduced the new Canadian flag.
> The production manager [*any person who occupies that position*] assigns schedules.

4

(h) Occupational titles used descriptively are normally followed by a complete personal name. They should **not** be capitalized in writing for general readers, although corporate requirements and the expectations of a specialized readership often result in a more liberal use of capital letters:

> manager Cito Gaston
> production superintendent Anna Chang
> technical writer John Lipon

(i) Do **not** capitalize adjectives derived from titles unless they are part of a title:

> episcopal
> papal
> ministerial correspondence
> presidential prerogative
> Rabbinical College of Telshe

(j) Capitalize titles of respect and forms of address, even when used in the plural:

Your Honour	Mr. Chairman
Your Grace	Their Royal Highnesses
Your Excellencies	Her Worship

4.09 Personifications and abstractions

Capitalize vivid personifications and metonymic nouns:

> the march of Time
> Fate's fool
> the Chair (*the person in charge of a meeting or assembly*)
> the Crown (*the person or agency representing a king or queen*)

Abstractions are sometimes capitalized when used in an ideal sense. As general concepts, however, they are lower-cased:

> We know that Justice is blind.

> Beauty is truth, truth beauty—that is all
> Ye know on earth, and all ye need to know.
> —John Keats

4.10 Family appellations

Capitalize family appellations only when the name of a person follows, when they are unmodified, or when they are used in direct address:

> Grandmother Smith
> Aunt Sarah
> I met Mother at the theatre.
> Tell me, Son, where you have been.

> **but**

> John's grandmother
> This is my aunt, Sarah Vick.

4.11 Races, languages and peoples

Capitalize nouns and adjectives referring to race, tribe, nationality and language:

Caucasian	Indian
Inuk (*plural*: Inuit)	Francophone
Métis	Anglophone
Amerindian	Arabic
Cree	French

Do **not** capitalize the word *allophone*, which refers to a person whose first language is neither English nor French and which is used with specific reference to Quebec.

The form of some words may vary depending on the meaning:

> Highlander (inhabitant of the Scottish Highlands)
> highlander (inhabitant of any highland area)

> Aborigine (one of the indigenous peoples of Australia)
> aborigine (indigenous inhabitant of a region)

> Pygmy (member of a group of African peoples)
> pygmy (small in stature; insignificant)

Capitalize the singular and plural forms of the nouns *Status Indian, Registered Indian, Non-Status Indian* and *Treaty Indian,* as well as the terms *Aboriginal, Native* and *Indigenous* when they refer to Aboriginal people in Canada.

The terms *Aboriginals* and *Natives* are **not** used as proper nouns. When *Aboriginal, Indigenous* and *Native* are used as adjectives, note the following noun forms:

> Aboriginal person (one individual)
> Aboriginal persons, Aboriginal people (more than one person)
> Aboriginal peoples (two or more Aboriginal groups)

Representatives from three Aboriginal peoples were present.
Any Native person in Alberta is eligible under this program.
The conference could not have succeeded without the help of almost a thousand Indigenous people from all over Saskatchewan.

For further information on the representation of Aboriginal (Native) peoples in written communications, see Chapter 14.

4.12 School subjects, courses and degrees

In keeping with 4.11 above, capitalize the names of languages. Do **not** capitalize the names of other disciplines when used in a general sense. Capitalize them when used to refer to school subjects or the names of particular courses:

This university requires French as a prerequisite.
She is interested in history.
He reads articles on economics and biology in his spare time.

but

He passed with a "B" in History this term.
She is taking Chemistry 101 and Economics 406.

Do **not** capitalize the name of a degree in general references, but do capitalize it when it follows a person's name and is written in full:

Janet is earning her master's degree
Ellen Compton, Doctor of Philosophy
He holds a Master of Arts degree from McGill University.

Do **not** capitalize terms designating academic years:

She held two jobs during her senior year.

Capitalize *grade* when followed by a number or letter:

My daughter has completed Grade 6.

4.13 Military terms

Capitalize the names and nicknames of military bases, forces and units of all sizes and of exercises:

the Canadian Forces	450 Helicopter Squadron
Mobile Command	Exercise Rapier Thrust
Canadian Forces Base Trenton	the Blue Berets

Note

In Department of National Defence documents, the specific part of an exercise name is written entirely in upper case, e.g. *Exercise SILENT DEFENDER.*

Use the lower case for general and informal references:

> the Fifth Army

> **but**

> the army

4.14 Modes of transportation

Capitalize the names of types of aircraft, the names of makes of cars and other modes of transportation, and the names of individual ships, locomotives, spacecraft, etc.:

> the Cessna-7
> a Boeing 747
> HMCS *Donnacona* (italics for the name; roman type for the abbreviation)
> the Bricklin
> *Mariner IV*

See 6.07 for further information about the italicization of such names.

4.15 Medals, awards, honours and decorations

Capitalize the official names of professional, academic and military medals, awards, honours and decorations:

> Distinguished Flying Cross   a Nobel Prize winner
> Order of Canada   Governor General's Award
> Nobel Peace Prize   Victoria Cross

Most common-noun short forms are lower-cased:

> No award was given this year.

However, they may be capitalized if the reference is clear:

> The Prize [*Nobel Peace Prize, mentioned in a previous sentence*] was her reward for a lifetime of effort.

4.16 Sporting events and trophies

Capitalize the official and familiar names of major sporting events and trophies:

> the Queen's Plate
> the XXVI Olympiad; the Olympic Games
> the Stanley Cup

Capitalize the short form in subsequent references:

> The second Series game will be played today.
> Her team won the Cup last year as well.

4.17 Time references and historical periods and events

Capitalize the names of months and days, of holidays and holy days, of historical and geological periods and events, and of parliamentary sessions:

Wednesday	the Ice Age
October	the Second World War
Thanksgiving Day	World War II
Passover	the Middle Ages
Christmas	the Gulf War
April Fools' Day	the Pleistocene Epoch
The First Session of	
the Thirty-second Parliament	

Do **not** capitalize the names of the seasons, centuries or decades unless they are personified or are part of special names:

spring
winter
the twentieth century
the fifties

but

the Roaring Twenties (name of an era)
the Winter Palace

Capitalize the names of events recorded in sacred writings and of historical events with a strong religious dimension:

the Flood	the Reformation
the Exodus	the Great Schism
the Immaculate Conception	the Hegira
the Crucifixion	the Diet of Worms
the Crusades	the Second Vatican Council

Terms that refer to events and periods are often capitalized when they refer to specific events or periods and lower-cased when used in a general sense:

the Ice Age	the most recent ice age
the First World War	the two world wars
the Quiet Revolution	She started a revolution.
the Crusades	a crusade against poverty
Stone Age hunting implements	He uses stone-age management techniques.

For the use of capitals with time zones, see 1.22.

4.18 Cultural periods, movements and styles

Capitalize nouns and adjectives designating literary, philosophical, musical, religious and artistic periods, movements and styles when they are derived from proper nouns:

Aristotelian logic	Romanesque architecture
Cartesian dualism	Arianism
the Bauhaus	Methodism
Gregorian chant	Hasidism

Otherwise, such terms are lower-cased except when it is necessary to distinguish a style or movement from the same word used in its general sense:

cubism	the New Criticism
existentialism	the Group of Seven
humanism	the Enlightenment
rococo	Scholasticism

4.19 Terms related to religion

The same principles apply to religious terms as to general vocabulary. Writers should resist the temptation to overcapitalize.

(a) Capitalize most adjectives and verbs derived from the names of organized religions:

Anglican
Roman Catholic
Shiite
Greek Orthodox
Christianize
Free Methodist

but

baptize
baptism
christen

(b) Capitalize the names and titles of holy and revered persons:

The Blessed Virgin	Saint Jerome
Our Lady of Sorrows	Maimonides
Mother Superior	Buddha

(c) Capitalize unique theological concepts:

the Fall	the Nativity
the Flood	the Chosen People
Original Sin	the Holy Grail
the Second Coming	the Holy of Holies

(d) Do **not** capitalize derived terms that are not used in a religious sense:

She is very catholic in her literary tastes.
His ideas are quite orthodox.

(e) Capitalize the titles of religious writings and documents, special prayers and devotional canticles, creeds and confessions:

the Bible	Deuteronomy
the Torah	the Apocrypha
the Koran	the Ten Commandments
the Vulgate	the Talmud

4.20 Deities

(a) Capitalize names, synonyms and personifications of deities and other supernatural beings:

God	Siva
the Creator	Minerva
the Almighty	Moloch
Mother Nature	Allah
Jehovah	Manitou

(b) Do **not** capitalize such words used as common nouns:

The child was an angel.
The adoring public regarded the film star as a god.

(c) Derivatives of these terms are normally lower-cased, as are similar terms used metaphorically:

christen
messianic
a saviour

(d) Capitalize personal pronouns that refer to deities when they are used as proper nouns, but do **not** capitalize relative pronouns:

Trust in Him whose strength will uphold you.

(e) Do **not** capitalize the words *god* and *goddess* when they refer to pagan deities, but capitalize the names of the deities themselves (*Baal, Woden, Zeus*).

(f) Do **not** capitalize words such as *heaven, paradise, purgatory, nirvana, happy hunting ground, devil* and *angel* when used in a non-religious sense:

After his wife died he went through purgatory.
War is hell.

but

God is in Heaven.
Many Buddhists seek to attain Nirvana.

4.21 Geographical terms

(a) Capitalize the names of countries, regions, counties, cities and other official and specified political, administrative and geographical divisions and topographical features:

El Salvador
the Northern Hemisphere
the International Boundary
the Prairies
the Canadian Shield
the Maritimes
the Atlantic provinces
the Ontario Region (sector of government department)
the Crow's Nest Pass

the Grassy Narrows Reserve
the Pacific
Lanark County
Sherbrooke
Pickle Lake
Elm Street West
the Okanagan Valley
the South Saskatchewan River
the Northwest Territories

(b) Capitalize a generic term when it is an accepted short form of the proper noun:

the Continent   the States

(c) Do **not** capitalize a generic term such as *city, county, state* or *province* when it precedes the proper noun or stands alone, unless it is used in a corporate sense:

She lives in the city of Regina. (*place*)
I have travelled all over the province of Ontario. (*place*)
The states of Switzerland are called cantons.
the newly created state of Palestine

but

Buy Province of Ontario bonds. (*provincial government*)
The City of Regina took him to court. (*municipal government*)
The State of New York has revamped its social assistance programs.
    (*state government*)

(d) Do **not** capitalize a generic term used in the plural unless it is part of a geographical name:

lakes Huron and Ontario
the Thompson and Fraser rivers

but

the Rocky Mountains
the South Seas

(e) In general, do **not** capitalize the names of compass points or similar descriptive terms unless they have taken on political or other connotations or form the titles of administrative regions:

northern New Brunswick
the west of Saskatchewan

but

the West
Western values
the Far North
the Eastern Townships
Northern Ireland

(f) Some terms are capitalized when they refer to specific regions and lower-cased when used descriptively:

the East Coast **but** the east coast of Nova Scotia
Arctic Ocean **but** arctic conditions

4.22 Buildings, monuments and public places

Capitalize the official names of specific buildings, monuments, squares, parks, etc.:

the National Gallery	Robson Square
the Peace Bridge	the O'Keefe Centre
the Plains of Abraham	the Brock Monument
the Toronto Public Library	St. Andrew's Church
the Vancouver International Airport	the Temple of Cheops

Do **not** capitalize words describing these features when they are used generically, in names that are not official, or in plural forms:

the city's war memorial
the international bridge
an Anglican church
an Egyptian temple
Yonge and Bay streets
the Vancouver airport

4.23 Astronomical terms

Capitalize the names of planets and other astronomical bodies and configurations. Capitalize *earth, sun* and *moon* only when they are mentioned in relation to other planets or heavenly bodies:

Venus
the Great Bear
The sun shines brightly.
Mercury is closer than the Earth to the Sun.

Do **not** capitalize generic words forming part of the name of a celestial object:

Halley's comet
the rings of Saturn

4.24 Biological terms

Capitalize the scientific name of a phylum, order, class, family or genus, but **not** common names or the epithets referring to a species or subspecies, even if they are derived from proper names:

> the phylum Arthropoda
> the order Rosales
> the genus *Sporotrichum*
> the species *Sporotrichum schenkii* (second word denotes species)
> The jaguar and the lion are members of the family Felidae.

See 6.11 for rules governing the italicization of biological classifications.

Capitalize proper nouns modifying a common name, except where usage has established the lower case:

> Grayson lily   Cupid's-delight
> Queen Anne's lace   Judas tree
> Canada goose   Dutch elm
>
> **but**
>
> malpeque oyster   timothy grass

4.25 Chemical, medical and pharmacological terms

In text, do **not** capitalize the names of chemical elements and compounds:

> krypton
> sodium bicarbonate
> hydrogen peroxide

The capitalization of chemical symbols should follow standard practice:

> H_2O
> $NaHCO_3$

Do **not** capitalize the names of conditions, syndromes and the like, but capitalize a personal name that forms part of such a term:

> diabetes insipidus
> Down syndrome
> Huntington's chorea

Capitalize the names of infectious organisms but **not** the names of conditions based upon such names:

> People attacked by *Salmonella* are likely to suffer from salmonellosis.

Do not capitalize the generic names of drugs:

> phenobarbital
> sulfasalazine

4.26 Scientific names with eponyms

In scientific terms composed of a common noun preceded by a proper noun, an adjective derived from a proper noun, or a proper noun with an apostrophe *s*, capitalize the adjective or proper noun but **not** the common noun. Do **not** capitalize the names of laws or theories or the names of minerals, particles or elements derived from personal names:

Hodgkin's disease	Becquerel rays
Reiter's syndrome	Gaussian curve
Bohr radius	Ohm's law

but

the general theory of relativity
the second law of thermodynamics
forsterite
boson
germanium

Note that certain personal names begin with a small letter:

van't Hoff equation
van Willebrand disease

4.27 Copyrighted names

Capitalize trade names of drugs and any other manufactured products unless they have become established as common nouns:

Plexiglas	Tylenol
Valium	Prozac

but

styrofoam	nylon

To determine proper usage, check the *Canadian Trade Index* or your dictionary.

Some industries, especially in the high-technology field, use capital letters within the name of a product. The names of all such terms and products, including those of computer languages, should be capitalized according to the manufacturer's preference:

WordPerfect
VisiCalc
Pascal
COBOL
BASIC

Wherever possible, do **not** use trade names as generic nouns or adjectives. For example, write *adhesive tape*, not *Scotch tape*. Some words, such as *frisbee* and *realtor*, are commonly used as generic terms, but they are in fact copyrighted. The word *Aspirin* is trademarked (and capitalized) in Canada, but not in the United States.

4.28 SI/metric units

Capitalize only the word *Celsius* when writing the names of SI/metric units in full. When using symbols, capitalize all those based on personal names and the letter *L* for *litre:*

30 m (metres)	12 V (volts)
475 g (grams)	30 L (litres)

Capitalize the symbols for the prefixes from *mega* to *exa.* The symbols for the others remain in lower case. Consistency is important here because the letters *m* and *p* are both used in symbols for two different prefixes:

mg (milligram)	Mg (megagram)
pm (picometre)	Pm (petametre)

See also 1.23.

4.29 Publications and works of art

In English titles of books, articles, periodicals, newspapers, plays, operas and long musical compositions and recordings, poems, paintings, sculptures and motion pictures, capitalize all words except articles, conjunctions of fewer than four letters, and prepositions of fewer than four letters. These exceptions are also capitalized when they immediately follow a period, colon or dash within a title and when they are the first or last word in a title:

book	*Virginia Woolf: A Biography*
book	*Under the Volcano*
book	*To Kill a Mockingbird*
book	*How to Succeed in Business Without Really Trying*
painting	*Rain in the North Country*
film	*Goin' Down the Road*
opera	*The Magic Flute*

Words that are normally prepositions are capitalized when they help form another part of speech:

Getting By While Getting On
Guide to On-Reserve Housing

In short titles, capitalize words that would be capitalized in full titles:

Appleton's General Guide to the United States and Canada, Illustrated With Railway Maps, Plans of Cities, and Table of Railway and Steamboat Fares, for the Year 1891 (full title)

Appleton's Guide for 1891 (short form)

I read about it in the *News.*

Even if some words appear in all capital letters on the title page, capitalize only initial letters, except in specialized bibliographies that must reflect the original typography.

Titles of ancient manuscripts are capitalized, even if the titles were assigned in modern times:

> the Dead Sea Scrolls
> Codex Alexandrinus

See the Appendix for capitalization of titles in French.

4

In titles containing hyphenated compounds, always capitalize the first element. Capitalize the second element if it is a proper noun or proper adjective or if it is as important as the first element:

> *A History of Eighteenth-Century Literature*
> *Anti-Americanism in Latin America*

4.30 Parts of a book or document

(a) Capitalize references to specific parts of a document. These include certain common nouns in the singular when they are used in text references with numbers or letters indicating place, position or major division in a sequence. Capitalize a letter following such a term:

Act II	Figure 7
Appendix B	Plate 4
Chapter 3	Scene iii
Chart 2	Table 3
Corollary 1	Theorem 3
Exhibit A	Volume 13

(b) Do **not** capitalize minor subdivisions such as *page, note, line, paragraph* and *verse:*

> See page 6, line 48.

(c) Do **not** capitalize *section* when used for part of a law or set of regulations, but capitalize it if it refers to a large subdivision of a report, book or other document:

> under section 23 of the Act
> Volume 10, Section 5

(d) Do **not** capitalize words referring to parts of a book when they are used in a general sense, are preceded by modifiers, or are in plural forms:

> The theory will be discussed in the next chapter.
> The appendixes outline other migration patterns.
> Even Miller's extensive bibliography is not complete.

(e) Capitalize cross-references within a book when they refer to a particular section:

> Further readings are listed in the Bibliography.
> See the Appendix for urban statistics.

(f) Informal references to chapter and topic titles may be capitalized and written without italics or quotation marks:

> His topics included Northern Travel, Survival on the Road, and Basic Maintenance.

See also 1.12.

4.31 Headings

In headings that begin at the margin, capitalize only the first word and any other words that require capitals in their own right. In centred headings, capitalize all words except for articles (unless they begin the heading) and any conjunctions or prepositions of fewer than four letters. Prepositions that are an inseparable part of the verb should also be capitalized.

For further information, see 11.16.

4.32 Terms indicating time or numbered sequence

Capitalize common singular nouns and abbreviations followed by a date, number or letter to denote time or sequence, or for the purpose of reference:

> It's Day 15 of the election campaign.
> The shortest route from Toronto to Montréal is along Highway 401.

Some idiomatic expressions containing common nouns followed by a letter or number are also capitalized. The numbers in such expressions are often spelled out:

> Back to Square One.
> He's on Cloud Nine.

4.33 Lists

Point-form lists make it easier for the reader to understand how the elements are related. Grammar and syntax determine the internal capitalization and punctuation of the initial letters of items in lists. It is more important for lists to be logically understandable and syntactically consistent than to look alike.

If the lead-in to a list is syntactically related to the points that follow, as in this list,

- do **not** capitalize the first words of items within the list, and

- except for the bullets or dashes, punctuate as if the entire sentence were not in point form.

Items in lists are sometimes capitalized. This list illustrates one possible set of conditions:

- It is made up of complete sentences, which do not depend on the lead-in sentence fragment and which end with a period.

- It contains points that are more easily grasped separately than together.

Incomplete sentences or single words entered as points in lists are normally lower-cased:

> Four issues are related to the economics of healthy housing:
> –affordability
> –adaptability
> –viability for the construction industry
> –marketability

Note that there is no period at the end of the list.

See also 7.70.

4.34 Legal usage

(a) Some common nouns referring to parties to an action, the names of documents or judicial bodies are capitalized:

> Counsel for the Plaintiff
> The Court (*meaning* the Judge) sustained the objection.
> the said Notary
> the aforementioned Agreement
>
> **but**
>
> The court was in session.

(b) Capitalize the official names of treaties, agreements, legal codes, pieces of legislation and other official documents, as well as their official short forms:

> the Treaty of Versailles
> the Financial Administration Act
> the White Paper on Taxation
> Order-in-Council P.C. 1354

(c) Short forms are normally capitalized only when they constitute proper nouns or refer to a document of great significance:

> An appeal was launched under the Charter (*full name*: Canadian Charter of Rights and Freedoms).

Do **not** capitalize short forms when they are used in a general sense, as adjectives or plurals, or with modifiers:

> Farmers objected to some of the treaty provisions.
> Parliament discussed the new white papers before it adjourned.
> Under this act, a subsidy was offered to transportation companies.

(d) Do **not** capitalize general references to pending and defeated legislation:

> Parliament is discussing a new privacy act.

4.35 The salutation and complimentary close

Use capitals for the first word and all nouns in the salutation of a letter, but only for the first word in a close:

> My dear Sir   Yours truly
> Dear Madam   Very sincerely yours

4.36 Compounds

A proper noun or adjective in a hyphenated compound retains the capital:

> Greco-Roman   neo-Nazi
> trans-Canada   Pan-American

In general, do **not** capitalize prefixes or suffixes added to proper nouns:

> The President-elect will tour the mid-Atlantic States in an American-made car.

Do **not** capitalize the second element of a compound if it simply modifies the first or if the hyphenated elements make up a single word:

> Sonata in E-flat Major
> Re-education for development
> Forty-second Street

4.37 The definite article

Capitalize *the* when it is part of a corporate name:

> *The Globe and Mail*
> The Pas
> The Canadian Red Cross Society

Do **not** capitalize *the* when it is used adjectivally:

> The Minister answered the *Globe and Mail* reporter.

The French definite article should be retained if it is part of a corporate name, and *the* should not precede it. If the French article is not part of the official title, replace it with *the*:

> an article in *Le Devoir*
>
> **but**
>
> a representative of the Office des professions du Québec

4.38 Single letters used as words

Capitalize a single letter used as a word, whether hyphenated or not:

C minor	U-turn
H-bomb	vitamin A
T-shirt	X-ray

4

Chapter Five

Numerical expressions

5

Numerical Expressions

5.01 Introduction

Numerical information should be conveyed in such a way as to be understood quickly, easily and without ambiguity. For this reason, numerals are preferred to spelled-out forms in technical writing. Except in certain adjectival expressions (see 5.05) and in technical writing, write out one-digit numbers and use numerals for the rest. Ordinals should be treated in the same way as cardinal numbers, e.g. *seven* and *seventh*, *101* and *101st*.

Many other factors enter into the decision whether to write numbers out or to express them in numerals. This chapter discusses the most important of these and presents some of the conventions governing the use of special signs and symbols with numerals. The rules stated should, in most cases, be regarded as guidelines for general use that may be superseded by the requirements of particular applications.

5.02 Round numbers

- Write out numbers used figuratively:

    a thousand and one excuses
    They may attack me with an army of six hundred syllogisms.
    　　　　　　　　　　　　　　　—Erasmus
    And torture one poor word ten thousand ways.
    　　　　　　　　　　　　　　　—Dryden

- Numbers in the millions or higher should be written as a combination of words and figures:

    23 million　　　　　3.1 million

    There were more than 2.5 million Canadians between the ages of 30 and 40 in 1971.

- When such compound numbers are used adjectivally, insert hyphens between the components (see 5.05):

    a 1.7-million increase in population

- Whether or not it is used adjectivally, the entire number (numeral and word) should appear on the same line.

- Numbers with a long succession of zeros should normally be rewritten. Thus *2.6 million* is preferable to *2 600 000*.

- Numbers are normally rounded to no more than three significant digits. Thus *2 653 000* becomes *2.65 million*, not *2.653 million*.

- The proper form for large numbers that must be written in full is as illustrated:

    one hundred and fifty-two thousand three hundred and five

- The practice of writing a number in numerals and then repeating it in full in parentheses should be reserved for legal documents:

    nineteen hundred and ninety-six (1996)

5.03 Consistency

Numbers modifying the same or similar items should be treated alike within a given passage. If numerals are to be used for any, they should be used for all:

> Of the firm's 318 outlets currently operating in Atlantic Canada, only 6 accept more than two major credit cards.

> Out of a population of 74 000 000, only 360 000 voted for the Socialist candidate.

> the 3rd, 6th and 127th items in the series

Where many numbers occur in close succession, as in scientific, technical or financial documents, express all of them in numerals.

5.04 Initial numbers

- Spell out a number—or the word *number*—when it occurs at the beginning of a sentence, as well as any related numbers that closely follow it:

    Three hundred persons were expected, but only twenty-three showed up.

    Number 6 was the last in the series; there was no number 7.

Where this would result in a cumbersome construction, recast the sentence. The first sentence above could be rewritten as

> A crowd of 300 was expected, but only 23 showed up.

- To avoid starting with a number, it may be possible to end the preceding sentence with a semicolon or to punctuate in some other manner. Instead of writing

    But that was now in the past. 1994 was another year.

you could insert a semicolon after *past* or write ". . . in the past, and 1994 . . . ."

- In accordance with 5.10, a number followed by a unit of measurement may have to be written in numerals. Thus, to avoid using numerals at the start of a sentence, rewrite

    18.3 cm/s was the best result we could obtain.

as

    A result of 18.3 cm/s was the best we could obtain.

    not

    Eighteen point three . . .

5.05 Adjectival expressions and juxtaposed numbers

- Normally, for numbers used in adjectival expressions, follow the rule given in 5.01, i.e. write out those from one to nine and use numerals for the rest:

    seven hour day
    two-metre-wide entrance
    a 10-year-old boy

- If the unit is represented by an abbreviation or symbol, use numerals (see 1.23):

    a 2.36 m high jump
    three 5-L containers

    or

    three 5 L containers

- Do **not** use a hyphen between a numeral and a non-letter symbol:

    a 90° angle
    four 100°C thermometers

- When a number immediately precedes a compound modifier containing another number, spell out the first or the smaller number:

ten 34-cent stamps	15 one-litre jugs
two 10-room houses	120 eight-page reports

5.06 Mathematical usage

Use numerals for numbers treated as nouns in mathematical usage:

multiply by 3	factor of 2	14 plus 6

Algebraic expressions used in association with units of measurement should be distinguished from the latter by means of italics, unless the units are written in full:

    3ab metres **or** $3ab$ m

5.07 Ratios

The usual forms are:

> 1 to 4 **or** 1:4
> 1:3:4 (1 to 3 to 4)
> 3:19::12:76 (3 is to 19 as 12 is to 76)

Certain types of ratios may be re-expressed as percentages or decimals. For example, *a slope of 1:10* (or *a slope of 1 in 10*) may be written as *a 10% slope*.

5.08 Fractions

In non-technical writing, spell out simple fractions, especially when used in isolation:

> half of one percent
> half an inch **or** one-half inch
> a quarter of an inch **or** one-quarter inch
> three quarters of an inch **or** three-quarters inch (**not** inches)
> three-quarter length

When a fraction is used adjectivally, place a hyphen between the numerator and the denominator unless either of these elements is itself hyphenated:

> four-fifths inch
> a three-quarters majority

Fractions such as the last two, which lend themselves to confusion, are better expressed in numerals.

For the use of hyphens with fractions, see 2.11.

It is incorrect to use *th* or *ths* after fractions expressed in numerals:

> 1/25 **not** 1/25th
> 3/100 **not** 3/100ths

A fraction expressed in numerals should not be followed by *of a* or *of an*:

> 3/8 inch **not** 3/8 of an inch

If the sentence seems to require *of a*, the fraction should be spelled out.

Mixed numbers (combinations of a whole number and a fraction) should be given in numerals:

> $2^3/_4$ **but** time and a half for overtime

5.09 Decimal fractions

In technical and statistical writing and with SI/metric units, decimals are preferred to fractions. Normally, no number should begin or end with a decimal point. A zero is written before the decimal point of numbers smaller than 1, while in whole numbers the decimal point should either be dropped or be followed by a zero:

> $0.64 **not** $.64
> 11 **or** 11.0 **not** 11.

Exceptions

> a .39 calibre revolver
> .999 fine gold

See also 5.16.

Zeros may be used to indicate the number of decimal places to which a value is significant: *0.60* implies significance to two decimal places, *0.600* to three.

Note 1
In many countries the decimal marker is the comma, not the period. In Canada, however, the period is the generally used decimal marker in English-language texts.

Note 2
The *Canadian Metric Practice Guide* (CAN/CSA-Z234.1-89) of the Canadian Standards Association specifies that groups of three numerals (triads) shall be separated by a space, except in the case of monetary values. It advises against the use of commas as separators. Although both commas and spaces are still widely used in Canada, *The Canadian Style* recommends that, except in financial documents, a space be used instead of a comma. Such a space is also to be inserted after groups of three digits to the right of a decimal point. Note that numbers of four digits only (on either side of the decimal marker) need not be so spaced unless used in combination with other numbers of more than four digits. The following examples illustrate the correct use of the space to separate triads of numbers:

whole numbers	decimals
5005 **or** 5005	5.0005 **or** 5.000 5
50 005	5.000 05
500 005	5.000 005
500 005 000	5.000 005 000

Omit the space in pagination, inclusive numbers, addresses, numbering of verse, telephone numbers, library numbers, serial numbers and the like.

5.10 Quantities and measures

(a) When quantities or measures consist of two or more elements, when they are used in a technical context, or when a decimal marker is involved, write them in numerals. Otherwise, follow the rule of writing the number out if it is less than 10 (see 5.01):

> three miles
> 5.6 km
> 20/20 vision

a magnification of 50 **or** a 50× magnification
two metres tall
1.6 m tall **not** 1 m 60 cm tall
six feet tall
5 feet 11 inches tall (*no comma between elements*)
8$\frac{1}{2}$ by 11 inch paper **or** 8$\frac{1}{2}$ × 11 inch paper
50 cm × 75 cm × 2 m (*unit repeated to avoid ambiguity*)

(b) Use of the International System of units (SI) is now the norm in technical writing. Basic information about SI symbols and their use is found in Chapter 1 of this guide. For more detailed information, consult the *Canadian Metric Practice Guide.*

As noted in 1.23, SI usage requires either that both the number and the unit be written in full or that both be abbreviated:

two metres **or** 2 m

not

2 metres **or** two m

Prefixed units should not normally appear as denominators in expressions of the form *g/cm³*, which should be re-expressed in terms of cubic metres. An exception to this rule is the symbol *kg*, since the kilogram is considered the base unit of mass.

(c) When one type of unit is converted to another in non-technical work, the converted value should normally be rounded to within five percent of the initial numeral and should be preceded by the word *about* or some other indication that the value is an approximation:

5 lb. or about 2.3 kg

(d) Note the following conventions for using the degree symbol:

40°   40 proof
30°–50°C (*symbol repeated*) **but** 30±2°C
10–15°C
−10 to −15°C **not** °10−15°C
10°C   10.5°C
300 K **not** 300°K
10° (*of arc*)
10.5° **or** 10.°5 **or** 10°30′ **or** 10°30′00″
36°N lat.   36th parallel
mm/degree **not** mm/° (° *not to be used alone in denominator*)

See 1.17 for use of the term *percent* and the percent sign.

5.11 Money

Sums of money are usually expressed in numerals, except when they refer to round or indefinite amounts or are used in a formal or legal context:

$5.98/m²   a few thousand dollars
a fare of 75¢   a twenty-dollar bill

Payments shall be made in equal instalments of two hundred and thirty dollars per month.

Use the following forms:

65¢ **or** $0.65 **or** 65 cents

not

$.65 **or** .65¢

two million dollars **or** $2 million **or** $2 000 000 **or** $2,000,000[1]
a two-million dollar loan

$100

not

$100. **or** $100.00 (*when standing alone*)

five dollars **or** $5

not

5 dollars

$5 worth **or** five dollars' worth

The abbreviations *B* for billion, *M* for *million* and *K* for *thousand* are often encountered, especially in newspaper headlines. Avoid them in formal writing. Note that there is no space between the numeral and the letter:

Foreign aid reduced by $5B in budget

When dollar amounts are used with SI symbols, the following forms are required:

$11.50/m²

not

$11.50/square metre

$3.99/kg

not

3.99/kilogram **or** $3.99/kilo

98¢/L

not

98¢ per litre

---

1. See 5.09, Note 2

Place the dollar sign before the numeral in question.

For representation of dollar amounts in Canadian and other currencies, see 5.26.

5.12 Representation of time in ordinary prose and with SI units

Except in descriptive text and in approximations, write the time of day in numerical form:

The program will be broadcast at 8:05 p.m.

but

He said that he would call after ten o'clock.

In a scientific or technical context, express precise measurements of elapsed time by means of the internationally recognized symbols of time *d* for *day*, *h* for *hour*, *min* for *minute* and *s* for *second*:

7 h 20 min flying time
The test run took 1 d 3 h 43 min 09 s precisely.

These symbols should also be used when units of time are expressed with SI units:

16 km/d	16 m/s
10 J/h	60 r/min

5.13 Representation of time of day

In documents presented in both official languages, and in all forms of international communication, it may be desirable to use the 24-hour system for representing time of day, in accordance with International Standard ISO 3307 and the Treasury Board *Federal Identity Program Manual*.

The hour is represented by a two-digit number ranging from 00 up to 23 (or 24), the minute and second are represented by a two-digit number ranging from 00 up to 59, and the colon is used as a separator between hour and minute and between minute and second, as illustrated:

24-hour representation

with seconds	without seconds
00:15:00	00:15
08:00:00	08:00
12:00:00	12:00 (noon)
24:00:00	24:00 (midnight)
07:15:00	07:15
11:37:00	11:37
14:12:26	14:12

Note

The instant of midnight should be represented (when seconds are included) as either 24:00:00, the end of one day, or 00:00:00, the beginning of the next day, according to circumstances.

5.14 Dates

For calendar dates, the common alphanumeric method remains acceptable, provided that cardinal numbers are used:

March 15, 1993 **or** 15 March 1993

not

March 15th, 1993 **or** March fifteenth, 1993

When the *day and month only* are given, cardinal or ordinal forms may be used:

recommended	not recommended
August 17	
August 17th	
the 17th of August	17 August
the seventeenth of August	

Note also the usage

He was on holiday from September 20 to 25 inclusive.

not

from September 20–25.

For the use of the comma in dates, see 7.20.

The all-numeric form of dating may be more appropriate for such purposes as office memorandums and chronological files and on documents such as certificates, forms and plaques that are presented in both official languages. The format prescribed below is in accordance with the Treasury Board *Federal Identity Program Manual*, National Standard of Canada CAN/CSA-Z234.4-87 and International Standard ISO 2014. The year, month and day should be separated by a space or hyphen, as illustrated:

1994 03 27 **or** 1994-03-27 (March 27, 1994)
1995 06 02 **or** 1995-06-02 (June 2, 1995)

The advantage of international standardization in this format is that, whereas *2/06/95* could mean either *June 2, 1995* or *February 6, 1995*, the form *1995-06-02* can mean only the former.

Dates are sometimes spelled out in cases such as the following:

the Fourth of July
during the seventies
He returned on the ninth of August. (*reported speech*)
I last saw him on November 11. By the morning of the twelfth he was dead.

Dates are spelled out in legal texts and in formal invitations and announcements:

Mr. and Mrs. Walter and Mary Chute
are pleased to announce
the marriage of their daughter
Janet Elizabeth
to
Donald Eric MacLeod
Saturday the tenth of October
nineteen hundred an ninety-six

Year designations take the following forms:

the class of '68
the 1880s
1300 BC
AD 1300

5.15 Age

Exact age is usually indicated in numerals, even if less than 10:

Jane, aged 9, and her brother Tom, 10, led the hike.

It is written out, however, in the case of approximate age and in formal contexts:

He's eighty if he's a day.
She was no more than seventeen at the time.
On the occasion of her retirement at the age of sixty-five.

5.16 Market quotations

Market quotations are invariably given in numerals:

wheat at 2.30
sugar, .05 **or** sugar, 0.05
Preferred stocks sell at 245.
Fastbuck Fortunes 5s at $17\frac{1}{4}$

5.17 Votes, scores, etc.

Give votes, scores and odds in numerals:

The vote was 51 to 3, with 6 abstentions.
The justices ruled 5 to 3 in his favour.
The Flames beat the Canucks 3 to 2 (3–2) in overtime.
The Netherlands was made favourite at 2 to 1.

5.18 Governmental, military and historical designations

(a) Write out numbers of dynasties, governing bodies, and sessions of Parliament or Congress as ordinals:

First International	Twenty-fourth Dynasty
Third Reich	Thirty-second Parliament
Fifth Republic	Ninety-seventh Congress

(b) Write out ordinal numbers below 100 designating political and administrative divisions:

Fifth Ward	Twenty-second District
Tenth Circuit Court	Fifteenth Precinct

(c) Designations of large military units, especially in a foreign or historical context, may be written out in ordinals; otherwise use cardinal numerals:

Sixth Fleet	First Canadian Army
5 Combat	422 Tactical
Engineer Regiment	Helicopter Squadron

(d) Write out numbers in historical, biblical or formal references:

the Thirteen Colonies	the Twelve Apostles
the Ten Commandments	the Third World

5.19 Names of organizations

Ordinals modifying the names of churches and religious bodies are usually written out:

First Baptist Church
Seventh-Day Adventists
First Church of Christ Scientist

Use Arabic figures in referring to union locals, fraternal lodges and similar organizations:

Teamsters Union Local 91
Loyal Order of Moose 1765
Royal Canadian Legion, Stittsville Branch 618

5.20 Numbers used as nouns

Use numerals when numbers are referred to as nouns:

Highway 3
Channel 3
Grade 4
Bulletin No. 40
Revolution No. 9
values of 0 and 1
Engine No. 9 is arriving on Track 3.
Air Canada Flight 67 now boarding at Gate 6.

5.21 Addresses

Street and avenue designations up to and including *Tenth* are usually spelled out, especially when this helps to prevent confusion with the building number. If the street name is written in numerals, modern usage tends to favour cardinal rather than ordinal numbers:

    9511 TENTH AVENUE   96 AVE   101 ST

In abbreviated form, apartment or suite numbers are written before the building number and are often followed by an en dash:

    107–6807 92 AVE N

Identify floors of a building as follows:

    Floor 11
    L'Esplanade Laurier

5.22 Reference numbers

Page numbers are usually written in Arabic numerals, but in prefatory material they may be written as lower-case Roman numerals:

    page vii of the Foreword
    page 7 of the Introduction

Within the body of the text, volume numbers may be indicated by Arabic or Roman numerals or be spelled out. Numbers of chapters and other major divisions of a book may be spelled out, but are more often written in Roman or Arabic numerals—the tendency being away from Roman numerals in the case of both chapter and volume numbers. Verse numbers and those of minor divisions of a book are written as Arabic numerals:

    I Kings 9:1–4
    Volume 18, Section 8

Paragraphs may be numbered 1, 2, . . . ; clauses within paragraphs, 1), 2), ... Groups of paragraphs may be numbered with Roman numerals. In citations from legislation and the like, numbers and letters designating parts of a section should be enclosed in parentheses, with no space between them:

    section 123(4)(*b*)(ii)

See also 4.30.

5.23 Plurals

Plurals of numerals are usually formed by adding an *s*:

    the 1960s
    five 55s
    The bonds are $4\frac{1}{2}$ s.
    Korolev scored 9.85s on the floor and pommel horse exercises.

In cases where this might cause misreading, add an apostrophe and *s* or italicize the numerals:

> Her performance earned her three 5.8's.
> His 5's look like 6's.
> His *5*s look like *6*s.

Whichever practice is adopted, consistency should be maintained in any one document.

Do **not** pluralize SI/metric symbols:

> 5 kg **not** 5 kgs

5.24 Comparative and inclusive numbers

(a) For general comparisons note the following:

> five times as great   **not**   five times greater
> one fifth as large   **not**   five times smaller

Note that "a four-to-one margin" is meaningless; "a margin of three" is correct.

(b) Consecutive numbers are joined by *or* or *and*, except where intermediate quantities are possible:

> rows 5 and 6
>
> **but**
>
> a range of 5 to 6
>
> **rather than**
>
> a range of 5 or 6

In references to successive pages, *p. 15, 16* indicates matter that is disconnected in the two pages, whereas *pp. 15–16* indicates that the subject is continuous from the first page to the second.

(c) Opinions differ on the proper forms for inclusive numbers written as numerals. To ensure clarity, abbreviate second numbers according to the following principles.

Repeat all digits in numbers below 100:

> 4–10   67–68   82–99

Repeat all digits where the first number is 100 or a multiple of 100:

> 100–138   700–706   1900–1901

Where the first number is in the range 101–109, in multiples of 100, use the changed part only and omit unnecessary zeros:

> 10–39   808–18   1007–8

Where the first number is in the range 110–199, in multiples of 100, use two or more digits, as needed:

435–37   1986–87   3740–75

With numbers of four digits, use all digits if three of them change:

1889–1915

Note the following special cases:

899–900 (*second digit with even hundred*)
398–396 BC (*all digits repeated in years BC*)

5.25 Roman numerals

Roman numerals are becoming increasingly rare, but they still have the following uses:

- names of rulers, aristocrats, and the names of ships, racing cars and space vehicles:

    Charles IV   *Bluenose II*
    Pius XII   *Apollo XIII*

- numbers of volumes, chapters, tables, plates, acts and other divisions of a book or play (now often replaced with Arabic numerals):

    Psalm XXIII
    Volume XII
    Appendix III
    Act II, Scene iii *(act number in upper case, scene number in lower case)*
    Iliad xi.26

- Government of Canada Statutes:

    Schedule IV
    Part III

- years, centuries and recurring events of major importance:

    MCMLXLV *(in very formal contexts)*
    XIX century (**or** 19th century)
    XXIII Olympiad

Do **not** use ordinal forms (*st, nd, th,* etc.) with Roman numerals.

Lower-case Roman numerals may be used for page numbers in preliminary matter (preface, foreword, table of contents, etc.), subclauses and subordinate classifications in a series.

Note that a bar over a letter in a Roman numeral multiplies its value by 1000:

$\overline{D}$ = 500 000 $\overline{V}$ = 5000

5.26 Other considerations

Clarity should be the primary consideration when communicating numerical information. Present it in such a way that it will be readily grasped by the reader. When writing for non-Canadians, make sure you are aware of the conventions used in the target country. Europeans, for example, who are steeped in the metric system, do not confine themselves as we usually do to multiples of 1000. They will more naturally write *3 dL* (decilitres) than *300 mL* or *0.3 L*. Material written for the European market should conform to this practice.

Remember, too, that in Europe—and in Quebec—*1,500* means "one and a half", and *1.500* means "fifteen hundred." The British "billion" is the equivalent of the American "trillion," while a British "trillion" is a million million million. In certain circumstances it may be advisable to write a *thousand million* or *10^9* or *giga-* instead of *billion*, and a *million million* or *10^{12}* or *tera-* instead of *trillion*, to avoid the risk of misinterpretation. For similar reasons, the abbreviation *ppb* (parts per billion) should not be used. Rewrite *100 ppb* as *0.1 ppm*.

Dollar amounts in different currencies should be distinguished from one another by some easily understood marker. A reference to $20 will be ambiguous to a non-Canadian reader and may be taken to refer to American or some other currency. No single system is universally accepted, but the following is the one used by the Department of Finance and the International Monetary Fund:

C$20	for Canadian dollars
US$20	for American dollars
A$20	for Australian dollars
NZ$20	for New Zealand dollars

If greater clarity is required, the abbreviations *CAN* and *AUS* may be used. Note that CAD and AUD are also becoming increasingly current.

Where the reader may be in doubt as to which conventions should be followed for writing numerical expressions, the safest course is to adhere to international conventions (see 5.09, notes 1 and 2).

5

Chapter Six

Italics

6

Italics

6.01 Introduction

Because italic (sloping) type *contrasts* with roman (vertical) type, a writer can require words or passages to be typeset in italics in order to call special attention to them, to give them special meaning, or to distinguish them from the rest of his or her text.

Use italics sparingly, or they lose their effectiveness.

When an entire passage is printed in italics, the punctuation (including parentheses) and any numbers (including footnote references) will also be in italics. If just a word or phrase is in italics, only the punctuation proper to it is printed in that typeface.

Note that when the main body of a text is printed in italics, roman type is used for emphasis and for the other purposes described in this chapter.

6.02 Emphasis

Italics can serve to indicate emphasis in the following cases:

• when the writer uses an unexpected word:

> What differences might we expect to see in human behaviour if honesty were shown to be the *worst* policy?

• when two words are contrasted:

> I did not say we *would* go: I said we *might* go.

• when the writer wishes to stress a word that would not normally be stressed in the sentence:

> Why was *he* chosen to chair the committee?

6.03 French and foreign words and phrases

Write these in italics if they are not considered to have been assimilated into English. A non-English pronunciation often indicates that a word or phrase has not been assimilated. Many such terms occur in legal, political and musical contexts:

> *allegro non troppo*   *mutatis mutandis*
> *caveat emptor*   *raison d'état*
> *laissez-passer*   *res ipsa loquitur*

When French or foreign words or phrases are considered to have been assimilated into English, italics are *not* used:

ad hoc	per capita
aide-de-camp	strudel
autobahn	tsunami

Most dictionaries do not indicate which words or phrases are to be italicized. Among those that do are *The Concise Oxford Dictionary*, *The Random House Dictionary* and the *Collins* dictionaries, but they are not always unanimous. Consult the *Concise Oxford* but also exercise your own judgment, with due regard for the type of text and intended readership. When in doubt, use roman type.

If an unfamiliar French or foreign term or phrase is used repeatedly in a text, it should be italicized at the first occurrence and accompanied by an explanation. Subsequently, it may be set in roman type.

6.04 Latin terms and abbreviations

Although there is a growing tendency to print Latin reference terms and phrases in roman type (especially when abbreviated), many are still italicized:

idem	*sic*
infra	*supra*
passim	*vide*

Do not italicize the following:

AD	et seq.	e.g.	loc.cit.
QED	ca., c.	i.e.	ibid.
NB	cf.	v., vs.	op.cit.
PS	etc.	viz.	et al.

6.05 Titles of publications and works of art

Italicize the titles of books, pamphlets, published reports and studies, plays, operas and long musical compositions, paintings, sculptures, novels, films, long poems, newspapers and periodicals:

book	*The Canadian Style*
pamphlet	*Keeping the Heat In*
report	*Public Accounts of Canada*
play	*Murder in the Cathedral*
opera	*Rigoletto*
symphony	the *Pastoral Symphony*
painting	*Voice of Fire*
novel	*Cabbagetown*
long poem	*The Rime of the Ancient Mariner*
sculpture	*David*
newspaper	*The Globe and Mail*
periodical	*Saturday Night*

Exception

Titles of scientific periodicals are usually abbreviated and set in roman type (see 9.08(c)).

Do **not** italicize unofficial titles:

A record of the debate can be found in Hansard.

Titles of articles, short poems and short stories, songs, arias and other short musical compositions, and radio and television programs are set in roman type and enclosed in quotation marks:

article	"The Life Beyond"
aria	"Pace, pace, Mio Dio"
musical composition	"Stille Nacht"
television program	"Street Legal"

6.06 Legal references

In legal texts italicize the names of statutes and court cases:

the *Official Languages Act*
the *Divorce Act*
Weiner v. The Queen
Robson v. Chrysler Corporation

Do **not** italicize short forms such as "the Act" or "the Charter."

See also 6.10.

6.07 Modes of transportation

Italicize the names given to individual ships, spacecraft, aircraft and trains but **not** abbreviations preceding them:

HMCS *Brunswicker*	the *Spirit of St.Louis*
the spacecraft *Challenger*	the *Rapido*

Note

In Department of National Defence documents, names of ships are written entirely in upper case and are **not** italicized:

HMCS ATHABASKAN   HMCS SACKVILLE

6.08 Letters and words referred to as such

These should be italicized:

Delete the second *and* from line 15.
There is only one *s* in *disappoint*.

Quotation marks (see 8.11), boldface type and underlining may perform the same function.

6.09 Peripheral matter in a text

Italics may be used to set off peripheral matter such as prefaces and dedications or epigraphs and quotations at the beginning of a book or chapter. Stage directions for a play are usually set in italics and placed within brackets or parentheses. Introductory matter setting the scene is also usually in italics, but not in brackets or parentheses.

Italicize the terms *See, See under, See also* and *See also under* when used in indexes, and the expressions *To be continued, Continued on p., Continued from p.*and *Continued on next page.*

Italicize editorial clarifications:

> Representatives from certain Carribean [*sic*] countries . . .
> [*My emphasis*]
> [*Translation*]

See 8.10 and 8.14 for further information on this point.

6.10 Identifying matter

Italicize:

- letters referring to subdivisions of a statute or other regulatory document:

  > Paragraph 42(2)*(e)* of the *Canada Business Corporations Act*
  > In accordance with paragraph (*f*) of CFAO 19-27/H . . .

- letters referring to lines of verse (rhyme schemes):

  > The Shakespearean sonnet has an *abab, cdcd, efef, gg* rhyme scheme.

- letter symbols or words used in legends to illustrations, drawings, photographs, etc. or within the body of the text to identify parts of the item concerned. Such words as *top, bottom, left, right, above, below, left to right* and *clockwise from left* are frequently encountered in this context:

  > United States envoy Holbrook, *left*, greets his Russian counterpart, Vitaly Churkin, in the Serbian capital.

6.11 Mathematical, statistical and scientific material

Italicize the scientific (Latin) names of genera and species in botanical, zoological and paleontological matter:

> The sugar maple (*Acer saccharum*) is a member of the family Aceraceae.

Do **not** italicize the names of the larger subdivisions (phyla, classes, orders, families and tribes):

> The order Primates includes modern man (*Homo sapiens*).

Italicize letters designating unknown quantities and constants, lines, etc. in algebraic, geometric and similar matter:

> Let *n* be the number of molecules . . .
> $5x \times a^2 - 2ab$

Note in the second example that no space is left between the numerical coefficients and the variables, and that the italics help to differentiate between the variable x and the multiplication sign. Correct spacing and italic type also help to distinguish between algebraic variables and SI/metric symbols:

> 10*x* m
> 6*a* cm
> 10*b* L

Italicize quantity symbols such as *l* for length, *m* for mass and *v* for velocity in order to distinguish them from unit symbols such as "L" for litre, "m" for metre and "V" for volt, which are normally printed in roman type:

> $60 \text{ N} = m \times 12\text{m/s}^2$
> *m* = 5 kg
> (N = newton, *m* = mass, and m = metre)

Italicize Latin prefixes and Greek and Roman letters used as prefixes to the names of chemical and biochemical compounds:

> *cis*-dimethylethylene
> *β*-lactose
> *N*-acylneuraminic acid
> *M*-xylene

A number of Greek and Roman letters used in statistical formulas and notations are italicized:

> *P*   probability of
> *μ*   population mean
> *ó*   population standard deviation
> *ó²*   population variance

6.12 Headings

Headings or subheadings of a document may be italicized in order to clarify its arrangement for the reader. See Chapter 11.16 for further information.

An example of an italicized run-in sidehead can be seen in 7.07.

Chapter Seven

7

Punctuation

7.01 Introduction

Punctuation serves primarily to help show the grammatical relationships between words, but it is also used to indicate intonation. Its role is to clarify, and this principle takes precedence over all precepts governing the use of individual marks of punctuation. In the interest of clarity, punctuation should be as consistent as possible within a given text. For clarity, too, some grammarians recommend the use of "close" punctuation—the insertion of all punctuation, required or optional, which can be legitimately used. Most readers, however, will be grateful to the writer who opts for a more "open" style, omitting punctuation when this can be done without creating ambiguity. Finally, punctuation should not be a chore; if a passage appears difficult to punctuate, it probably needs to be rephrased.

Quotation marks are discussed extensively in Chapter 8.

7.02 Spacing

As a general rule, in English there is no space before and one space after a punctuation mark. Exceptions follow.

Period

No space before or after a decimal period between numerals:

    10.6 million Canadians $7.45

A space before and none after a decimal period not preceded by a numeral:

    a .22 calibre rifle

A space after a period following a person's initial:

    W. S. Avis

No space before or after a period in multiple numeration:

    subsection 2.5.12

No space before or after a period when followed by a closing quotation mark, parenthesis or bracket, or a comma:

    John Fraser Jr., Ellen Putniak and George Zeller were nominated.
    (See Chapter 21.)

No space before the periods following the capital letters in the official abbreviations of provinces and territories and no space after such periods except the last one:

> P.E.I.   Y.T.

Ellipsis points

A space before, between and after ellipsis points:

> There was little he could say . . . so he said nothing.

See also 7.05 and 8.09.

Question mark and exclamation mark

No space before or after a question or exclamation mark when followed by a closing quotation mark, parenthesis or bracket:

> The delegate added, "Is it not high time we tightened our belts and dealt with the deficit?"

Comma

No space before or after a comma when followed by a closing quotation mark:

> "Stop procrastinating," she said.
> The terms "interfacing," "conferencing" and "downsizing" are now part of the language of business.

No space before or after a comma used to separate triads in numbers (see Note 2 in 5.09):

> $12,670,233

Colon

No space before or after a colon when used to express ratios or the time of day using the 24-hour clock, or to separate chapter and verse, volume and page, act and scene in references to books, plays, etc.:

> a slope of 1:4   We arrived at 15:30   Psalms 39:5

Parentheses and brackets

One space before and none after an opening parenthesis or bracket within a sentence; no space before or after a closing parenthesis or bracket when followed by a punctuation mark:

> Please read the enclosed booklet (*Using Your Modem*); it will help you take full advantage of your new communication tool.

No space before or between parentheses enclosing sections or subsections in citations from legislation:

> section 123(4)(*b*)(ii)

Em dash, en dash and hyphen

No space before or after these marks when they are inserted between words, a word and a numeral, or two numerals:

I will support you in any way I can—even to the point of silence.

—Eugene Forsey

a few 90-cent stamps

pp. 134–200

Oblique

No space before or after an oblique when used between individual words, letters or symbols; one space before and after the oblique when used between longer groups which contain internal spacing:

n/a   *Language and Society / Langue et société*

Apostrophe

No space before or after an apostrophe within a word.

One space before and none after an apostrophe used to indicate omitted figures in dates:

the committee's report   the employees' suggestions
the class of '79

Quotation marks

One space before and none after an opening quotation mark within a sentence; no space before or after a closing quotation mark when followed by a punctuation mark:

The Minister spoke of "a full and frank discussion with all parties"; a resolution to the conflict is expected within the week.

The Period

7.03 Main purpose

The period marks the end of an affirmative sentence or sentence fragment:

The executive assistant was hired on the strength of his curriculum vitae. No interview or examination. Just an analysis of his file.

The period is a "full stop." It stops the reader more fully than the colon, semicolon, comma or dash. Each of these marks of punctuation may, in many circumstances, be used in place of one of the others in order to lessen or intensify a break in the flow of the sentence or passage. In the following examples the period has replaced a weaker mark of punctuation in order to slow the reader down and focus his or her attention:

The wheels of government grind exceeding slow. And with good reason. I don't know if you know the mental effect of a bromoseltzer.

> But it's a hard thing to commit suicide on.
> You can't.
> You feel so buoyant.
>   —Stephen Leacock

In the following examples, the period has itself been replaced by a weaker mark of punctuation in order to bring the elements into a closer relationship:

> He never drew the wrong conclusions—he never drew any conclusions at all.
> The parliamentary process is either exciting or efficient; efficient is better.

7.04 Imperatives, exclamations and indirect questions

Use a period after a mild imperative or exclamation:

> If you want to know who is going to change this country, go home and look in the mirror.
>   —Maude Barlow

> U-turn if you want to. The lady's not for turning.
>   —Margaret Thatcher

A sentence that is interrogative in form may be imperative in function and thus take a period (see 7.10):

> Will you come this way, please.

Indirect questions are affirmative sentences and take a period, not a question mark (but see 7.10):

> It is important for managers to ask why annual performance objectives have not been met.

7.05 Ellipsis points

Use three ellipsis points (. . .) to indicate a silence in dialogue, hesitation or interruption in speech, a pause in narrative, or the passage of time. Used in this way, they are sometimes also referred to as suspension points:

> "What is your approach to self-actualization?"
> " . . . "
> "Let me rephrase that."

> The Minister's speech dragged on and on . . . until, finally, the TV announcer's voice broke the monotony.

Ellipsis points may be substituted for *etc.* and similar expressions at the end of a list:

> nuts
> bolts
> screws
> . . .

Do **not** use ellipsis points to imply hidden meanings or to separate groups of words for emphasis, as is often done in advertising.

For the use of ellipsis points to indicate omissions in quotations, see 8.09.

7.06 Leaders

A row of dots (or short dashes), called leaders, is used in indexes and tables, including tables of contents, to help the reader align material separated by a wide space:

> 1. Period 10
> 2. Leaders 11

A series of dots is sometimes used in place of underlining to indicate where information (or a signature) is to be entered on a form:

> Suggestion No. ....
> Approved by ....

7.07 Other uses

Periods may replace parentheses after numerals or letters used to introduce items in a vertical list (see 7.67):

> 1. Logic
> 2. Grammar
>   a. relative clause
>   b. subordinate clause

A run-in sidehead should be followed by a period:

> *Punctuation.* Punctuation is the art of . . . .
> Fig. 3. Human resources by sector

7.08 Periods properly omitted

Do **not** use a period at the end of any form of heading (other than run-in sideheads), legend or the like, or after a date line or signature:

> Summary of Expenditures   June 22, 1996

Short signboard messages do not require a final period:

> No Trespassing   Employees Only

Do **not** use periods with acronyms and initialisms and with abbreviations of compass directions (except in street addresses), degrees, memberships and distinctions, SI/metric unit symbols, chemical symbols or mathematical abbreviations:

NATO	OECD	NE
BSc	MA	FRSC
cm	NaCl	cos

The Question Mark

7.09 Main purpose

A question mark is placed at the end of a direct question, sometimes even if the sentence is declarative or imperative in form:

> Doctor Livingstone, I presume?
>
> Surely not?
>
> Give him more time? Don't make me laugh.
>
> I don't suppose you'd have another one in the same colour?

A question mark may be used for each query within a sentence:

> Managers must ask themselves: How will this proposal affect cost? productivity? employee satisfaction?

7.10 Requests, indirect questions and other uses

Opinions differ as to whether a polite request of the type *May I . . . , Would you . . .* or *Will you . . .* requires the question mark. However, a question mark will look out of place after longer requests of this kind, especially if the sentence embodies straightforward affirmative elements:

> May I escort you to your car?
>
> Will you come this way, please.
>
> Will you please go—before I have you thrown out.

Although the question mark is normally omitted after indirect questions, one may be added if the sentence has the force of a request:

> I wonder if you could give me two dollars for the bus ride home?

Occasionally a question will incorporate an exclamatory element. The writer must then decide whether the interrogative or the exclamatory element is to be given greater prominence:

> What hath God wrought!
> How many times must I tell you?

A question mark in parentheses (italicized in square brackets in quoted material) is inserted after information about which the writer is uncertain:

> The explorer William Kennedy, a strong advocate of the annexation of Rupert's Land to Canada, was born at Cumberland House (?), Rupert's Land, on April 26, 1814.

Indicate missing digits with a question mark:

> Henri Potvin (1615–165?)

See Chapter 8 for the use of the question mark with quotation marks and other punctuation.

The Exclamation Mark

7.11 Main purpose

The exclamation mark is an intensifier. It is used to indicate surprise, urgency, finality and the like. It is most often found after interjections, but also after ellipses, contractions and inversions and after certain onomatopoeic words:

> Crash! went the filing cabinet.

but

> The crash of the filing cabinet was heard far down the hall.

Sometimes the exclamation mark is used to convey a special intonation that the reader would not give the words if they were punctuated normally:

> And I thought he was joking!

The exclamation mark is also used after forceful requests, wishes, invocations and commands:

> Would that I could!
>
> Follow my white plume!
>
> —Sir Wilfrid Laurier

7.12 Miscellaneous

An exclamation mark, usually in parentheses (italicized in square brackets in quoted material), is sometimes used to indicate incredulity on the part of the writer. As with the analogous use of the question mark, this is a technique easily overdone:

> Mr. Jones asserted that never in his long and distinguished (!) political career had he taken a bribe.

When exclamations occur in a series they are usually separated by commas:

> **Several honourable members:** Hear, hear!

However, two interjections may be combined with no intervening punctuation:

> Oh no!

Where the words themselves suffice to convey the emphasis, or where the sentence or clause is more properly a question, do **not** use an exclamation mark:

> Another project failure like this, and we are finished.
>
> Who knows? Who cares?

Exclamations are of necessity short. An exclamation mark should never appear at the end of a long sentence unless it is intended to intensify only the last word or words.

The exclamation mark should be used as sparingly as possible. Emphatic wording is usually more effective than emphatic punctuation.

The Comma

7.13 General

The comma is the most frequently misused punctuation mark, and many of the rules governing its use are vague and riddled with exceptions. The writer must frequently rely on personal judgment and should be guided by considerations of clarity more than by any particular set of rules.

Note that, as a general rule, commas interrupt the flow of a sentence and should therefore not be used where they do not contribute to clarity. A sentence requiring a large number of commas for clarity is probably a poorly constructed one in need of rephrasing. Yet the comma is also the mark most often incorrectly omitted.

7.14 Restrictive/non-restrictive

Most difficulties with the use of the comma hinge on the distinction between restrictive and non-restrictive sentence elements. A restrictive word, phrase or clause adds to the words it modifies a "restrictive" or defining element that is essential to the meaning of the whole; it should therefore not be separated by a comma or other mark of punctuation. A non-restrictive element provides incidental or supplementary information which does not affect the essential meaning; it should be set off by a comma or commas.

Compare

> The senators who had objected most strongly to the shift in policy were quick to acknowledge the error in their thinking. (*restrictive*)

and

> The senators, who had objected most strongly to the shift in policy, were quick to acknowledge the error in their thinking. (*non-restrictive*)

(a) Introductory elements

There are exceptions to the general rule for punctuating restrictive and non-restrictive elements. An introductory phrase or clause, especially if it is a long one, is often followed by a comma whether it is restrictive or not:

> Of all election issues, the place of minorities in society is the most sensitive.

> When choosing between two approaches, it is important to consult experts in the field.

but

In the course of the conference some provincial leaders reversed their position on Native rights.

Each of the above sentences could have been correctly punctuated with or without the comma. But if an introductory subordinate clause is followed by a conjunctival *now*, *then* or *still*, the comma should be retained in order to avoid having these words read as adverbs of time. In the following example

When there are enough good Moslems in a society, that society will inevitably become an Islamic society. If that Islamic society establishes itself and endures then, no less inevitably, it will produce an Islamic state.

the word *then* appears to be an adverb of time belonging to the *if* clause, but it in fact introduces the main clause and should be preceded by a comma.

After introductory adverbs and short phrases indicating time, frequency, location or cause, the comma is omitted unless needed to avoid ambiguity or add emphasis:

By next week the new budget will have been thoroughly analysed.

but

In 1994, 1457 employees started using the new operating system.

Introductory adverbs or phrases used to mark transition or to express a personal comment are usually set off by commas:

Nevertheless, the program will go ahead as scheduled.

In short, no hiring is currently taking place.

The introductory phrase may also consist of an adjective or participle separated from its noun by the definite or indefinite article:

Unprepared, the team was no match for its opponents.

Clearly upset by the heckling, the speaker stopped for a moment to regain his composure.

Conversely, it is sometimes possible to omit the commas that ordinarily set off non-restrictive elements, without obscuring the meaning. This is especially true of short adverbial expressions:

Her words went of course unheeded.

All the same he had no compunction about slipping the waiter a few dollars to be on the safe side.

In such sentences the addition of commas not strictly needed for clarity gives emphasis to the elements thus enclosed:

Her words went, of course, unheeded.

(b) Absolute expressions

One form of non-restrictive expression is the **absolute**[1] construction: a participial phrase grammatically unconnected with the rest of the sentence. Such phrases are followed by a comma:

> Weather permitting, the conference will be held as planned.

> The chapter completed, I returned to my former duties.

Note the following errors in the punctuation of absolute expressions:

> The investigation had been completed, and the results, having been known for some time, the public was anxiously waiting for heads to roll.

> (*remove comma after* results)

> We were unable to answer her questions.The truth being that we hadn't given the matter much thought.

> (*replace the period after* questions *with a comma or dash*)

(c) Parenthetic expressions

Parenthetic expressions are non-restrictive and therefore require commas:

> We could see that the plan, if not actually rejected out of hand, was far from popular with senior management.

If a parenthetic expression is removed from the sentence, the remainder of the sentence should read as a coherent, grammatically correct whole. For example, the sentence

> The task force wanted to show that it was as good, if not better, than its predecessors.

is unacceptable because "as good . . . than" is incorrect English. The sentence should be recast as follows:

> . . . it was as good as, if not better than, its predecessors.

Occasionally it may be expedient to omit the first of the pair of commas around a parenthetic expression:

> But without realizing it, he had sparked a whole new controversy.

The parenthetic phrase here is "without realizing it."

Both commas can sometimes safely be omitted; under no circumstances, however, should the second comma be omitted while the first is retained:

> But without realizing it he had sparked a whole new controversy.

> **not**

> But, without realizing it he had sparked a whole new controversy.

---

1. Do not confuse *absolute* constructions with those involving *dangling* or *unrelated* participles:
   Listening to his speech, it felt as if he would drone on all day.
   This common problem is avoided if the sentence is recast so that the subject of both clauses is the same:
   Listening to his speech, I had the impression that he would drone on all day.

Parenthetic expressions may be set off by parentheses or dashes instead of commas, depending on the degree of emphasis or pause desired, or the length of the expression. Compare:

> Jane (evidently) had no stake in seeing the dispute continue.
>
> Jane evidently had no stake in seeing the dispute continue.
>
> Jane, evidently, had no stake in seeing the dispute continue.
>
> Jane—evidently—had no stake in seeing the dispute continue.

A common error occurs with parenthetic phrases following the conjunction *that*. The comma that belongs after the conjunction is often placed before it instead:

> The odd thing was, that no matter how he tried, he couldn't remember where he had left the document.

(d) Appositives

Restrictive and non-restrictive appositives should be carefully distinguished. The latter are set off by commas, whereas the former are not:

> St. John of the Cross
>
> Graham St. John, of Hoary Cross
>
> Her painting *Reflections* drew a poor response from the public.
>
> Her first painting, *Contrasts*, has been little studied.

As in the case of parenthetic expressions, the comma following a non-restrictive appositive cannot be omitted. Thus the sentence

> The statement by the Government House Leader, Herb Gray that no changes would be made to salaries paid to Parliamentarians was not unexpected.

is incorrect. A comma is required after "Gray."

Non-restrictive appositives in final position are usually preceded by a comma:

> Our supreme governors, the people.

Often, however, the comma is replaced by a colon or dash:

> Tact: a quality that no skilled diplomat can do without.
>
> Margaret Laurence—perhaps the greatest writer to come out of Manitoba.

If the appositive contains internal commas, it is best introduced by a mark other than the comma. In the following example, a colon would be an improvement over the comma after *legacy*:

> The Pearson government left behind a remarkable legacy, a pension plan, a universal medicare plan and a new flag.

(e) Annunciatory expressions

The annunciatory expressions *namely, that is* and *for example* are usually followed by a comma. They may be preceded by a comma, a dash, a semicolon or a period, or the matter that the expression introduces may be enclosed in parentheses, depending on the emphasis desired:

> Plans for Senate reform should be honestly and objectively assessed, that is, bearing in mind only the public good.

The abbreviations *i.e.* and *e.g.* should be preceded by a comma, a dash or an opening parenthesis, but need not be followed by a comma.

Note that the expression *such as* is used to introduce an example, not an appositive, and therefore is not followed by a comma. It may be preceded by a comma or other punctuation, as required in the sentence.

(f) Vocative forms

Vocative forms are non-restrictive and are set off by commas:

> Gentlemen, where I come from, a black-hearted bastard is a term of endearment.
> —Donald Gordon

> Awake, my country, the hour is great with change!
> —Charles Roberts

Similarly, exclamations and interjections are set off by commas (or exclamation marks):

> God, what a lot we hear about unhappy marriages, and how little we hear about unhappy sons and daughters.
> —Robertson Davies

7.15 Co-ordinate elements

Elements of equal rank or relation in a sentence are said to be co-ordinate. The co-ordinate elements may be words or phrases in a series, or they may be entire clauses.

(a) Nouns and noun phrases

Items in a series may be separated by commas:

> Complacency, urbanity, sentimentality, whimsicality

They may also be linked by co-ordinating conjunctions such as *and* or *or*:

> economists, sociologists or political scientists
> the good, the bad and the ugly

Opinions differ on whether and when a comma should be inserted before the final *and* or *or* in a sequence. In keeping with the general trend toward less punctuation, the final comma is best omitted where clarity permits, unless there is a need to emphasize the last element in the series. This comma is usually omitted in the names of firms and always before an ampersand:

> Deeble, Froom & Associates Ltd.
> Cohen, Hansen and Larose

On the other hand, it is usually inserted if the items in the series are phrases or clauses of some length, or if omission of the comma might lead to ambiguity or misunderstanding:

> Tenders were submitted by Domicile Developments Inc., East End Construction, Krista, and Ryan and Scheper.

A comma is also required before *etc.*:

> He brought in the wine, the glasses, etc.

A more complex situation occurs when apposition commas are used together with co-ordinating commas, as illustrated below:

> Carla Tavares, a recent MBA graduate, three students and a technician set up the experiment.

The sentence should be rephrased so that no non-restrictive appositive occurs within a co-ordinate element:

> A recent MBA graduate named Carla Tavares, three students and a technician set up the experiment.

Alternatively, semicolons may be used to separate elements in a complex series (see also 7.23):

> Jane Stewart, MP for Brandt, Ont.; Stan Keyes, MP for Hamilton West, Ont.; John Nunziata, MP for York-South Weston . . .

(b) Clauses

A comma is normally used to separate two main clauses in a compound sentence when they are joined by a co-ordinating conjunction (*and, but, or, nor, yet* or *for*):

> They are often called individualists, and in economic matters they were, but in social matters, the dominating concept was that of good neighbourliness.
> —M. M. Fahrni

If the clauses are short or closely related, the commas may be omitted before *and, but, or* or *nor*:

> He opened the letter and then he read the contents.
> Life is short but art is long.

Co-ordinate clauses **not** joined by a co-ordinating conjunction are usually separated by a heavier mark of punctuation than the comma:

> When the white men came we had the land and they had the Bibles; now they have the land and we have the Bibles.
> —Chief Dan George

A comma will suffice, however, if the clauses are short, or if the writer wishes to emphasize a contrast or lead the reader on to the following clause as quickly as possible:

> There are good regulations, there are bad regulations.
> It was not the duration of the pilot project that caused concern, it was the size of the project team.

When a number of independent co-ordinate clauses follow one another, a comma should be used after each one except (usually) the last, in accordance with the rule for items in a series (see 7.15(a)):

> She investigated the matter, wrote a report, presented it to the committee and answered everyone's questions satisfactorily.

It is a common error to confuse a simple sentence having a compound predicate with a compound sentence requiring a comma between clauses. Note the difference between the following examples:

> She investigated the matter and then wrote a detailed report. (*simple sentence*)
> She investigated the matter, and then the committee began its work. (*compound sentence*)

Where the clauses of a compound sentence are joined by a conjunctive adverb (such as *however, instead, meanwhile, otherwise, similarly, so, still, then, therefore* or *yet*), a semicolon is usually called for, though a comma will often suffice before *so, then* and *yet*:

> Much of English-speaking Canada has been populated . . . by a highly literate people, drawn in part from the educated classes of the Old Country, yet in its two hundred years of existence it has produced few books and not a single great one.
> —E. A. McCourt

(c) Adjectives

A series of adjectives modifying a noun may or may not be co-ordinate. The adjectives are co-ordinate if their order does not affect the meaning, in which case they should be separated by a comma. If they are not co-ordinate, that is, if one adjective modifies the phrase formed by the following adjective(s) plus the noun, then they should **not** be separated by a comma:

> a rich, creamy sauce
> **but**
> a naive domestic burgundy

Adjectives of both types may of course occur together:

> a tender, succulent young chicken

The rule stated above, however, is not an infallible guide. When in doubt omit the comma, as in:

> The plain honest truth is that he is a liar.

The final adjective in the series should **not** be separated from the following noun by a comma:

Nations require strong, fair, open, decisive government.

(d) Antithetic expressions

Antithetic expressions are usually separated by a comma:

This proposal is not to be tossed lightly aside, but to be hurled with great force.

However, short expressions of this type may not require a comma:

The more wit the less courage.

7.16 Clarity and emphasis

Sometimes the reader will be led astray by a word or phrase which appears at first to be used in one sense but turns out from the context to be used in another. In all the following examples, commas should have been used in order to prevent misreading:

In all his efforts were quite laudable.
(*comma after* In all)

He was taken to the cleaners and left without any money, he soon grew desperate.
(*comma after* and)

In the presence of Sir Henry James began to quiver.
(*comma after* Sir Henry)

I was high up and far below I saw the globe of the earth.
(*comma after* up)

The comma can be a useful device for securing a pause or emphasis:

I am sure the contract will be signed, eventually.
Senior management had, once again, put itself in a no-win situation.
The end had come, but it was not yet in sight.

7.17 Omitted words

A comma may be used to indicate that words have been omitted:

The African countries sent six representatives; the Asian countries, five.

Again, the comma may be omitted if clarity is not compromised.

See also 7.22 and 7.23.

7.18 Quotations, etc.

Place a comma after words introducing short direct quotations, declarations and direct questions (a colon is needed to introduce longer sentences):

> A politician once remarked, "Life is short; live it up."
> I repeat, No milk today.
> Ask yourself, Can I afford this?

Note the capital letter and the absence of quotation marks in the last two examples.

If the quotation or question follows a form of the verb *to be*, is in apposition to a noun, or is worked naturally into the syntax of the sentence, no comma is needed:

> What he actually said was "Play it, Sam."
> Did I give a satisfactory answer to the chairperson's question "Why are there so few women in management?"
> She asked us to "rephrase the question to make it less offensive."

It is also acceptable to omit the comma before quotations introduced by verbs of saying:

> He said "Have a nice day," fired a few shots, and ran.

The use of punctuation in quotations is discussed in 8.03.

7.19 Names and titles

Commas are used around titles and degrees within the body of a sentence:

> Charles Peabody, MD, PhD, was the first to arrive.
> Judith Foster, Chairperson of the Foreign Affairs Committee, made the opening statement.

A comma is placed between a surname and a given name or initials if the surname is written first:

> Mammouri, Muhammad
> Grove, F. P.

Chinese and Vietnamese names are an exception. They are written with the family name first and no comma:

> Deng Xiaoping
> Nguyen Tranh

7.20 Dates, geographical names and addresses

Use a comma to separate the day of the week from the date and the place from the date:

> Friday, February 13 **but** Friday the thirteenth
> Hull, February 13

If the date is written in the order day-month-year, no commas are required before, after or between the components of the date:

> The meeting of 10 January 1996 did little to allay tensions.

If, however, the order given is month-day-year, the day and year are separated by a comma, and the year should normally be followed by a comma within the body of a sentence or sentence equivalent:

> February 20, 1995, marked the beginning of a new era.

> On April 16, 1985, certain additional provisions of the Charter took effect.

If you are stating only the month and the year, do **not** insert a comma:

> Treasury Board approved the submission in February 1995.

Similarly, a comma separates a place name from the name of a province or the abbreviation for that province, and the province's name or abbreviation is normally followed by a comma within the body of a sentence or sentence equivalent:

> Swift Current, Saskatchewan, has applied to host the event.

> We arrived at Corner Brook, Nfld., the following day.

Use commas to separate address components, as illustrated:

> Our address is 340 Laurier Ave. West, Ottawa, Ontario K1A 0P8, and our telephone number is (613) 999-9900.

Note that the postal code is followed, but not preceded, by a comma when the address forms part of a sentence, and that two spaces separate the provincial name from the postal code.

7.21 Commas properly omitted

Do not use commas between the name and the number of an organizational unit:

> Teamsters Union Local 91
> Loyal Order of Moose 1765

Do **not** insert commas in numerical expressions such as the following:

> 2 years 6 months 7 days
> a 2-year 6-month sentence
> a 3-minute 50-second mile
> 1 h 12 min 55 s

The Semicolon

7.22 Between independent clauses

The semicolon is used between independent clauses not joined by a co-ordinating conjunction but too closely related to be separated by a period:

> Inflation makes misery unanimous; it is universal poverty.
> —Arthur Meighen

> When I was younger I used to worry about having enough money for my old age; now I worry about having enough old age for my money.
> —Helen Stimpson

> In theory the Commons can do anything; in practice, it can do little.
> —John Turner

If the clauses are short and parallel, a comma may replace the semicolon:

> I'll talk, you listen.

Clauses joined by a co-ordinating conjunction may also be separated by a semicolon (instead of a comma) if they are the last two of a series of clauses separated by semicolons:

> It is easy to jump on the bandwagon; it is easy to wash one's hands of an issue; but it is not easy to take a position contrary to that of the majority and to defend it at all costs, to the bitter end.

Use a semicolon if a sharper break is required than could be achieved with a comma (for emphasis or to convey antithesis):

> The politician proclaims that we live in the best of all possible worlds; and the unemployed worker fears this is true.

Clauses joined by a conjunctive adverb usually require a semicolon between them, though a comma may suffice if the clauses are short:

> He loved his country; therefore he fought and died for it.

> I think, therefore I am.

Elliptical clauses are conventionally separated from each other and from the introductory clause by semicolons, with commas often marking the ellipsis (see 7.17):

> To err is human; to forgive, divine.

The semicolon can be replaced by a comma, however, provided that the comma marking the ellipsis can be dropped:

> One best seller makes a successful writer, ten a great one.

7.23 Co-ordinate elements

Semicolons may be used in place of commas to separate parallel elements in a series if these elements are complex or contain internal punctuation, or if greater emphasis is desired:

> Genesis 2:3; 4:15,17; 5:9–14
> Nature is often hidden; sometimes overcome; seldom extinguished.

Even a series of parallel subordinate clauses may be separated in this manner, provided that the resulting punctuation is not apt to confuse the reader.

7.24 Misuse and overuse

Although most writers tend to underuse rather than overuse the semicolon, a writing style that employs a large number of semicolons is likely to be heavy and dull. Consider using the dash, colon or comma instead.

The Colon

7.25 Between independent clauses

The colon may be used between two independent clauses not joined by a conjunction if the second clause explains, illustrates or enlarges upon the first. In such sentences a semicolon would also be correct, but less effective:

> Put most simply, the colon looks forward or anticipates: it gives readers an extra push toward the next part of the sentence.
> —*The Canadian Writer's Handbook*

> We are now at the point when an awakening bitterness follows a night of intoxication: an ebb of retribution now follows in the wake of a flood-tide of railway construction.
> —Arthur Meighen

A colon may be used between two clauses in antithesis:

> Man proposes: God disposes.

The work of the colon could have been done by a period or even a comma in the above example.

7.26 Annunciatory function

The colon is used primarily to introduce the words that follow it. It introduces a formal quotation or a formal statement:

> The first sentence of the circular was unequivocal: "The purpose of this circular is to announce the termination of the policy respecting federally administered prices."

> Simply put, the directive says this: Employees may smoke in designated areas of the cafeteria, but nowhere else.

Short quotations or declarations, however, are usually introduced by a comma (see 7.18).

The colon is also used for the question-and-answer format, to introduce dialogue and in transcriptions:

> **Some Hon. Members:** Hear, hear!

The colon introduces a list, but should not be used after "such as," "for instance" or "for example," or if the list is the object or complement of an element in the annunciatory statement:

> There are three kinds of lies: lies, damned lies, and statistics.

but not

The subjects covered were: bonds, mutual funds and global investments.

or

The memo was sent to: directors, section managers and human resources managers.

In cases such as the last two, use no punctuation after the annunciatory statement or insert a phrase such as "the following," "as follows" or "as illustrated," which then takes a colon.

The colon can be used to introduce vertical lists, even if the series is a complement or object:

The teleworking issues before the working group included:
human resources
technology
space and accommodation
financial implications

However, here too, an introductory phrase ("the following," etc.) is preferable.

7.27 Miscellaneous

In business letters and printed speeches, a colon follows the salutation:

Dear Mr. Fox:

In personal letters, the colon is usually replaced by a comma:

Dear Susan,

The colon is used to separate titles from subtitles. It is followed by a single space:

Canada: A Story of Challenge

In references to books, plays, etc., colons separate chapter and verse, volume and page and act and scene, with no space on either side of the colon:

Numbers 7:11
History of Upper Canada, II:791
Fortune and Men's Eyes, I:i

Location and name of publisher are also separated by a colon. The colon is followed by a single space:

Ottawa: University of Ottawa Press

See Chapter 9 for further information on the use of the colon in reference matter.

See Chapter 5 for uses of the colon with numerical expressions.

7.28 Misuse

Do **not** use a colon followed by a dash (:—).

Do **not** place a colon at the end of a title or heading standing on a separate line from the text it introduces.

Parentheses

7.29 General

Parentheses, or round brackets, are used to enclose additional information serving to explain, amplify or provide comments on adjacent material. Commas and dashes are also used for this purpose (see 7.14(c), 7.42 and 7.44). Parentheses, however, are generally used for words that are less closely related to the rest of the sentence than material which would be set off by dashes or commas. They are also more convenient for parenthetic elements which run to some length or contain internal punctuation, although it is best to avoid lengthy parentheses wherever possible.

7

7.30 Clarification

Parentheses may save the writer from other punctuation problems, such as the confusion created when apposition commas and enumeration commas appear together, as illustrated below:

> Carla Tavares (a recent MBA graduate) , Lisa Thompson and three students

> **not**

> Carla Tavares, a recent MBA graduate, Lisa Thompson and three students

7.31 Punctuation with parentheses

A parenthesis consisting of a complete sentence does not take an initial capital and final period unless it stands alone between complete sentences:

> To achieve the best possible results, adopt a combination of the CPM and PERT methods. (See a model of such a combination in the attached paper.) This will provide you with an effective, low-cost control mechanism.

An opening parenthesis should not be preceded by any other mark of punctuation unless the parentheses are being used to enclose numbers or letters of enumeration (see 7.35):

> I am (I hope) reliably informed that a new president has been appointed.

After the closing parenthesis, any punctuation which would be appropriate in the absence of the parenthesis should still be used:

> I am (I hope), always have been and always will be an honest judge.

Before a closing parenthesis only a period, question mark, exclamation mark or quotation mark is permitted:

> I have always been willing (do you not agree?) to hear both sides of the issue.

7.32 Afterthoughts and asides

Parentheses de-emphasize the words they contain, which often take the form of an afterthought or aside:

> The premier (no mean orator himself) was enthusiastic in his praise of the minister's speech.

An important afterthought, however, should be preceded by a dash or other mark of punctuation:

> Finally the Computer Operations Branch agreed to follow through on the auditor's recommendations—which is what it should have done six months earlier if it had had the best interests of the organization at heart.

In transcripts, use parentheses to enclose information on one of the speakers:

> **The Hon. John Manley (Minister of Industry)**:
> Mr. Speaker, I support this initiative.

Parentheses should not alter the flow of the sentence in which they are inserted; the rest of the sentence should make sense if the parenthetic element is removed. The following is incorrect:

> She had to forfeit her acting appointment (not to mention her bilingualism bonus) and she got no sympathy on either count.

7.33 Parentheses within parentheses

If you cannot avoid placing parenthetic material within other parenthetic material, use square brackets within the round brackets (see 7.37) or use a combination of parentheses and em dashes:

> He worked hard—twelve hours a day (and no bonus for overtime), seven days a week—until the task was completed.

7.34 Legal documents

In legal texts, parentheses are used to enclose numerals previously written out:

> one thousand nine hundred and ninety-nine (1999)

7.35 Letters and numerals

Individual letters or groups of letters may be enclosed within parentheses:

Language(s) spoken in the home _____

Numerals or letters of enumeration may be enclosed in parentheses (or be followed by a period):

4. Work plan
   (a) Evaluation
   (b) Training

Guidelines for writers: (1) Be concise. (2) Write idiomatically. (3) Proofread carefully.

See 5.22 and 6.10 regarding references to sections of legislation. See Chapter 9 for the use of parentheses in reference matter.

Square Brackets

7.36 General

Square brackets, often simply called *brackets*, are more disconnective than parentheses. They are used to enclose material too extraneous for parentheses. Use brackets for editorial comments or additional information on material written by someone else. To use ordinary parentheses for this purpose would give the impression that the inserted words were those of the person quoted. Square brackets should also enclose translations given immediately after short quotations, terms and titles of books or articles. See 8.14 for detailed information and examples.

7.37 Use within parentheses

When one set of parentheses is to be placed within another, replace the inner parentheses with square brackets (though dashes may be used instead—see 7.33). Parentheses within parentheses should be used sparingly, however, except in legal and scholarly texts and specifically for letters and numerals referring to subsections of a document:

Acadia (from *Algatem* ["dwelling here and there"])
(See section 14(i)(*c*))

Square brackets may also be used in place of round brackets where two or more sets of the latter would otherwise occur in succession:

in 3(a) [according to Bixby's enumeration] . . .
Here, f(x) [c. s. 8.3] reaches a maximum when . . .

Braces

7.38 Use

Braces are used to link two or more lines of writing:

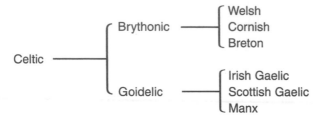

They are also used to group items in formulas and equations. See 7.39.

7.39 Multiples

In mathematical usage, the preferred order for multiple brackets is as follows:

$$\{[(\{[(\quad)]\})]\}$$

Note that square brackets enclose round brackets, in contrast to the practice in non-mathematical usage.

The Em Dash

7.40 General

In most of its uses the em dash ("long dash") is a substitute for the colon, semicolon or comma, but it indicates a more emphatic or abrupt break in the sentence, or a less formal style.

7.41 Enumerations

Use a dash, not a colon, to enclose a list of terms that does not end the sentence:

A number of processes—gassing, electroplating, soldering, casting, etc.—are used in the copper industry.

not

A number of processes: gassing, electroplating, soldering, casting, etc., are used in the copper industry.

7.42 Interruptions, pauses, afterthoughts, clarifications and emphasis

Like parentheses, a dash may be used at the end of an unfinished or interrupted statement or a pause, as in transcripts:

I have indicated that the appointment of the judge was terminated—or rather was not terminated but came to—

Some Hon. Members: Oh, oh!

Here the dashes are used to indicate, first, a pause and clarification and, second, an interruption.

The dash may be used to introduce an afterthought, correction or repetition:

> Who will oppose—who are now opposed to the union?

It may similarly be used to set off an emphatic ending or one that contrasts with the remainder of the sentence:

> To write imaginatively a man should have—imagination.

Dashes give greater emphasis to parenthetic material than do commas or parentheses. If the parenthetic material contains internal punctuation or forms a complete sentence, the commas that might have been used to enclose it should be replaced by dashes or parentheses, depending on the degree of emphasis desired or the closeness of the relationship to the rest of the sentence. Parentheses are generally used to enclose material more remote from the main thrust of the sentence, dashes for material more closely related:

> This country is something that must be chosen—it is so easy to leave—
> and if we do choose it we are still choosing a violent duality.
> —Margaret Atwood

The em dash is also used to attribute a quotation, as in the example above.

7.43 Summarizing

A dash is sometimes inserted before the final portion of a sentence to clarify its relationship to the rest of the sentence, often with the help of a summarizing pronoun such as *all* or *these* or with the repetition of key words:

> Rich stores of minerals, good agricultural land, forests stretching over
> millions of acres, and energetic and enterprising people—all these
> assure Canada a bright future.

7.44 Material in apposition

Explanatory material in apposition may be set off by dashes to secure greater emphasis than would be achieved with a colon or commas or to avoid confusion with commas within the apposition:

> Increased government funding—once hailed as a panacea for all
> society's ills—is today no longer an option.

7.45 Headings

A dash may be used to separate the heading of a chapter or the like from the description of its contents or to separate subheadings within a chapter or section, as in a catalogue:

> Gelatin Membrane Filters, White, Plain, Sartorius—A water soluble filter developed solely for . . .
>
> Appendix A—Table of Symbols
>
> ISO 2382-1994 Information-processing systems—Vocabulary—Part 14: Reliability, maintenance and availability

7.46 Lists and tables

It is sometimes used in place of bullets, numerals or letters in vertical lists:

> 3. Service to the public
>   —enquiries answered
>   —brochures sent out
>   —complaints investigated

It can represent *nil* or *unknown* in a list of figures:

	Atomic weight	Density	Melting point
Actinium	227	—	—
Aluminum	26.98	2.7	660

7.47 Punctuation with em dash

Do **not** combine the dash with any mark of punctuation other than quotation marks, the question mark, the exclamation mark and occasionally the period. In particular, do **not** use the colon-dash (:—) to introduce a quotation or a list.

The En Dash

7.48 Numerals

Use the en dash ("short dash") to join inclusive numbers:

> pages 9–12
> 3–7°C **but** -3 to -7°C **not** -3–7°C
> Robertson Davies (1913–95)

7.49 Compound expressions

Use the en dash to join the names of two or more places:

> the riding of Kenora–Rainy River
> the Québec–Windsor corridor

The Hyphen

7.50 Compound words

The hyphen is used in certain compound nouns, adjectives and verbs, and to join prefixes to proper nouns. It is also used in word division at the end of a line. See Chapter 2.17.

7.51 Spelling and enunciation

Use the hyphen to spell out a word:

s-p-e-l-l
Where did you put the c-a-n-d-y?

Hyphens also indicate slow, deliberate enunciation:

im-pos-si-ble
Rai-aid!

For use of the hyphen with numerical expressions, see 2.10, 2.11, 2.15, 5.05 and 5.08.

The Oblique

7.52 General

The oblique is also known as a *solidus, slant (line), bar, virgule, diagonal, stroke* or *slash.*

Do **not** use the oblique instead of a hyphen at the end of a line of ordinary prose to indicate word division.

7.53 Abbreviations

The oblique is used in certain abbreviations:

c/o	care of	i/c	in charge
w/o	without	n/a	not applicable
a/c	account	A/Director	Acting Director

It can be used as a symbol for *per*:

km/h N/m^2

Do **not** use the oblique to represent *per* more than once in a single expression:

$2.7\ m{\cdot}s^{-2}$ **not**   2.7 m/s/s

Do **not** use it with expressions of quantity written out in full:

metres per second **not** metres/second

7.54 Numerals

The oblique is sometimes used in fractions, especially when set into running text, or when they would be ungainly in the form $\frac{a}{b}$:

> She covered 2 1/3 lengths in 70 seconds.

Use it with ellipsis points and a numeral at the lower right-hand corner of a page to indicate that the text continues on the following page:

> . . . /2

7.55 Alternatives and headings

An oblique may indicate alternatives:

> Send in your cheque/money order without delay.
> and/or
> Parent/Guardian: _____

The expression *and/or* may be redundant and should be used with caution:

> The engines will be manufactured in Canada and/or the United States.
>
> **but**
>
> renovations or repairs **not** renovations and/or repairs

A similar use is seen in bilingual titles such as *L'Actualité terminologique / Terminology Update*.

Oblique strokes may separate headings on a form:

> Division/Branch
> Series/Cert. No.

The oblique is used increasingly to indicate complex relationships between words, a role traditionally filled by the hyphen:

> the student/teacher ratio (the student-teacher ratio)
> labour/management relations (labour-management relations)
> owner/manager (owner-manager)
> the total Boston–Montréal/Montréal–Toronto air mileage

The Apostrophe

7.56 Possession

The primary use of the apostrophe is to indicate possession. A word which does not end in a sibilant (*s* or *z* sound) forms the possessive by the addition of *'s*:

> a dog's breakfastToronto's CN Tower

To form the possessive of French words ending in a non-sibilant *s* or *x*, add an *'s*:

> Duplessis's cabinet   Malraux's art

Note that it is the pronunciation, not the spelling, which determines the possessive form. The word *conscience* ends in a sibilant; *Illinois* does not. Plural forms which do not end in a sibilant are no exception to the general rule:

> women's   children's

- Plurals ending in a sibilant take only the apostrophe:

> the ministers' responsibilities
> developing countries' needs

Regarding the appropriate form for singular words that end in a sibilant, pronunciation is again the determining factor. If it would be natural to pronounce an extra *s*, add *'s*; if an additional *s* would be difficult to pronounce, add only an apostrophe:

> Joyce's *Ulysses*   Brussels' bureaucrats
> Ulysses' wanderings   the boss's office

- Since awkwardness of pronunciation is the basic criterion, the decision to add or omit a possessive *s* ultimately depends on the writer's own sensitivities. One option is to rephrase:

> the tourist industry of Mauritius
> the ramblings of Joyce's Ulysses

> **rather than**

> Mauritius' tourist industry
> Joyce's Ulysses' ramblings

7.57 Inanimate possessors

With inanimate "possessors," especially abstract concepts, the apostrophe is generally not used to denote possession. Use an "of" construction instead:

> the incidence of conjugal violence
> the priority of tourism

> **not**

> conjugal violence's incidence
> tourism's priority

However, certain expressions of time and measurement do take the apostrophe:

> a month's vacation   ten dollars' worth

7.58 Compounds

Figurative compounds of the sort *bull's-eye* or *crow's-nest* retain *'s* in the plural:

> bull's-eyes   crow's-nests   shepherd's pies

When the possessive of a compound noun or a noun phrase is formed, add *'s* to the last word only, unless there is a possessive relation between the words within the phrase itself:

> someone else's problem
> her brother-in-law's address
>
> **but**
>
> John's father's problem

7.59 Two nouns (group genitive)

If possession is shared by two or more subjects, add *'s* to the last word only:

> Adam and Eve's progeny
> the Prince and Princess's visit
> Rodgers and Hammerstein's musicals

To indicate individual possession, *'s* is added to each element in the series:

> Abraham's and Lot's descendants
> Rodgers' and Hammerstein's private lives

7.60 Geographical names

The apostrophe is often omitted in geographical names:

> Gods Lake   Humphreys Mills
>
> **but**
>
> St. John's   Land's End

Note also *Saint John* (city in New Brunswick) and *Hudson Bay*—but *Hudson's Bay Co.* Consult the *Gazetteer of Canada* when in doubt.

7.61 Institutions and organizations

The *'s* is often omitted in names of institutions, especially in the case of plural nouns that are adjectival rather than strictly possessive:

> teachers college **but** inmates' committee
> veterans hospital **but** officers' mess

The official or customary form should be used, whatever it may be:

> Eaton's   Canadian Forces Headquarters

7.62 Its

Note that there is no apostrophe in the possessive forms *yours*, *hers* and *its*. *It's* is always a contraction of *it is*. See also 12.03.

7.63 Contractions

Apostrophes represent omitted letters in contractions or omitted numerals in dates:

It's the best of its kind.	the recession of '82
Treasury Board didn't agree.	the crash of '29

7.64 Plurals

Certain plurals are sometimes written with *'s*:

* abbreviations whose appearance would otherwise be ambiguous or confusing (see 1.04) and the plurals of lower-case letters, symbols and numerals:

c.o.d.'s	x's	+'s and -'s
POW's	a's and w's	6's

Another solution is to italicize the letter, symbol or numeral in question (see 6.11).

* cited words:

an overabundance of is's and which's

It is not necessary to use the apostrophe in set expressions such as "the dos and don'ts," "no ifs and buts," "the whys and wherefores."

* words not conveniently pluralized:

all the Toms, Dicks, Harrys and Louis's
all the Lao's in Laos

Vertical Lists

7.65 General

Vertical lists can be punctuated in a number of ways, but the writer should ensure that punctuation is consistent throughout the text.

7.66 Use of colon

The colon is generally used to introduce vertical lists. When the sequence of a list is random or arbitrary, the various elements may be simply indented or set off with bullets or em dashes:

These factors should determine committee size:
* Number of employees at the work site
* Variety of functions
* Number of trade unions
* Number of shifts

7.67 Numbering

Numbers and letters, enclosed in parentheses or followed by a closing parenthesis or period, are used to introduce items in lists where precedence or sequence is important:

> The tasks assigned to the committee are as follows:
> (a) setting up safety programs
> (b) monitoring the programs
> (c) dealing with employee complaints
> (d) maintaining complete records
> (e) making recommendations

Punctuation can be omitted after each item if the items are brief. Otherwise, a comma, semicolon or period is generally used.

7.68 Use of semicolon

Use a semicolon after each item (and a period at the end of the list) if one or more items contain internal punctuation, or after each item of a list ending in *and* or *or*, even if the items contain no internal punctuation:

> The Bureau has set the following priorities for the coming year:
> 1. Determining customer needs;
> 2. Improving teamwork and internal communication;
> 3. Updating equipment to increase turnaround time; and
> 4. Initiating quality-assurance procedures.

7.69 Complete sentences

Items made up of sentences should begin with a capital letter and end in a period (or question mark):

> The following factors affected grain yield:
> —Rainfall was exceptionally low in June and August.
> —The hailstorm of September 12 damaged crops in southern Alberta.

If a comma or semicolon is used after each item, put a period after the final item. See also 7.07, 7.26, 7.35 and 7.46.

7.70 Capitalization

Practice regarding capitalization of items in vertical lists varies. The first word of each item is usually capitalized when the item is a complete sentence or when the annunciatory statement is a complete sentence.

The first word of each item is usually lower-cased if the items in the list are syntactically linked to the introductory statement, especially if the list is not introduced by a colon:

> This versatile program can be applied to
> —personal development
> —management development
> —career counselling
> —team building

Chapter Eight

Quotations and quotation marks

8

Quotations and Quotation Marks

8.01 Introduction

The main use of quotation marks is to set off the exact words of a speaker or written source from the main body of a text. The quotation may consist of one or more complete sentences or paragraphs, parts of a sentence or paragraph or as little as one word. As an alternative to the use of quotation marks in the **run-in** format (quotations integrated into the text), direct quotations may be indicated by means of indention and/or reduced leading (space between lines) or font size, called the **block** format. Whichever format is adopted, the quoted matter should normally be faithfully reproduced in every detail: the spelling, punctuation and other characteristics of the original may not be changed without good reason (see 8.10 for information on insertions in and alterations to quoted matter).

Bear in mind, too, that the excessive use of quotations can mar the appearance of a page and make it difficult for the reader to follow the ideas being presented; it is often better to paraphrase, use indirect speech or give a summary of the ideas concerned in your own words—in each instance accompanied by a footnote providing the source of information. Quotations are justified if the intention is to demonstrate a particular characteristic, style or wording, or to compare quotations; if the material is striking, memorable or well known; or if the quotation itself is an example or proof of what is being discussed, as in the case of legal evidence.

In this chapter, we shall follow the predominant Canadian practice of placing the period or comma within closing quotation marks and using double rather than single quotation marks (except for quotations within quotations, as illustrated in 8.08).

8.02 Run-in format

Use the run-in format when the quoted matter is not more than fifty words or five lines long (longer quotations should be set in block format):

> The Minister said, "Prospects for growth are not good."

The quotation remains within the body of the paragraph.

Because the run-in format does not require indention, the writer enjoys some latitude in positioning the clause or phrase that introduces the quotation, also called the **annunciatory** element.

Note that when a quotation is interrupted by other matter, the quotation marks are repeated before and after each part of the quotation:

> "In a narrower sense," the Minister added in her report, "governments are becoming increasingly worried about large spending deficits. The chances of still higher deficits, as tax revenues falter and spending pressures mount in a weak economy, are very great."

If you decide to insert the annunciatory clause between two items that were separate sentences in the original or have become separate sentences in the quotation, capitalize the first word of the second sentence, i.e. of the second part of the quotation:

> "In a narrower sense governments are becoming increasingly worried about large spending deficits," the Minister added in her report. "The chances of still higher deficits, as tax revenues falter and spending pressures mount in a weak economy, are very great."

Note that in the second example the annunciatory clause ends with a period and not a comma.

When a quotation within a sentence is preceded by *that*, do **not** capitalize the first word (unless it is a proper noun or adjective):

> The Minister added in her report that "the chances of still higher deficits, as tax revenues falter and spending pressures mount in a weak economy, are very great."

8.03 Punctuation and grammar in run-in quotations

(a) Place commas and periods within closing quotation marks, whether or not they were included in the original material:

> **Original**
> Literature's world is a concrete human world of immediate experience. The poet uses images and objects and sensations much more than he uses abstract ideas; the novelist is concerned with telling stories, not with working out arguments.

> **Run-in quotation**
> "Literature's world is a concrete human world of immediate experience," according to Northrop Frye. "The poet uses images and objects and sensations much more than he uses abstract ideas; the novelist is concerned with telling stories, not with working out arguments."

(b) However, when a very high degree of accuracy is required (as in a legal context), it may be desirable to place any punctuation not part of the original document outside the quotation marks:

> This part of section 2 reads as follows: "real and personal property of every description and deeds and instruments relating to or evidencing the title or right to property".

(c) Place a closing dash, question mark or exclamation mark inside the closing quotation marks if it applies to the quoted material and outside if it applies to the entire sentence:

> If I hear one more word about "political correctness"—
> Stop telling me to "relax"!
> All she kept saying during the trip was "Are we there yet?"

(d) Note that when a statement or question ends with a quotation that is itself a question or exclamation, no period, exclamation mark or question mark is required after the closing quotation marks:

> Isn't it time we stopped asking "How much does it cost?"

(e) A closing semicolon or colon should normally be dropped and replaced with a period, a comma or ellipsis points.

(f) When introducing a quotation with the word *that*, do **not** use a comma or a colon. Quotations that follow annunciatory clauses ending in *that* also require grammatical changes—from first-person to third-person pronouns, possessive adjectives and verbs. Neither the third person pronoun nor *that* is ever enclosed in quotation marks or square brackets:

Original

I want to consider one sort of semantic change, the kind of generalization that has affected *literally* and hundreds of other words. It has been occurring for a long time, often draining meaning until no echo of the word's roots remains, and I suspect that it is occurring more rapidly in this age of electronic communication. I want to consider it from a particular point of view—as a usage problem, but also as an aspect of what Edward Sapir, more than seventy years ago, described as "drift."
—Robert Gorrell, "Language Change,
Usage and Drift," *English Today*

Restructured version

Gorrell discusses one sort of semantic change, the kind of generalization that has affected *literally* and hundreds of other words. This semantic change has been occurring for a long time, he believes, and he suspects that "it is occurring more rapidly in this age of electronic communication." In this work, he "[considers] it from a particular point of view—as a usage problem, but also as an aspect of . . . 'drift.'"

Note that if several changes of this kind need to be made within the same quotation, the material should be presented entirely in indirect speech (see 8.04). For information on how to use ellipsis points to indicate omissions from quoted passages, see 8.09.

(g) In-text notes, that is, author and page number references following a run-in quotation and enclosed in parentheses, should be placed between the closing quotation marks and the required final punctuation:

> Recently researchers have examined the sociological aspects of tourism and people's travel habits in the past century: "Scholars have attempted to deconstruct tourism by asking why sites and practices become designated as culturally desirable to 'do,' (such as Niagara Falls, the Canadian Rockies, Peggy's Cove or the West Edmonton Mall), and others (there are plenty of waterfalls, mountains, fishing villages and shopping malls in the world) do not" (Dubinsky 1986).

For further information on in-text notes, see 9.25.

(h) When quoting poetry in running text, use a slash (/) to indicate the end of a line:

> "Language, the fist/proclaims by squeezing/is for the weak only," says Margaret Atwood in *Power Politics*.

For further information on the use of a comma or colon before opening quotation marks, see 7.18 and 7.26.

8.04 Indirect (reported) speech

Another way of reproducing someone else's words without repeating them exactly is through indirect or reported speech. By adding a reporting verb (*said, stated, exclaimed, declared,* etc.) and shifting tenses as required, you can integrate the original speaker's statement grammatically into the new sentence. Adverbs and adjectives expressing nearness in place or time (*here, this, now, next,* etc.) become the corresponding adverbs or adjectives of remoteness (*there, that, then, the following,* etc.) in indirect speech. Examples are given on the following pages.

In indirect speech, the first example in 8.02 would be restructured to read as follows:

> The Minister said that prospects for growth *were* not good.

The verb in the subordinate clause shifts from the present tense of direct speech (*are*) to the past tense (*were*) in keeping with the rules of tense sequence. Likewise, a verb that was in the future tense in direct speech often takes the conditional form in indirect speech. Thus if the Minister's words had been

> "There *will* be no growth for some time."

the indirect form would be

> The Minister said that there *would be* no growth for some time.

However, the present and future tenses are retained and demonstratives are not modified if the actions or situations referred to are still current or future at the time of quotation:

Direct quotation
"There will be no growth this year."

Indirect speech (statement reported in the same year)
The Minister said that there *will* be no growth this year.

Indirect speech (statement reported in a subsequent year)
The Minister said that there *would* be no growth *in that* year.

Alternatively, a blend of direct and indirect speech may be preferred when a particular part of the original statement is to be highlighted:

The Minister said that prospects for growth were not good and that "governments [were] becoming increasingly worried about large spending deficits."

Because the first subordinate clause verb (*were*) is in the past tense, the tense of the verb within the quotation must be altered. This time, because direct speech is being retained and the speaker did not actually use the past tense, the editorial change has to be indicated by means of square brackets (see also 8.10 on altering quotations).

The table below shows the corresponding tense and other changes when direct speech is converted to indirect speech:

Direct speech	Indirect speech
Simple present "I hate this film," she said.	*Simple past* She said that she hated that film.
Present progressive "I'm watching the fireworks," he said.	*Past progressive* He said that he was watching the fireworks.
Present perfect "I've found a new job," she said.	*Past perfect* She said that she had found a new job.
Present perfect progressive He said, "I've been running around all day."	*Past perfect progressive* He said that he had been running around all day.
Simple past "I saw Maria in Saskatoon last Saturday," he said.	*Past perfect* He said that he had seen Maria in Saskatoon the previous Saturday.
Future She said, "I'll be in Nova Scotia by Friday."	*Conditional* She said that she would be in Nova Scotia by Friday.
Future progressive "I'll be needing the car on the fifteenth," Paul said.	*Conditional progressive* Paul said that he would be needing the car on the fifteenth.
Conditional "I would really like to go," he said.	*Conditional (no tense change)* He said that he would really like to go.

8.05 Paragraphing: run-in format

If you are using the run-in format to quote two or more consecutive paragraphs from the same source, place quotation marks at the beginning of each paragraph and at the end of the last:

> The Minister outlined his vision of the new Department of Fisheries and Oceans (DFO) and its role in ocean and marine resource management: "Our mission is to manage Canada's oceans in close co-operation with other federal departments and stakeholders . . . .
>
> "Stewardship of oceans and coastal resources is a responsibility that must be shared by all levels of government, business, unions and other interested parties.
>
> "Sustainable development requires decision making that is open, transparent and based on sound environmental management principles. It must apply multidisciplinary approaches and integrate economic, environmental and social considerations."

Similarly, material quoted from a letter should carry quotation marks before the first line (usually the salutation) and after the last line (usually the signature), as well as at the beginning of each new paragraph. However, block quotations would be more appropriate in such cases.

8.06 Block format

A block quotation set off from the text is not enclosed in quotation marks. However, it requires indention, single spacing, and double spacing above and below the passage to set it off. Smaller font size is an alternative to single spacing or indention. Use a colon at the end of introductory phrases:

> In "Keeping Our Words," Burkhard Bilger examines the rapid extinction of most Native American languages and concludes that, although traditional field work might be the only way to save these languages, linguists are running out of time and financial support:
>
> > Endangered languages, like endangered species, might be infinitely valuable, but funding and linguistic expertise are finite. They could resort to triage, ignoring both the healthiest languages and the lost causes to concentrate the money where it will make the most difference. Saving a language, however, is more unpredictable than saving a battlefield casualty. A single committed speaker can resuscitate a language, whereas a million suppressed or indifferent speakers can let their language die in a generation.[1]

Note that in this case the source is mentioned at the beginning of the passage and further information is given in footnotes or endnotes. Place any in-text reference notes (see 9.25) at the end of the block, immediately after the period.

8.07 Paragraphing: block format

If the block quotation begins with a complete sentence—whether or not this was the first sentence of the paragraph in the source document—the first line may be indented further in order to match the format of subsequent paragraphs in the quotation:

The Auditor General's report brings out a major contradiction in the way finances are being handled:

> There have been major initiatives in public administration in the last fifteen years: the emergence of value-for-money auditing, the creation of the Office of the Comptroller General, Part III of the Estimates, the emphasis on internal audit, the advent of program evaluation, and emphasis on the three E's of economy, efficiency and effectiveness. Many of these had their origins in the government itself.
>
> Yet, despite these many initiatives, Canada's finances are not in any better shape. Changes in process have not solved the fundamental problem of balancing expenditures with revenues. As early as 1976, the Auditor General was "deeply concerned that Parliament, and indeed the government," had lost, or was "close to losing, effective control of the public purse."

8.08 Quotations within quotations

Material that was already a quotation in the source document or speech should be enclosed in single quotation marks when run into text and in double quotation marks within block quotations. The same rules of punctuation apply (see 8.03):

Run-in

In his article "The Grand Illusion," Robert Fulford states: "Television news responds to one of our most profound needs: it reduces the chaos of the day to something approaching order. The anthropologist Clifford Geertz has explained that human beings are 'symbolizing, conceptualizing, meaning-seeking' animals who wish to 'make sense out of their experience, to give it form and order.'"

Block

In his article "The Grand Illusion," Robert Fulford writes as follows:

> Television news responds to one of our most profound needs: it reduces the chaos of the day to something approaching order. The anthropologist Clifford Geertz has explained that human beings are "symbolizing, conceptualizing, meaning-seeking" animals who wish to "make sense out of their experience, to give it form and order."

In the rare event that a further quotation within a quotation occurs, enclose it in double quotation marks:

> He answered, "I was told, 'Keep the document marked "Secret" in a safe place.'"

8.09 Omissions

Omissions of material from a quoted passage, whether run-in or block, should be indicated by ellipsis points (three spaced dots) positioned on the line and separated by one space from the preceding text or from any punctuation marks that follow it.

Note

There is an alternative format. It requires no spaces before, between or after the ellipsis points (*economic...developments*).

The use of ellipsis points can vary, depending on whether they indicate an omission in the middle of a sentence, at the beginning or at the end.

(a) In the middle of a sentence

Use other punctuation marks together with ellipsis points only if they are essential for clarity:

Original sentence
Interviews, often disparaged for their judgmental subjectivity, have been more successful than alternative selection methods.
—Optimum

Quoted sentence with omission
According to *Optimum*, "Interviews . . . have been more successful than alternative selection methods."

Note that the comma after *Interviews* has been dropped[1] and that the word itself begins with a capital *I* because the quotation, even with the omission, is still a complete sentence.

(b) At the beginning of a sentence

To represent omission of the beginning of a sentence, use three dots followed by a space. If, in a quoted passage, one or more preceding sentences have been left out, use four dots—a period immediately following the preceding word and then three spaced dots:

Complete quotation
The Canadian committee system is much less effective than it could be because of the high rate of substitutions and turnover permitted. Much of the problem with the Canadian committee system is that membership turnover is so high that few committees ever develop the continuity, expertise and mutual trust that make a committee effective. A change of attitudes and habits is required and we suggest a new parliamentary convention that committee membership be stable.
—Royal Commission on Financial Management and Accountability,
Final Report

Quotation with omissions
The Canadian committee system is much less effective than it could be because of the high rate of substitutions and turnover permitted. . . . We suggest a new parliamentary convention that committee membership be stable.

The four dots in this case represent omission of a whole sentence and the beginning of the next. Note that the first letter after the ellipsis is capitalized, even though it does not begin a new sentence in the original. In legal writing, indicate any such change by enclosing the capitalized letter in square brackets.

---

1. The example illustrates the care that must be taken in presenting partial quotations. The omitted qualifying phrase is non-restrictive, that is, it is not required for the rest of the sentence to be syntactically correct and to make perfect sense on its own. Had the commas not been placed around it in the original, the phrase would have been restrictive: it would have defined a certain type of interview and could not have been dropped without altering the meaning of its antecedent, *Interviews*, and misrepresenting the facts in the quotation. See also 7.14.

(c) At the end of a sentence

To represent omission of the last part of a quoted sentence, use four dots, but this time the ellipsis points come first, followed by a period to indicate the end of the sentence:

> **Quotation with omissions**
> The Canadian committee system is much less effective than it could be because of the high rate of substitutions and turnover permitted. Much of the problem with the Canadian committee system is that membership turnover is so high that few committees ever develop the continuity, expertise and mutual trust that make a committee effective. A change of attitudes and habits is required . . . .

Ellipsis points can also indicate that a sentence has been interrupted or deliberately left incomplete:

> **M. Fulton:** Oh, one minute. Perhaps we could expand a little bit, then, into the forestry job question for B.C. I am sure Mr. Reed is abundantly aware of the . . .
> **The Vice-Chairman:** The answer will have to be given in writing.

> The critic said, "I realize the play has its good qualities, but . . ."

(d) If one or more paragraphs have been omitted, use four dots, that is, three spaced dots immediately following the period at the end of the preceding paragraph. If the next paragraph in the quotation begins with a sentence that does not open a paragraph in the original, it should be preceded by three ellipsis points after the usual indention.

(e) A complete line of dots from the left-hand margin to the right-hand margin is used to indicate the omission of one or more lines of poetry quoted in block format. The same rules of omission as for prose apply to the omission of one or more lines of poetry quoted in run-in format.

> In the poem "Bushed," Earle Birney says:

>> But the moon carved unknown totems out of the
>> lakeshore owls in the beardusky woods derided him
>> . . . .
>> then he knew though the mountain slept the winds
>> were shaping its peak to an arrowhead poised.

8.10 Insertions, alterations and parentheses

While every quotation must be scrupulously exact, you may wish to provide the reader with information to clarify items in the quotation. For example, you may feel it advisable to indicate to whom the possessive adjective refers in the following:

> The official insisted: "We foresee no change in their environmental policy in the near future."

155

The clarification is made by means of square brackets:

> The official insisted: "We foresee no change in [United States] environmental policy in the near future."

If you need to indicate an error in the original, such as a misspelling, insert the Latin word *sic*, italicized and enclosed in brackets, immediately after the word concerned. The addition of [*sic*] assures the reader of the accuracy of the quotation.

When used in this way, [*sic*] should not be followed by a period or an exclamation mark. Avoid implicit comments on peculiarities of form or content by means of an exclamation mark or question mark enclosed in parentheses.

If you wish to draw attention to specific parts of a quotation, underline or italicize them. The reader must be informed in a footnote, or in parentheses or brackets immediately following the quotation, by means of a phrase such as *Italics mine*, *Underlining mine* or *My emphasis*, that the emphasis was not in the original.

8.11 Reference to words as such

When referring to a word's form rather than its meaning, use quotation marks to draw the reader's attention. Usually these words are preceded by terms such as *means, marked, specified, as, referred to as, the word, the phrase, entitled* and *designated*. Most writers prefer to place words referred to as such in italics or to underline them rather than to use quotation marks, but consistency in form is the golden rule (see 6.08). Words being defined, French terms and foreign words are set in italics, and their definition or translation is placed in quotation marks:

> The Canadian International Development Agency will be referred to as "the Agency" in this Agreement.

> The French word *dotation* means "staffing."

> *Ibid.*, short for *ibidem*, meaning "in the same place," is used when references to the same work follow each other without any other intervening reference.

See 6.03 for information on the use of italics with French or foreign words and phrases.

8.12 Words used in an ironic or special sense; slang and technical terms

(a) Slang and colloquial terms are often peculiar to one region and should be enclosed in quotation marks if they are foreign to the normal vocabulary of the intended readers:

> The prairie fire was finally "gunnybagged" with the help of local farmers.

Vernacular terms used for effect in administrative documents and reports are treated in the same way.

However, the enclosure of supposed slang or colloquial words in quotation marks is often unnecessary. First, ascertain whether the term is now part of the standard language. If it is, quotation marks are not required. If the term is still a slang term, determine whether using it, rather than a synonym that is standard, is warranted—for rhetorical effect or in order to demonstrate a person's or group's speech or style, for example.

(b) Technical terms may be enclosed in quotation marks in non-technical writing:

> The steel has to be "cold-rolled" before further processing.

> A research team headed by Luigi Luca Cavalli-Sforza, a geneticist at Stanford, completed a global survey of "genetic markers"—variations in proteins and enzymes, for example, that reflect data in a person's DNA.

This practice is often unnecessary, however, in an era when the educated lay reader has some knowledge of modern science and engineering. Depending on the target readership, technical terms may not need special treatment.

8

(c) Quotation marks can also enclose words used ironically:

> Many "experts" were called in for consultation.

> The party whip called the five renegade MPs in for a "full and frank discussion" of the issue.

Here again, it is often possible to avoid quotation marks by using the preceding text to prepare the reader for the irony.

(d) Words used in a special sense or juxtaposed to terms with which they are not usually associated require quotation marks:

> The mayor was considered a "stuffed shirt."

> There is a high-technology spillover which makes human communication with machines easier and is helping to create "intelligent" robots.

8.13 Titles

Quotation marks should enclose the titles of the following when those titles are presented within the body of the text, in footnotes and in bibliographies:

- articles from newspapers, magazines and periodicals
- chapters of books
- short stories published in collections
- lectures and papers
- songs and short musical compositions
- short poems, and poems from collections

- dissertations and theses
- unpublished manuscripts
- radio and television programs

See 6.05 for titles of works that are italicized.

8.14 French and foreign-language quotations

When including a quotation (as opposed to individual words or phrases) from French or foreign-language documents in your text, do **not** use italics. The material can be quoted as it stands, without a translation, as long as the Roman alphabet is used, the intended reader has sufficient knowledge of the source language and the context is explicit enough for the quotation to be understood. If you do provide a translation, however, you must enclose it in quotation marks. There are several ways to proceed.

Once the decision to give a translation has been made, it is preferable to quote from a translation that has already been published or gained credibility in some other way (in a thesis, for example) rather than to provide one of your own.

Place the translation of a short quotation or title (itself enclosed in quotation marks or italicized if it is the title of a published work) in square brackets immediately after the original, as in the examples below:

> Chapter 5, "Die Benennung" ["Terms"], contains an extensive description of rules for the construction of German words and terms.
>
> Chapters 6 and 7 contain an elaborate classification of *Zeichen* [signs].
>
> Wüster states: "Ein Schriftsonderzeichen ist jedes Zeichen, das kein Schriftgrundzeichen ist." ["A special writing character is any symbol that is not a main writing character."]
>
> The reader should consult Choul's article "Approches de la traduction technique" ["Approaches to Technical Translation"] for further information.

For a long quotation, give a translation in a footnote on the same page.

Whether you are presenting both the original and the translated quotation, a quotation from a published translation, or your own translation, do not forget to identify the translation in a footnote or immediately before or after the quotation, as illustrated below:

> Belorgey goes on to say:
>
> *[Translation]*
> The considerable growth in governments' powers has won general acceptance because it is seen as the best way of providing the services needed by the community.

or

Belorgey goes on to say:

The considerable growth in governments' powers has won general acceptance because it is seen as the best way of providing the services needed by the community.

[Translation]

In all cases, the source of the original must be referred to in a footnote.

An alternative to a source-language or translated quotation is an English paraphrase of the passage concerned, presented within the body of the paragraph and introduced by a phrase or clause such as *According to X* or *X notes that*. This approach is appropriate if emphasis is to be placed solely on the ideas contained in the source material, not on any special characteristics that can be communicated only through direct quotation.

Whether the passage finally presented is a paraphrase, a quotation from a published translation, or your own translation, take great care to ensure that the content of the original has been rendered accurately. Even translations from prestigious publishing houses often contain serious translation errors.

8.15 Abuse of quotation marks

Quotation marks should not enclose titles at the beginning of papers or articles, chapter headings, epigraphs, well-known literary expressions, the words *yes* or *no* (except in direct speech), proverbs or well-known sayings, matter following *so-called*, or mathematical or scientific symbols.

8

Chapter Nine

9

9

Reference Matter

9.01 Introduction

The purpose of this chapter is to provide guidelines for the organization and presentation of bibliographies, footnotes, endnotes and indexes.

Bibliographies and reference notes are the means used by authors in all fields to document the source of any quotations or ideas that are not their own. Footnotes and endnotes may also contain a reference to information found elsewhere in the book or article, or provide supplementary or background data that cannot easily be incorporated into the body of the text. Indexes, on the other hand, never contain information; they guide the reader to information in the text.

Bibliographies

9.02 General

Bibliographies are indispensable research tools that list books and articles related to a general or highly specialized field of study in order to help the reader locate and consult a particular book or article. Reference works should always be listed in the same manner within a single bibliography, for reasons of precision, uniformity and clarity. Bibliographic standards have been established for the translation of a reference work listing from one language to another. The bibliographic style presented here is based on International Standard ISO 690 entitled *Documentation—Bibliographic References—Content, Form and Structure* and on ISBD (International Standard Bibliographic Description) protocols.

9.03 Types of bibliography

Various types of bibliography are possible, depending on the nature of the book or document in which they are to appear. A bibliography may list all the works consulted by a writer, as well as others the writer believes readers will find useful, or it may be restricted to a listing of works actually cited in the text. An **annotated bibliography** contains comments made by the author concerning the scope, usefulness or other features of the works listed. A bibliography may appear at the end of a book, report or other document (before the index, if any), at the end of a chapter, or as a separate document.

9.04 Arrangement

If a book covers a broad subject, or if each chapter in it is devoted to a different topic, it may be more practical to break the source material down into a general bibliography of works covering the subject as a whole and a number of separate listings of works referring to specific chapter topics or fields. *The Canada Year Book*, for example, contains a listing of general reference works as well as separate listings, at the end of each chapter, on such topics as geography, health, the legal system, art and culture, banking and finance, and transportation. Other arrangements are possible—separate listings for books and articles, for example. In most cases, however, a straightforward, alphabetical, letter-by-letter arrangement (see 9.42) will suffice. Choose an arrangement that presents the source works in as clear, orderly and logical a manner as possible.

9.05 Romanization

Romanization is the transcription of characters of another alphabet into Roman characters so as to make a text, and specifically a bibliographic entry, readable. The Library of Congress and the International Organization for Standardization have published conversion tables to facilitate transcription.

9.06 Translation

If the translated (English) title appears on the title page of a publication in another language, it follows the primary title in the bibliographic entry and is italicized, with a period separating the two elements:

> Von Keitz, S., and W. von Keitz. *Bibliotheks- und Informationswissenschaft. Library and Information Science.* Weinheim, Germany: VCH Verlagsgesellschaft, 1989.

If you yourself must provide a translation, insert the English version of the title (no italics) in brackets after the primary title, capitalize the initial word, and place a period after the closing bracket:

> Chang-Rodríguez, Eugenio. *Latinoamérica: su civilización y su cultura* [Latin America: its culture and civilization]. Boston: Heinle and Heinle, 1991.

For a publication in which French and English titles are given, both languages should be included:

> Canada. Department of Canadian Heritage. *Convention on the Rights of the Child. First Report of Canada / Convention relative aux droits de l'enfant. Premier rapport du Canada.* Ottawa, May 1994.

Note the space on each side of the oblique.

The publisher's name should not be translated, but for the benefit of the unilingual reader the place of publication may be:

> *L'Europa mediterranea: Spagna, Portogallo, Francia.* Arnoldo Mondadori, ed. Milano (Milan): Panorama, 1990.

When no translation is given on the title page, check whether translations of the work are already on record at the National Library of Canada, the Canada Institute for Scientific and Technical Information (CISTI) or elsewhere before translating the primary title. Accuracy of translation is essential.

9.07 Principal source of information

The principal source of information when listing a work should be the work itself. In the case of a monograph (book, pamphlet), the title page and overleaf are the sources of information, whereas for a work published in a series (periodical), the main source is the title page or, in the absence of a title page, the cover, the running title or the copyright page. In the case of a computerized document, information for the bibliographic entry is found on the sticker on the disk, diskette or packaging. For films and videotapes, the main sources of information are the credits and the packaging. If any bibliographic details are missing and cannot be found in the principal source of information, scan the document itself or check library records.

9.08 Compiling a bibliographic entry

(a) Books

A bibliographic entry for a book should generally comprise the following:

- Author's name (one or several authors; corporate author; editor or compiler, if there is no author; translator or illustrator, if either is the focus of the study)
- Title (includes title and subtitle)
- Secondary responsibility (includes editor, translator, compiler, preface writer, etc.)
- Edition (other than the first)
- Publication data (place of publication, publisher, date)

These components are separated by periods and a space, and the second and subsequent lines of an entry are indented.

(b) Articles

An entry for an article in a periodical should contain the following:

- Author's name
- Title of the article
- Name of the periodical

- Volume and issue number (if any)

- Date

- Page number(s) (inclusive)

The article title is enclosed in quotation marks and followed by a period inside the closing quotation marks. Note that the date is placed in parentheses and no comma separates it from the volume or issue number. In accordance with International Standard ISO 690: 1987, the abbreviation *p.* or *pp.* may be omitted, and a colon then precedes the page number(s). However, if the volume number has not been given, the abbreviation is used and is preceded by a comma:

> Moore, Jason. "Understanding Old Age." *Popular Medicine* 7,3 (August 1991): 210–14.

> Luna, James. "Allow Me to Introduce Myself: The Performance Art of James Luna." *Canadian Theatre Review* 68 (Fall 1991), pp. 46-7.

(c) Specialized periodicals

Bibliographic, footnote and endnote entries for articles in specialized periodicals in the natural, applied and social sciences are generally presented as follows:

- Only the first word in the article title and proper nouns and their derivatives are capitalized.

- Since most scientific publications use the author-date system in references, the date of publication is placed directly after or below the author's name.

- No quotation marks are used for the title of the article.

- The title of the publication is invariably abbreviated and in most cases not italicized.

- The volume or issue number is followed by a colon, and *p.* or *pp.* is not used.

> Ivanovic, M., and K. Higita. 1991. Advances in cellular and development biology. Can. J. Biochem. 125: 539-41.

Note the use of periods with the abbreviations.

See 9.25 for the author-date system and 9.29 for title abbreviations.

9

9.09 Author's name

List a maximum of three names of people or groups of people responsible for the content of the work. Give the author's name exactly as it appears on the title page of the work. Do **not** abbreviate a name that has been given in full.

Omit an author's titles, affiliations or degrees.

See 9.42 and 9.45 on how to alphabetize names in a list.

(a) One author

The author's name may be that of a person or persons or of a corporate body. A person's surname precedes a given name or initials. The article (*A*, *An* or *The*) at the beginning of a corporate author's name is usually omitted, as is any term identifying the nature of the enterprise, such as *Inc.* or *Co.*:

> Carpenter, Thomas. *Profiles in Canadian Genius*. Camden East, Ont.: Camden, 1990.
>
> Canada. Public Service Commission of Canada. *Selection Standards*. Ottawa, 1989.

If there are multiple entries by the same author, begin the second and subsequent entries with a 3-em dash and a period:

> Atwood, Margaret. *Wilderness Tips*. Toronto: McClelland and Stewart, 1991.
>
> ———. *The Robber Bride*. Toronto: McClelland and Stewart, 1993.

(b) Two or three authors

Open the entry with the first name mentioned in the document. Only the first name listed is inverted; the rest are transcribed as they appear in the document, separated by a comma:

> Eagleson, Alan, and Scott Young. *Powerplay: The Memoirs of Hockey Czar Alan Eagleson*. Toronto: McClelland and Stewart, 1991.

(c) More than three authors

When there are four or more authors responsible for a single work, the entry should begin with the name of the first author, inverted, followed by a comma, a space and "et al." (short for *et alii*), meaning "and others":

> Klassen, Paul, et al. *The Butterflies of Manitoba*. Winnipeg: Manitoba Museum, 1989.

(d) Editor

An editor may have primary responsibility for a work or may share it with a writer. In the former case, the editor's name is placed first in the bibliographic entry, followed by a comma and the abbreviation *ed.* (*eds.* for more than one editor). In the latter case, the editor's name, preceded by "Edited by," follows the title of the work:

> Tortelli, Anthony B., ed. *Sociology Approaching the Twenty-first Century.* Los Angeles: Peter and Sons, 1991.

> Moodie, Susannah. *Roughing It in the Bush, Or, Life in Canada.* Edited by Carl Ballstadt. Ottawa: Carleton University Press, 1990.

(e) Corporate author

List documents lacking a specified author or editor under the title of the sponsoring body, which may be a country or its government; a department, board, agency or commission; an association, company, institution or firm; or even a sporting event or exhibition.

In the interest of clarity, cite the full name of the corporate author, **not** its abbreviated form. If the organization is better known by its acronym or by some other shortened version of its name, choose the more familiar, reduced form, as in "Unesco" instead of "United Nations Educational, Scientific and Cultural Organization."

The name of a superior governing authority is usually listed first in a bibliographic entry, unless the corporate author's name includes a term indicating the organization's dependence. Therefore, list

> Unesco. Adult Education Section.

not

> United Nations. Unesco.

In the case of government publications, begin the entry with the name of the country, province, state or municipality issuing the document:

> Canada. Department of the Environment. *Trademarks on Base-Metal Software.* Ottawa: Canada Communication Group, 1991.

When listing a court of law, indicate the political entity under which it exercises its power, as in "Canada. Supreme Court" or "Manitoba. Court of Queen's Bench."

(f) Pseudonyms and anonymous works

Authors better known by a pseudonym than by their real name should be listed under that pseudonym. Where required, give the author's real name or place "pseud." in brackets after the pseudonym. In the case of anonymous works for which the author's identity has been established, place the author's real name in square brackets. Otherwise, list the work by its title followed by the rest of the bibliographic information. Do **not** use "anonymous" or "anon." unless the author really is unknown:

> Carroll, Lewis [Charles Lutwidge Dodgson]. *Through the Looking Glass.* New York: Random House, 1946.

Eliot, George. *Middlemarch*. Norton Critical Editions. New York:
W. W. Norton, 1977.

[Horsley, Samuel]. *On the Prosodies of the Greek and Latin Languages.*
1796.

"Summer is Icumen In." In *Immortal Poems of the English Language.*
Edited by Oscar Williams. New York: Pocket Books, 1954.

9.10 Order of precedence

Note the following conventions for the order of bibliographic entries:

- A single-author entry precedes a multiple-author entry beginning with the same name.

- An author's own volume precedes one that he or she has edited or compiled.

- Corporate authors are alphabetized according to the first key word in the name (not *A*, *An* or *The*).

- A list of works by the same author is presented in chronological order.

The rules given in 9.42 for alphabetizing index entries also apply to bibliographies.

9.11 Title

Transcribe the title as it appears on the title page; the original capitalization and punctuation need not be retained. Italicize titles of published works such as books or periodicals. If the work being listed is published within another document, such as an article in a periodical, set the title off in quotation marks:

Horsman, Jenny. *"Something in My Mind Besides the Everyday": Women and Literacy in Nova Scotia.* Toronto: Women's Press, 1990.

Clement, Lesley D. "Artistry in Mavis Gallant's 'Green Water, Green Sky': The Composition of Structure, Pattern, and Gyre." *Canadian Literature* 129 (Summer 1991), pp. 57–73.

If the title is in two or more languages, transcribe the titles as they appear, separating them with an oblique (/) and a space on each side of the oblique:

The Future of Canadian Programming and the Role of Private Television: Keeping Canada on the Information Highway / L'avenir des émissions canadiennes et le rôle de la télévision privée: Maintien du Canada sur l'autoroute électronique. Report to the Minister of Canadian Heritage. March 1995.

See 9.06 for information on translated titles.

Any subtitle should follow the title after a colon and a space. If the title and subtitle are italicized, so is the colon:

Schwartz, Ellen. *Born A Woman: Seven Canadian Singer-Songwriters.*
Vancouver: Polestar Press, 1988.

9.12 Secondary responsibility

Mention the name of the writer of the preface, foreword or introduction only if there is specific reference to that part of the book and if the writer is not the same as the author of the rest of the work. List the author of the cited preface, foreword or introduction, then the title of the book, followed by the name of the author of the book itself:

> Atwood, Margaret. Afterword to *A Jest of God*, by Margaret Laurence. Toronto: McClelland and Stewart, 1993.

Place the name of a person or group who is not primarily responsible for the work itself, such as a compiler, editor, translator or illustrator, after the title, using the appropriate term or abbreviation ("Comp. by," "Edited by," "Trans. by," "Illus. by"):

> Wood, A. J. *Errata: A Book of Historical Errors*. Illus. by Hemesh Alles. Stewart House, 1992.

> Laferrière, Dany. *Eroshima*. Trans. by David Homel. Toronto: Coach House, 1991.

If no author is mentioned, the name of the editor, translator or compiler takes the place of the author:

> Bryden, Philip, Steven Davis and John Russell, eds. *Protecting Rights and Freedoms: Essays on the Charter's Place in Canada's Political, Legal, and Intellectual Life*. Toronto: University of Toronto Press, 1994.

9.13 Edition

When citing an edition other than the first one, indicate the edition used in Arabic numerals and abbreviate the word "edition" as "ed.":

> Werther, William B., et al. *Canadian Human Resource Management*. 3rd ed. Whitby, Ont.: McGraw-Hill Ryerson, 1990.

The words "reprint," "printing" and "impression" do not indicate a new edition.

9.14 Place, publisher and date

(a) Place of publication

If a document has more than one place of publication, choose the Canadian city, if any, or the first city mentioned. When it is necessary to differentiate a place of publication from others with the same name or to identify one that is not well known, add a geographic identifier (name of country, province or state), in an abbreviated form:

> Willmot, Elizabeth. *When Anytime Was Train Time*. Erin, Ont.: Boston Mills, 1992.

If the place of publication is not given, insert "N.p." for "no place of publication," in square brackets.

(b) Publisher

Listed after the place of publication, the publisher's name is preceded by a colon and a space, and followed by a comma. The publisher's name should be transcribed as it appears in the document, but articles and abbreviations such as *Co.*, *Ltd.* and *Inc.* are usually dropped:

> Harris, R. Cole, and John Warkentin. *Canada Before Confederation: A Study in Historical Geography.* Ottawa: Carleton University Press, 1991.

The publisher's name may be given in full or in an acceptable abbreviated form. For abbreviations of publishers' names, consult *Canadian Books in Print* and *Books in Print*.

If the name of the publisher is not provided, insert "n.p." for "no publisher," in square brackets.

(c) Date of publication

The date of publication is preceded by a comma and is always written in Arabic numerals. If the date of publication is not provided, add the copyright date instead.

If neither the date of publication nor the copyright date can be ascertained, check library records for the missing information. You can either give an estimated date of publication followed by a question mark, enclosing both in square brackets, or add "n.d." for "no date of publication." Give inclusive dates for a multivolume work:

> Banicek, Edward. *A History of Indonesia.* 3 vols. Philadelphia: Ross and Kittredge, 1988–93.

If a multivolume work has yet to be completed and all the volumes in print are listed, indicate the date of the first volume, followed by an en dash:

> Skelton, Margaret. *A Critical History of Modern Dance.* 2 vols. to date. Chicago: Terpsichore Press, 1987–.

9.15 Series

This item is reserved for works that are a part of a special collection. Include any number that has been assigned to the document cited. The name of the collection, followed by a comma, the abbreviation "No." and the number of the document are placed after the title:

> Martin, Robert, and G. Stuart Adam. *A Sourcebook of Canadian Media Law.* Carleton Library Series, No. 51. Ottawa: Carleton University Press, 1989.

9.16 Examples of specific entries

(a) Conference proceedings

Conference proceedings are identified by the title of the conference:

> *Cultural Economics 88: A Canadian Perspective.* Proceedings of the 5th International Conference on Cultural Economics, Ottawa, September 27–30, 1988. 3 vols. Edited by Harry Hillman-Chartrand, et al. Akron, Ohio: Association for Cultural Economics, 1989.

(b) Lectures

Give the speaker's name, the title of the lecture in quotation marks, followed by a descriptive identifier (seminar, address, lecture, etc.), the sponsoring organization, the location and the date:

> Massé, Marcel. "Partners in the Management of Canada: The Changing Roles of Government and the Public Service." John L. Manion Lecture, Canadian Centre for Management Development. Ottawa, February 18, 1993.

(c) Dissertations

List a published dissertation in the same way as other books, but identify the work as a dissertation and mention the academic institution:

> Collard, Janice. *The Theme of Rebirth in Canadian Drama.* Master's thesis. McGill University, 1989. Montréal: McGill-Queen's University Press, 1992.

Leave the title of an unpublished dissertation in roman type and enclose it in quotation marks:

> Monks, Ashley Andrew. "Gypsy Wanderings: Dialectal Differentiations in the Romany Language." Master's thesis. University of British Columbia, 1995.

(d) Electronic documents

Documents stored on a CD-ROM, computer disk or database are generally listed by title. The citation must specify, in square brackets, the type of document being listed and include information needed to identify and retrieve the work:

> "Acquired Immunodeficiency Syndrome." In MESH vocabulary file [database on-line]. Bethesda, Md.: National Library of Medicine, 1990 [cited October 3, 1990]. Identifier No. D000163. [49 lines.]

For further information regarding the listing of electronic sources, refer to International Standard ISO 690-2 *Information and Documentation— Bibliographic References—Electronic Documents or Parts Thereof.*

(e) Film and videotape

Depending on the focus of your study, a film or videotape can be listed under its title or the name of the director, producer, screenwriter or principal actor. Whatever the first component of the bibliographic entry may be, specify the medium of the work in square brackets at the end of the entry:

> Borsos, Phillip, dir. *Dr. Bethune.* With Donald Sutherland and Helen Mirren. 1990. [Film.]

(f) Musical recordings

Give the name of the composer, title of the recording (or works on the recording), artist's name (where applicable), manufacturer, catalogue number (if known), year of issue, and any other pertinent information:

> Prokofiev, Sergei. *Romeo and Juliet* (excerpts). Montreal Symphony Orchestra. Cond. Charles Dutoit. London: Decca Records, 1991.

> Somers, Harry. *The Fool.* With Roxalana Roslak, Patricia Rideout, David Astor and Maurice Brown. Cond. Victor Feldbrill, RCA, LSC 3094 (CBC, 272), n.d.

Bibliographic entries for published musical scores are similar to those for books.

(g) Interviews

Enter the name of the interviewee, the type of interview (personal, telephone, etc.), and the date:

> Egoyan, Atom. Personal interview. November 27, 1994.

(h) Radio and television programs

List the entry under the title of the program and include the network or local station, the city, the broadcast date, together with other pertinent information. Note that titles of television and radio shows are italicized and that segments and episodes are set off in quotation marks:

> *You Be the Doctor.* "The Lifestyle Crisis." With Valerie Pringle. Prod. by Jack McGraw. CTV Toronto Film Production. August 1,1995.

(i) Theatrical performances

In addition to the title of the play, the playwright, director and principal actor, give the name of the theatre, the city and the date of performance, along with any other pertinent information:

> Caird, John, and Trevor Nunn. *Les Misérables.* By Victor Hugo. With William Solo. Royal Shakespeare Company. National Arts Centre, Ottawa, 1994.

(j) Legislative documents

Acts, regulations and legal notices are published in federal and provincial government gazettes, which should be listed as follows:

> *The Canada Gazette. Part II.* Vol. 125, No. 1 (2 January 1991)–Vol. 125, No. 17 (14 August 1991).

Note that the title of the gazette is italicized and that the jurisdiction and legislative body need not be mentioned.

Adopt the following order for order papers and notices: name of government; name of department, agency or institution; title of document; legislature and session numbers; volume and issue numbers (if any); issue date; and publication data:

> Canada. Parliament. House of Commons. *Order Paper and Notices.* 33rd Parliament, 1st Session. No. 134 (28 June 1985). Ottawa: Queen's Printer, 1985.

9.17 Secondary source citations

When referring to a work that has been cited within another, list as the first component of your entry the work that is the focus of your text: either the work that has been quoted or the work in which it is quoted. The first-mentioned work, or **primary reference**, should be listed in the standard fashion. For the second document, or **secondary source**, the bibliographic data should be separated by commas. If the secondary source is a book, enclose the publication data in parentheses:

> Burns, Robert. *Epistle to a Young Friend.* 1786. Quoted in Robertson Davies, *The Deptford Trilogy: The Manticore* (Toronto: Macmillan, 1987).

> **or**

> Davies, Robertson. *The Deptford Trilogy: The Manticore.* Toronto: Macmillan, 1987. Quoting Robert Burns, *Epistle to a Young Friend*, 1786.

Reference Notes

9.18 General

Reference notes may be found within a text (**in-text notes**), but are usually presented at the foot of a page (**footnotes**) or at the end of a chapter or document (**endnotes**). Reference notes pertain to works that have been directly cited or paraphrased, whereas a bibliography lists the works consulted. Footnotes and endnotes are generally referenced by means of a raised (superscript) numeral, letter or symbol immediately following the item in question. The superscript follows all punctuation marks except the dash:

> As Kenneth Dyer points out in a recent article,[1] the ambassador's criticism of the countries involved[2]—India, Pakistan and Bangladesh—upset a number of delegates.

The principal differences between notes and bibliographies are as follows:

• Reference note entries are numbered.

• The author's name is not inverted.

• Components of the entries are separated by commas rather than periods, and there is a space but no punctuation between the title and the opening parenthesis before the publication information.

• The publication data is placed within parentheses.

• Page numbers indicate the exact position of the citation.

9.19 Books

If it is not included in a bibliography, cite the source work in detail the first time it is noted. A footnote or endnote description of a book should contain the same information as a standard bibliographic reference (see 9.08(a)).

The place of publication, publisher's name and date of publication should be enclosed in parentheses, but page references should remain outside the parentheses. The author's name is followed by a comma, the name of the place of publication is followed by a colon and one space, and the publisher's name is followed by a comma. A comma follows the parentheses:

> 1. Michael Ondaatje, *The Cinnamon Peeler* (Toronto: McClelland and Stewart, 1992), p. 13.

If the source material is listed in a bibliography at the end of the text, reference notes may not require elaborate treatment. The first reference to a book may comprise only the author's initials and surname, the title of the work, and the relevant page number(s).

9.20 Subsequent references

Subsequent references to a work may be shorter still. Only the last name of the author, key word(s) in the title, and the page number(s) are required. Thus the entry for Ondaatje is reduced to

> 5. Ondaatje, *Cinnamon Peeler*, p. 13.

If only one work—book or article—by the author is quoted, his or her name and the page number(s) will suffice. For the use of the abbreviations *ibid., loc. cit. and op. cit.*, see 9.27.

9.21 Articles

Information in a note reference to a periodical or journal article should include the name of the author(s), the title of the article, the name of the periodical or journal, the volume and issue numbers, the date and the page number(s):

> 1. George E. Wilson, "New Brunswick's Entrance into Confederation," *Canadian Historical Review* 10, 1 (March 1928): 23–24.

> 2. Laura Lush, "Fishing," *Antigonish Review* 68 (Fall 1990), pp. 111–2.

Note that the abbreviation *p.* or *pp.* may be omitted (see 9.08 (b)).

9.22 Newspapers and magazines

References to newspapers and magazines require the name of the writer, article title, name of the publication, date of issue and page number. Give the name of a newspaper as it appears on the masthead:

> 1. Charles Gordon, "Hats Off to Observers Who Can Interpret the Important Events of Our Era," *The Ottawa Citizen*, June 21, 1995, p. 4.

If the city is not identified as part of the newspaper's name, give it in square brackets after the name.

9.23 Footnotes

If only a few notes are required in an article or chapter and the note material is succinct, use the footnote format. A footnote may do more than simply refer the reader to another work or page for further information; it may give information on how facts presented in the text were ascertained or confirmed. Such a note is useful for conveying supplementary data, as in the following example:

> In the United States, by contrast, approximately 49% of psychologists name either teaching or research as their principal activity, compared with only 31% for service functions.[1] Table 15 shows the numbers and proportions of English- and French-speaking[2] Canadians and of American and other foreign respondents in each of the principal work functions. It is estimated that 13–14% of Canadian psychologists are French-speaking.[3]
>
> ---
>
> 1. 1986 National Register of Scientific and Technical Personnel.
> 2. French-speaking Canadians were identified by their request for or return of the French version of the questionnaire. Further identification and response rates were confirmed through follow-up telephone contacts with non-residents (see Appendix 3).
> 3. But see discussion by Dr. Bélanger on p. 127.

Number your footnotes page by page or chapter by chapter and thereby avoid the possibility of triple-digit references.

Occasionally two distinct series of footnotes are required: an author's notes on the one hand and a translator's or editor's notes on the other. Use asterisks and a different typeface for the translator's or editor's notes, which should end with the appropriate abbreviation (*Trans.* or *Ed.*):

> *The "commission" referred to is the Canada Labour Relations Board (Ed.).

Use special symbols or letters to indicate notes within the body of mathematical, statistical and other scientific documents, and particularly with tables and graphs, as illustrated below, since superscript numerals could be confused with mathematical indices:

	1990	1995	2000[a]
Haiti	35	19	2
Canada[b]	1080	920	3005

[a]projected [b]including Quebec

9.24 Endnotes

Where notes are numerous and lengthy and include extensive comments by the author, use the endnote format to facilitate word-processing and cross-referencing and enhance the appearance of the text.

Number your references consecutively throughout the article or chapter, as in the case of footnotes, and present the notes in a reference list at the end of the article or chapter:

Notes to Chapter 2

1. M. Fleming and W. H. Levie, eds., *Instructional Message Design: Principles From the Behavioral and Cognitive Sciences*, 2nd ed. (Englewood Cliffs, N.J.: Educational Technology Publications), 1993, pp. 34–57.

2. Fleming and Levie, p. 66.

3. B. Joyce, B. Showers, and C. Rolheiser-Bennett, "Staff Development and Student Learning: A Synthesis of Research on Models of Teaching," *Educational Leadership* 45, 2 (1987): 11–23.

9.25 In-text notes

Also known as the **author-date system**, in-text notes are found in running text or at the end of a block quotation, and consist of the author's last name (where that is the name under which the work has been listed) and the date of publication of the work, both enclosed in parentheses. This brief form of citation is meant to identify the work being cited, while full bibliographic information is reserved for the list of works cited:

(Fleming and Levie 1993)

(Joyce, Showers and Rolheiser-Bennett 1987)

Note that there is no punctuation separating the two elements of the note, unless there is a reference to a specific page, volume or other division of the work. Insert a colon, but no space, between volume and page references, and start with the volume number. Unless there is a risk of confusion, omit the abbreviations *p., pp.* and *vol.*:

(Suzuki 1990, 3:45)

(Wiebe 1993, 27)

9.26 Author-number system

This alternative involves a numerical arrangement of bibliographic references. Within the body of the text the writer merely cites the name of the author of each source work, along with a key number in parentheses on the same line:

As Craven (2) has demonstrated, there is no evidence that extensive feedback played a more significant role in improving students' writing.

In an accompanying bibliographic reference list, arranged numerically, the first reference to a work contains full details—except in a book with a main bibliography at the end, in which case a shortened note is required—and subsequent notes are as brief as possible, in accordance with the guidelines given in 9.20. The bibliographic entry for the preceding example is

> 2. Craven, Mary Louise. "Chinese-Speaking University-Level ESL Students' Changes to Essay Drafts." Paper presented at TESL Conference, Toronto, November 1988.

The advantage of the author-number system is that footnotes are required only for comments by the writer, examples and allusions. The inherent difficulty is that the writer must keep a running list of source works and appropriate page numbers at the first draft stage in order to ensure that each work is assigned the same number in every pertinent note reference.

9.27 *Ibid., Loc. cit., Op. cit.*

It is now more common to give the shortened form of previously listed reference notes, but you may want to avoid unnecessary repetition by using the Latin abbreviation *ibid.*, short for *ibidem*, meaning "in the same place," for consecutive references to the same work:

> 1. Weiss, Leon, ed., *Cell and Tissue Biology* (Baltimore, Md.: Urban and Schwarzenberg, 1988), p. 1144.
> 2. Ibid.
> 3. Ibid., 1062.

Note

Reference 2 is to the same page number. Reference 3 is to another page number of the same work.

Avoid using *loc. cit.* (*loco citato*, "in the place cited") and *op. cit.* (*opere citato*, "in the work cited") when you are making a reference to a previously cited work and when references to other documents have intervened. Tracing that earlier reference can be frustrating for readers; use of the short form of the reference note gives them the required information immediately.

9.28 Legal references

Legal documents require note and bibliography formats that differ from those of general works and government publications. Lawyers and legal scholars adopt many abbreviations in their references. Use these abbreviations if the intended reader has specialized knowledge of law, but use only familiar abbreviations when writing for a general audience.

Monographs. Books on legal topics may be presented in the same format as works in the humanities. However, because of the many footnotes in legal writing, specialists tend to omit the author's initial, place of publication and publisher's name in order to save space:

> 1. Linden, *Canadian Negligence Law* (1972), at 259.

Note the use of "at" in legal references. The abbreviation *p.* or *pp.* may be dropped in the interest of brevity.

Articles. Provide information in the following order: surname of author, title of article in quotation marks, year of publication in parentheses, periodical volume number, abbreviated periodical title, the number of the first page of the article, and the actual reference page number:

> 2. Castel, "Some Legal Aspects of Human Organ Transplantation in Canada," (1968) 46 Can. Bar Rev. 345, at 361.

Court decisions. For volumes of the *Supreme Court Reports* from 1923 on, give the case name in italics, followed by a comma, the year of publication in square brackets, the issue number (if desired), the abbreviation for the Reports, the number of the first page of the judgment, and the reference page number:

> 3. *Higgins v. Comox Logging and Ry. Co.*, [1927] 1 S.C.R. 359, at 360.

For volumes prior to 1923, cite the case name in italics and the year the judgment was rendered in parentheses, followed by a comma, the volume number, the abbreviation for the Reports, and the number of the first page of the citation:

> 4. *Burland v. Moffat* (1885), 11 S.C.R. 76.

For the *Federal Court Reports* use the same format as for post-1922 S.C.R. volumes:

> 5. *Canadian Pacific Air Lines, Limited v. The Queen*, [1979] 1 F.C. 39, at 40.

For the *Dominion Law Reports* give the case name in italics and, if desired, the date of judgment in parentheses before the comma, the volume number, the abbreviation for the Reports, the series number in parentheses, the number of the first page of the judgment, the reference page number and, if desired, the abbreviation for the court in parentheses:

> 6. *Beim v. Goyer* (1966), 57 D.L.R. (2d) 253, at 256 (S.C.C.).

The reference is complete without the date; the reader could find Volume 57 of the second series without knowing the date of judgment, which is therefore an optional addition for information purposes alone. However, there is an alternative D.L.R. format which incorporates a date as part of the reference:

> 7. *Nova Mink v. TCA*, [1951] 2 D.L.R. 241, at 254 (N.S.C.A.).

Here the date, which is the date of publication and therefore not necessarily the date of judgment, is in effect part of the volume number, while the number following is that of the issue.

Note that the *v.* in such references need not be italicized.

Statutes. When citing acts of Parliament, give the short version of the title of the act, the abbreviation for the Statutes and the year, the chapter number (each statute is a separate chapter of the *Statutes of Canada*), and the section referred to:

8. *National Sports of Canada Act*, 1994, c. 16, s. 5.

For further information on legal references, consult *The Canadian Guide to Uniform Legal Citation*.

9.29 Common abbreviations in notes and bibliographies

Abbreviations can help make your footnotes, endnotes and bibliographic entries more concise. For lists of relevant abbreviations see International Standard ISO 832, *Documentation–Bibliographical References— Abbreviations of Typical Words* and the latest edition of the *MLA Handbook*.

Guidelines for the creation of title abbreviations for serial and non-serial publications are provided in International Standard ISO 4-1984, *Documentation—Rules for the Abbreviation of Title Words and Titles of Publications*. Extensive lists of abbreviations for words commonly found in scientific periodical titles can be found in the *World List of Scientific Periodicals*, and for the social sciences, in the *World List of Social Science Periodicals*.

Indexes

9.30 Definition

An index is a systematic guide to significant items or concepts mentioned or discussed in a work or group of works; the items and concepts are represented by a series of entries arranged in a known or searchable order, with a **locator,** which is an indication of the place(s) in the work(s) where reference to each item or concept may be found.

9.31 Scope and complexity

An index may be **general** or **specific**. A **general** one lists subjects, authors, persons or corporate bodies, geographical names and other items. A **specific** index is limited to a particular category of entry, such as one of the items in the above list, abbreviations and acronyms, or citations.

A work may contain a general index and one or more specific indexes. The *Dictionary of Canadian Biography,* for example, has three: an index of identifications (occupational sectors of those listed), a geographical index and a nominal index. Multiple listings are designed to help readers research a particular aspect of the subject concerned.

The complexity of indexing has fostered the development of a number of computerized indexing methods (see bibliography). Human intervention is nonetheless required for hierarchical arrangement, alphabetization, choice of terms, word order, capitalization and cross-referencing.

9.32 Arrangement

The order of entries is usually alphabetical, and each entry is followed by a locator. The arrangement may vary, however, depending on the contents of the work being indexed. A chronological arrangement would be suitable for an index of historical events and persons, for example, and a numerical one might be required for lists of chemical elements, patents or highways.

9.33 Length

Agreement must be reached beforehand with the publisher on the length of the index. Normally, an index should not exceed five percent of the number of pages in the work itself. The need for completeness should be tempered by consideration of the extent of the prospective reader's knowledge of the subject matter.

9.34 Referenced material

Do **not** index the title page of a work, its table of contents and dedication, epigraphs, abstracts of articles, or synopses at the beginning of chapters. Include references to illustrations, photographs, graphs, tables and figures only if they give pertinent information not provided in the body of the text.

On the other hand, the index should, in addition to the text proper, cover introductions, addenda, appendixes and substantive notes, forewords and prefaces that contain pertinent information, and—in the case of newspapers and periodicals—book reviews and letters to the editor.

9.35 Simple entry

A **simple entry** is composed of an **identifier,** which is the heading, and a **locator**—the page or section number(s) where reference to the item may be found:

> Domino theory, 911
> Drainage basins, 4–6
> Drugs, control of, 180–82
> Duties, customs and excise, 802, 812, 818, 824

Each item is listed according to the key word, so inversion of phrases is often necessary, with a comma separating the two elements of the inversion. The key word should be the one that the reader is likely to look up in order to find the information required. The full heading is followed by a comma. The page numbers are given without *p.* or *pp.*, and inclusive numbers should be presented in accordance with the rules enunciated in 5.24, e.g. 47–48, 10–16, 213–18, 1653–1703. Avoid the use of *f., ff.* and *et seq.* in place of numerals.

9.36 Complex entry

A **complex entry** is composed of a main entry (with a main heading) and one or more subentries (subheadings), each with a locator. The complex entry may be presented in run-in or indent format:

run-in	**indent**
Maritimes, English in, 21, 32, 39; French in, 80; surveys in, 119	Maritimes, English in, 21, 32, 39 French in, 80 surveys in, 119

The two formats reflect the same inverted word order, a comma follows the heading in each case, and the second and subsequent lines of the entry are indented. In the run-in format, however, the entry is presented in paragraph style, each subentry being followed by a semicolon. In the indent format the presentation is columnar: the main entry and each subentry stand on a separate line, so semicolons are not required. In neither case does a period close the entry.

The advantage of the run-in format is that it saves space and can provide a seminarrative, chronological outline of events in a biographical or historical context, as shown in the following listing for a Canadian ship that was engaged in action in World War II:

> Haida, 197, 250; action of April 26/44, 251; action of April 29/44, 253, 258; 266; action of June 9/44, 286, 300; U-boat kill, 302; Channel and Biscay actions, 340, 348, 359, 401, 406

The advantage of the indent format is that it is more legible and makes the relationships between items more readily apparent to the reader. Use it when such relationships are to be highlighted, as in the case of scientific indexes:

> Muscles, skeletal
> congenital defects of, 342
> contracture of, 326
> diseases of, 226
> dystrophy of, 326, 896
> enzootic, 893, 896, 1015
> foals, 424
> hypertrophy, inherited, 1052

The example, taken from the field of veterinary medicine, illustrates the use of sub-subentries. In such circumstances a columnar presentation is essential.

9.37 Combined entries

In order to keep your index as short as possible, combine entries for closely related concepts. For example,

> Financial management, 35, 45
> Financial systems, 56, 67

can be amalgamated to form one entry:

> Financial management and systems, 35, 45, 56, 67

If the number of subentries is particularly long, the index may be too detailed, as in the following example:

> Engineering courses
> > chemical, 46
> > civil, 47
> > electrical, 48
> > marine, 49

A combined entry suffices:

> Engineering courses, 46–49

9.38 Double posting

Because readers do not necessarily look up the same term or expression as the one selected by the indexer, you can provide multiple access points to facilitate retrieval of a given piece of information:

> Editing, principles of, 62–73
> Revision, principles of, 62–73
>
> *Hodgson v. Matthews*, 266
> *Matthews v. Hodgson*, 266

9.39 Choice of terms

The wording of the entry should be as specific as possible for the prospective reader's purposes. Popular or specialized terms may be used, depending on the reader and the nature of the work. When preparing an index, you can glean established nomenclature from the indexes of previous publications on the same subject or from thesauri, or you can create your own headings on the basis of the work at hand. In doing so, check the author's terms for consistency and accuracy and, if necessary, use a standard term instead (e.g. when indexing medical publications).

9.40 Syntax of heading

Definite and indefinite articles, adverbs, and finite and infinitive verbs should not be included in headings or subheadings except in the case of headings comprising titles of publications and works of art. The only verb form permitted is the gerund. Retain conjunctions and prepositions essential to establishing a semantic link within the headings. Some latitude is possible here, however. Note that there is no prepositional link between the heading "Muscles, skeletal" (see 9.36 above) and the subheading "hypertrophy, inherited"; the reader will understand the semantic relationship between the two items, and the columnar presentation shows that one is an aspect of the other.

In determining the word order of a heading, the first step is to select a key word or phrase under which to list the entry. For example, an indexable subject in a social science manual might be the sources and collection of statistical data. *Statistical data* would be the key term and the entry would appear thus:

Statistical data, sources and collection of, 57

Sources and collection cannot be used as a key phrase because it is not specific enough. Accordingly, the normal word order has to be inverted and a comma is required after the key phrase. Inversion serves to reduce scattering of related headings and page numbers throughout an index because headings with the same key word will be located close together, e.g. *Heating, electric* and *Heating, oil-fired*.

An action word (gerund) in a heading is normally brought to the fore if the entry is listed under a noun:

Mean, determining standard error of, 35

In the interest of brevity, however, the gerund in the above example could be dropped, since the reader will realize what is entailed in the reference.

Another way of achieving conciseness is to drop prepositions. In the following example, the key phrase is followed by a logical sequence of modifiers:

Copper ores, mining, grinding, screening, pulverizing and floating

With the key phrase in boldface type, the preposition *of* can be dropped without causing the reader any problems of comprehension.

An adjective is inverted unless it is part of a name and the noun itself is non-specific:

Oral cavity
Pulmonary disease

9.41 Entry v. subentry

The indexer is constantly faced with the problem of whether to list references to a topic in a series of simple entries or as one main entry with a number of subentries. For example, references to the various types of statistical mean are scattered throughout a statistical work. They could be indexed in one large, complex entry:

Mean
    arithmetic, 28
        for grouped data, 29, 135
        properties of, 29, 136–37
    geometric, 31
        for chained ratios, 32, 138
        properties of, 31, 139–41
    harmonic, 32, 142

Since the document is a specialized one, however, it makes more sense to create main entries for each type of mean, with a cross-reference (see 9.52) from *Mean,* thereby obviating the need for sub-subentries and the repetition of page number references.

In general, avoid single subentries and sub-subentries. In the interest of conciseness, the complex entry

> Spasticity
>> neonatal, inherited, 1046
>> periodic, inherited, 1046

can easily be reduced to

> Spasticity, inherited neonatal and periodic, 1046

9.42 Alphabetical arrangement

Headings may be alphabetized letter by letter or word by word:

letter by letter	word by word
Laurence, Margaret	Laurence, Margaret
Leacock, Stephen	Le Jeune, Père
Leechman, Douglas	Le Pan, Douglas
Le Jeune, Père	Leacock, Stephen
Le Pan, Douglas	Leechman, Douglas

In the word-by-word listing, the position of the two-word names is determined by the first word; the second part of the surname comes into play in determining which of the two names is listed first. In the letter-by-letter arrangement, the number of words in the heading is irrelevant.

Use the letter-by-letter format for an index of acronyms, letters and symbols with technical meanings, as in a scientific work.

List organizations by their acronyms or abbreviations if they are usually referred to in that way. The short form should be alphabetized letter by letter and followed immediately by the full title in parentheses or a cross-reference to that title.

A word-by-word arrangement is often used in a proper noun listing of geographical names:

North Umpqua	Northumberland Strait
North Valley Stream	Northumbria
North Vancouver	Northvale
North Vernon	Northville
North Versailles	

In a letter-by-letter listing, the entries with the word *North* would not have been grouped together.

The word-by-word listing provides for a clear grouping of related headings, e.g. *book, book jacket, book label* and *book list,* which would otherwise be separated by a heading such as *bookkeeping.* Its disadvantage is that a related term may have to be separated from the grouping because it is one word, hyphenated or unhyphenated. For example, words such as *booklet* and *bookmark* might well be separated from the above group, even though they belong to the same subject field. This shows the advantage of a letter-by-letter listing: a compound occupies the same position, whether it is unhyphenated, hyphenated or written as two words.

Note that, whichever arrangement is adopted, prepositions at the beginning of a subentry or sub-subentry must be disregarded for alphabetization purposes.

9.43 Listing of subentries

Subentries are generally listed in alphabetical order of the first noun in the subheading, but a chronological, mathematical or other listing may be appropriate, as in the case of popes, kings, element numbers in chemistry, geological eras and highway numbers. See 9.36 for an example of chronological listing in a historical work.

9.44 Capitalization

The first letter of a main heading is capitalized, except in certain French and foreign names, the names of chemical compounds with an italicized prefix, and standard symbols with a lower-case first letter:

> van Willebrand disease
> *p*-Aminobenzoic acid
> pH

In scientific texts it is important to distinguish between common and proper nouns. The first letter of a generic or family name in biology is capitalized, but that of a specific epithet or common name is not:

> spirochetes
> Sporotrichinaceae
> *Sporotrichum schenkii*

9.45 Personal names

When an article or preposition is part of an English name, it is alphabetized without inversion, e.g. *de la Roche, Mazo; De Quincey, Thomas.* Names beginning with *Mac, Mc or M'* are alphabetized as if spelled *Mac.* Ignore the apostrophe in treating an Irish name such as *O'Flynn;* alphabetize it as if it were one unpunctuated word.

French surnames beginning with an article or a contraction of an article and a preposition are listed without inversion, e.g. *Le Rouge, Gustave; Du Pont, Georges.* Similarly, names beginning with *d'* are generally not inverted, e.g. *d'Arcy, Jules.* There is no standard method for alphabetizing names beginning with *de* or *de la.* Adopt the personal preference of the individual concerned or the traditional presentation of his or her name, e.g. *Balzac, Honoré de; La Fontaine, Jean de.* Christian saints should be alphabetized by their given names, with an identifier added if necessary:

> John, Saint
> John Chrysostom, Saint
> John of the Cross, Saint

The choice between *Saint-* and *St-* and between *Sainte-* and *Ste-* in personal names depends on the traditionally preferred presentation. When an abbreviated form is used, it should be alphabetized as if spelled out.

For detailed information on the presentation of English, French and foreign-language names, see the *Anglo-American Cataloguing Rules.*

9.46 Government departments and agencies

Invert the titles of government departments, e.g. *Justice, Department of.* It may be necessary to include a general cross-reference from *Department* informing the reader that each department is listed under the name of the field for which it is responsible.

Sometimes it is worth adding a geographical identifier in parentheses for the sake of clarity:

> Sociedad Nacional de Minería (Cuba)
> Sociedad Nacional de Minería (Peru)

9.47 Geographical names

Alphabetize geographical names according to the main noun *(Ontario, Lake; Robson, Mt.)*, except where the generic noun is part of the title *(Lake of the Woods)*. Alphabetize non-English names under the article if there is one *(La Prairie; La Tuque; Los Angeles)*, but list English names with articles under the main noun *(Eastern Townships, The; Pas, The)*.

List items under the names most commonly or officially used or most recently adopted, with a cross-reference from the alternative or former title:

> Dahomey. *See* Bénin
> Moldavian S.S.R. *See* Moldova
> Rhodesia. *See* Zambia; Zimbabwe

For information about the official versions of Canadian place names, see Chapter 15.

The English version of a French or foreign place name should be used. When there are two non-English names for the same place, use the one more commonly found in written English, e.g. *Bruges*, not *Brugge*.

In the English-speaking world the same name is used for many geographical entities. Use modifiers in parentheses when necessary:

> Hull (Quebec)
> Paris (Ontario)

The same word may be listed several times:

> Québec (city)
> Quebec (government)
> Quebec (province)

When listing the numbers of the pages where reference to a place is made, remember that it may also be referred to by its generic noun alone—*the lake, the mountain,* etc.—and that such references should be included in the index entry.

9.48 Newspapers and periodicals

List an English-language newspaper under the name of the place of publication if it is part of the title and, if not, under the first word of the title after the definite article, e.g. *Gazette, The.* List French-language and foreign-language newspapers under the first noun, e.g. *Journal de Montréal, Le.* The article may be dropped unless the omission will cause difficulty or will appear curious, e.g. *Droit, Le.*

List periodicals under their full title, without the article, e.g. *Canadian Journal of Chemistry.* In periodical citation indexes the abbreviated forms of titles are used (see 9.08 and 9.29).

9.49 Scientific names

Arabic numerals, Greek letters, capital letters with a special meaning, and modifiers prefixed to the names of chemical compounds should be disregarded for alphabetization purposes unless they constitute the only difference between entries:

> *N*-Acryloneuraminic acid
> *O*-Acryloneuraminic acid

When a Greek letter stands by itself as a separate entry, Romanize it, c.g. *Pi, Gamma.*

Abbreviations for scientific terms should generally not be used at the beginning of a main entry except (i) in a cross-reference, (ii) as part of the name of an enzyme or compound, or (iii) when more than one species is listed for a biological genus:

> i) CO_2. *See* Carbon Dioxide
> ii) mRNA, 16, 56
> iii) *Ambystonia maculatum*, 15
>   *A. mexicanum*, 17

Generic names in biology should in any case be abbreviated after the main entry and alphabetized by epithet as a space-saving device:

> *Triticum sp.*
>   *T. aestivium*
>   *T. durum*

9.50 Homonyms

Adopt the following order of entry for homonyms—person or organization (forenames precede surnames); place (cities and towns precede administrative areas, which precede physical features); subject; title of publication:

> Hull, Robert (hockey player)
> Hull (Quebec)
> Hull, population of
> *Hull, A Short History of*

Within a list of personal names an alphabetical *(John, Pope; John, Saint)*, hierarchical *(John, Saint; John, Pope)* or chronological/numerical *(John XXII; John XXIII)* arrangement is possible. The usual hierarchical order is saints, popes, emperors and empresses, kings and queens, surnames:

> John, Pope
> John, Augustus

Include modifiers in parentheses after each common noun in order to distinguish it from its homonyms:

> Character (literature)
> Character (psychology)

9.51 Abbreviations and other reference tools

References to material not contained within the body of the text, such as bibliographies, glossaries, illustrations and tables, require a locator in letters as well as in numbers. The numeral can be printed in boldface type, while the element in letters is presented in italics, usually as an abbreviation:

367 *bibliogr.*	bibliography
54 *(fig. 21)*	figure
345 *glos.*	glossary
68 (fn. 2)	footnote
54 *ill.*	illustration
36 (hn.)	headnote
facing **60**	plate

When more than one significant reference to an item is made on the same page of a text, and each piece of information is useful, the words *bis* (twice) and *ter* (three times) may follow the page number in the index:

> War of 1812–14, 78 *(bis)*, 87 *(ter)*

In indexing works with many words on a page, make the reader's search for information easier by assigning a letter or number to each part of the page. For example, in the *Encyclopaedia Britannica*, the letters *a, b, c* and *d* refer to the top, upper middle, lower middle and bottom of the left column of a page, and *e, f, g* and *h* to the same parts of the right column *(23a, 23b, 23c,* etc.).

Explain all abbreviations and special reference codes in an introductory note to the index.

9.52 Cross-references

Cross-references are required to guide readers from a given heading to a related heading that will lead them to the information required or to additional information on the same subject. The cross-reference is printed in italics, except when the subject heading referred to is itself normally presented in italics:

> Archaisms. *See* Relic forms; Historical forms
> Ryan, Claude, 234–65. See also *Devoir, Le*

There are five ways of indicating cross-references: *See, See also, See under, See also under* and *q.v.*

(a) *See* immediately follows the heading. No page numbers are given in the entry. A semicolon is used to separate headings if more than one entry is referred to:

> Reference matter. *See* Bibliographies; Endnotes; Footnotes; Indexes

It is sometimes impractical to list a whole series of cross-references, however. If so, make a non-specific reference. For example,

> Education, Department of. *See under government of appropriate province*

is a more succinct entry than one including the names of all the provinces.

The *See* cross-reference is appropriate in the following situations:

- When there is an acceptable synonym for the heading chosen:

  > War of 1812–1814. *See* Invasion of Canada

- When an entry is listed under a different letter from the one the reader might expect:

  > La Mare, Walter de. *See* de la Mare, Walter

- When a person is known by a title or pseudonym as well as by a first name and surname:

  > Beaverbrook, Lord. *See* Aitken, Max

- To refer the reader to an antonym of the entry:

  > Peace movement. *See* War, nuclear

- To refer the reader to a modern or popular term for the same concept:

  > Ceylon. *See* Sri Lanka
  > Latter-day Saints. *See* Mormons

- To refer the reader from a specific to a more general heading required by the nature of the subject field treated in the work. For example, in a chemistry text, an entry under *Algebra* might be too specific, and a cross-reference

  > Algebra. *See* Mathematics

  would be used. Conversely, in a work dealing primarily with mathematics, there would be a separate entry for algebra, but chemistry headings would be more general, e.g.:

  > Organic compounds. *See* Chemical compounds

(b) *See also* is used when at least one page number is not common to the two entries concerned. It guides the reader to additional information on a subject and is placed after the page numbers:

> Coinages, Canadian, 68, 153. *See also* Slang

9

(c) *See under* is used to direct the reader to a subentry:

Mandatory supervision. *See under* National Parole Board

(d) *See also under* is used in the same way as *See also,* except that it refers the reader to a subentry:

New Brunswick, 8, 14, 162, 170. *See also under* Maritimes

(e) The abbreviation *q.v.* applies to a particular word or expression within a heading or subheading, indicating that it can be turned to as a separate heading in the same index:

Acadians
    settlement of Port-Royal (now Annapolis Royal, *q.v.*), 116–27, 244–47

9.53 Blind references

Careless editing of indexes can result in circular cross-referencing of the type illustrated below:

Atlantic provinces. *See* New Brunswick; Newfoundland; Nova Scotia;
    Prince Edward Island
Maritimes. *See* Atlantic provinces
Nova Scotia. *See* Maritimes

Trace all cross-references to ensure that each of them leads the reader to real information.

9.54 Continued headings

Each page of a printed index contains at least two columns of entries. For the reader's benefit, it is important to ensure that a main heading is repeated—Industry, Department of *(cont.)*—at the top of the right-hand column or of the left-hand column of the next page if further subentries are to be listed.

9.55 "Dangling" entries

The first line of an entry should never be left at the bottom of a column. Any such entries found at the editing stage should be placed at the top of the next column at the head of the rest of the entry.

Chapter Ten

Letters and memorandums

Letters

Memorandums

Electronic mail

10

Letters and Memorandums

Letters

10.01 Introduction

The underlying principle of all forms of communication, not just letter writing, is the following: say what you have to say clearly and succinctly (see Chapter 13, "Plain Language"). The layout of the document should be such that the reader can quickly determine who the sender and intended recipient are, when the document was written or sent, what it is about, and what follow-up, if any, is required of the recipient.

Since the first edition of *The Canadian Style* was written, the personal computer has replaced the typewriter. This has had an impact on not only formatting, layout and editing but also the method of communicating written information itself. Hence a section on Electronic Mail has been included at the end of this chapter.

10.02 Block style

Letters are laid out in two basic styles or variations thereof: the block style and the indent style. The one recommended by the Canadian government's Treasury Board for administrative correspondence is the block style. (The Board recognizes that the full block style may not be suitable for all types of correspondence.) In it all lines begin flush with the left margin, including the sender's address, the date, the complimentary close and the signature, as illustrated in the example below (10.25).[1]

10.03 Indent style

In the indent style the sender's address, if not given in the letterhead, appears at the top right-hand corner with the date below it. The complimentary close and signature block are at the bottom right. The first line of each paragraph in the body of the letter is indented. Some feel that this style lends a more personal touch.

10

---

1. The federal government authority for document layout is the Treasury Board, acting through the Federal Identity Program (FIP) in accordance with Chapter 470 of the Board's *Administrative Policy Manual.* Guidelines on layout, paper and envelope size, and related items may be found in the *FIP Manual.* Any future recommendations and directives on document layout issued through the FIP will take precedence over recommendations made in this chapter.

10.04 Margins

Margins may be adjusted to make a short letter appear longer or a long one look shorter. The left margin must be absolutely straight and the right one as straight as possible without splitting words too often. Do **not** justify the right margin; otherwise distortions in spacing may occur.

10.05 Spacing

While recognizing that it may not be appropriate for all correspondence, the *FIP Manual* recommends five vertical spaces between the recipient's address and the salutation, two between the salutation and the body of the letter and five between the complimentary close and the sender's name. Leave one blank line between paragraphs.

Do **not** carry over fewer than three lines of text to a new page.

Names of people, numbers and dates should stay on the same line:

> Approval was given by Mr. Ranald A. Quail, Deputy Minister, Public Works and Government Services Canada.

> **not**

> As regards implementation, approval was given by Mr. Ranald A. Quail, Deputy Minister, Public Works and Government Services Canada.

> Subject to the limitations clearly spelled out in section 92(1)(*c*)(i) of the *Financial Administration Act*, ...

> **not**

> Subject to the limitations (. . .) clearly spelled out in section 92(1)(*c*) (i) of the *Financial Administration Act*, ...

10.06 Length

A letter should generally not exceed two pages. If three or more pages are required, consider preparing a separate report for attachment to the letter.

If a letter contains two or more pages, use page numbering: an indicator (. . . /2) at the bottom of each preceding page, flushed right, and page numbers themselves, centred at the top of each page.

The maximum length of an address is six lines.

10.07 Punctuation

Punctuation must be consistent throughout the document and should be used only where clarity demands it. Enter a colon after the salutation (see 10.16) and a comma after the complimentary close (see 10.20).

10.08 Consistency

For uniformity and consistency, put the parts of the letter, as applicable, in the order in which they are presented below (10.09–25). Each part will start two-to-five lines below the preceding part.

10.09 Letterhead

The heading or letterhead identifies the department or agency that produced the letter. The identification of federal organizations and position titles in the letterhead should be in accordance with FIP guidelines.

If the sender's address appears in the letterhead, there is no need to repeat it elsewhere. Otherwise, include a return address below the letterhead or below the signature.

10.10 Date

See 5.14 for the representation of dates.

The date appears at the left margin in full block style (see example), but it can be placed on the right-hand side of the page to help fit in all the pieces of information required and make it easier to find correspondence filed by date.

10.11 Delivery (mailing) notation

The logical place for notations such as *Personal, Confidential, Registered* or *Hand-delivered* is at the left margin, just below the date line, where the reader would probably look first upon opening the letter. Such notations may be in capital letters or with an initial capital and boldface.

10.12 Reference line

The reference line, on the right-hand side of the page, will give the sender's file number and the line below it the recipient's file number, as shown in the example.

10

10.13 Inside address

Place the recipient's address below the date and at the left margin, unless it must be moved to fit properly into a window envelope. Except in purely personal mail, the addressee's full address must be used. Note the following conventions:

• There is no punctuation at the end of address lines.

• The address should be single-spaced.

• When both a street number and a post office box are provided, use only the box number.

• When the terms *east, west, north* and *south* are used with street addresses, they are written with initial capital letters.

• The postal code is the last item in the address; enter it two spaces after the symbol or name of the province or on a separate line below the names of the municipality and province:[2]

---

2. For further information about addresses, see Canada Post Corporation, *The Canadian Addressing Standard Handbook.*

VESNA SOUKER
MANAGEMENT SERVICES
EXPORT DEVELOPMENT CORPORATION
151 O'CONNOR ST
OTTAWA ON K1A 1K3

Jacob Devine
Administration Branch
Atlantic Canada Opportunities Agency
664 Main Street
Moncton, New Brunswick
E1C 9J8

10.14 Official languages in addresses

See the *FIP Manual* for detailed information and guidelines on the presentation of addresses in letters and on other stationery. The *Manual* specifically covers use of the official languages in addresses and makes the following main points:

- Generally, words indicating a type of public thoroughfare such as *Street, rue, Avenue* or *avenue* are translated into the other official language because they do not form part of the official name of the thoroughfare.

- When the word is considered to be part of the official name of the thoroughfare, e.g. *Avenue (1re, 2e,* etc.), *Chaussée, Chemin, Montée, Circle, Square, (Fifth, 25th,* etc.) *Avenue,* do not translate it.

- When an address such as *100, boulevard de Maisonneuve* is translated, capitalize it in accordance with English usage:

    100 De Maisonneuve Boulevard

- Enquiries concerning the official name of a thoroughfare should be directed to the appropriate municipality.

- Names of government buildings and complexes that do not lend themselves easily to translation should not be translated, e.g. *Les Terrasses de la Chaudière, Place du Portage, L'Esplanade Laurier*.

- The names of provinces and territories are translated. In English, a comma is used to set off a place name from that of the province or territory (see 7.20), whereas in French parentheses enclose the name of the province or territory.

Note that an address can often be left untranslated.

See Chapter 15 for further information on the translation and spelling of such names.

10.15 Name of person, title, name of organization

Put the person's name on one line and his or her title and organization on the next line:

    J. Doe
    Chief, Co-ordination Division

10.16 Attention line

This line begins with *Attention of, Attention* or *Attn.,* ends with a colon and is placed flush with the left margin. It specifies the intended recipient within the organization when the letter is addressed to the organization or to the intended recipient's superior.

10.17 Salutation or greeting

The salutation will vary depending upon the person addressed and the nature of the letter. The following are some appropriate salutations for various circumstances:

Sir **or** Dear Sir Madam **or** Dear Madam	(for formal correspondence)
Dear Mr. **or** Mrs. **or** Ms. Jones	(for a more personal letter)
Dear S. Jones	(if sex of recipient is not known)
Dear Sir/Madam Dear Sir **or** Madam	(where a title is used but the person's name is not known)

If the person's name or title is not known, the expression *To whom it may concern* may also be used. It is not recommended that *Mr., Mrs.* or *Ms.* be used with a title as a salutation, as in "Mr. Premier."

The salutation begins at the left margin. For capitalization in a salutation, see 4.35; for punctuation, see 7.27.

10

10.18 Subject line

A subject line specifying the topic of the letter, if included, comes between the salutation and the body of the letter. The introductory word *Subject* may be used, but is not essential. The terms *Re* and *In re* should be reserved for legal correspondence. The subject line is entered either wholly in upper case or in boldface. It may begin flush with the left margin or be centred for emphasis. It is not used in personal correspondence, where the subject is usually referred to in the first paragraph.

10.19 Body of the letter

The body of the letter contains the message. Here, more than anywhere else, the general principle of communication applies: say it clearly and succinctly, so that the reader will understand the message properly and quickly. Letters are normally single-spaced, with one blank line left between paragraphs. If a letter is very short, it may be double-spaced. When double spacing is used, the first line of each paragraph must be indented. Avoid writing paragraphs of more than ten lines. By the same token, do not divide a letter into many very short paragraphs.

10.20 Complimentary close

The complimentary close consists of such expressions as *Yours truly* or *Yours sincerely*. It is followed by a comma.

10.21 Signature

The handwritten or stamped signature comes first, followed by the title of the sender and of the organization. If someone else signs for the nominal sender, the order is as shown below:

J. Doe
for F. Buck
Chief, Publications Division

or

F. Buck
Chief, Publications Division
per J. Doe

10.22 Reference initials

The initials of the sender and of the transcriber are separated by a colon or oblique. The initials may be all in capital letters, all in small letters, or, most commonly, as follows:

AB:cd

The information is not always needed but may be useful at a later time.

10.23 Enclosure notation

The notations *Enclosure(s), Encl., Attachment(s)* and *Att.* indicate that the envelope contains one or more documents in addition to the letter or attached to the letter. The number of such documents, if there are more than one, should appear after the notation.

10.24 Carbon copy notation

Although carbon is now rarely used for copies, the convenient initials *c.c.:* (or *cc:*) followed by a colon and the names of the recipients of copies of the letter is still the preferred copy notation. An alternative is *Copy to:*. It corresponds to the distribution list of documents such as memorandums and minutes, and lets the recipient know who else is receiving the message.

10.25 Postscript

A postscript is useful if the writer wishes to emphasize some point in the letter or if a point worthy of mention arises after the letter has been written. The use of a postscript obviates the need to rewrite the letter. However, if the postscript sheds a completely new light on the message conveyed, the letter should probably be rewritten. Similarly, a postscript should not be used to attempt to compensate for a poorly organized letter.

The notation *PS:* should be placed before the first word of the postscript and be indented if that is the letter format used. The postscript should begin on the second line below a carbon copy notation.

10.26 Model letter

I✦I Public Works and   Travaux publics et
      Government Services   Services gouvernementaux
      Canada   Canada

Our reference
3696-11

November 18, 1996

Your reference
675-21

Carol Robertson
Co-ordinator
Translation Studies
University of Ottawa
Ottawa, Ontario
K1N 6N5

Dear Ms. Robertson:

Thank you for your letter of October 15, 1996, concerning the possibility of the Translation Bureau accepting students from your program for spring practicums. It gives me pleasure to inform you that the Bureau will again be hosting students interested in one-to-three-month practicums in our organization.

I should point out, however, that owing to budgetary constraints, there may be fewer places available this year.

To facilitate matters, I would ask you to have the attached forms filled in by candidates and to return them to me by February 21, 1997, either by fax (my number is 997-7743) or by mail.

Please do not hesitate to contact me by telephone at (819) 997-7733 for further information.

Yours very truly,

Leopold Covacs
Linguistic Services Division
Translation Bureau
Public Works and Government Services Canada
Ottawa, Ontario
K1A 0S5

Encl.

c.c.: C. Dupont

Canadä

10

Memorandums

10.27 Format

A memorandum is a short letter, note or report. The format most often used for memorandums within the federal public service is illustrated in the example (10.28).

In the upper left part of the form appear the indications *To, From* and *Subject*. On the right are given the security classification (where applicable), the sender's and receiver's file references, if any, and the date.

If required, an indication of any attachments and a distribution list *(Distribution* or *c.c.:)* appear at the end of the document. This list can make communication more efficient because it tells the recipient who else is receiving the document.

10.28 Model memorandum

I✦I Public Works and   Travaux publics et
Government Services   Services gouvernementaux
Canada   Canada

Memorandum

TO	Simon Ferrand	SECURITY
	Director, Information Technology	unclassified
	and Systems	
		OUR FILE
		1024/3
		YOUR FILE
FROM	Irene Corrigan	6814/1
	Director General	
	Finance and Administration	DATE
		January 3, 1996

SUBJECT   Renewal of agreement between Regional Operations and Administrative Services

Following discussions between representatives of Regional Operations and Administrative Services, senior management has decided that the above-mentioned agreement will be renewed.

I would therefore appreciate your providing me, by January 15, with full details on Regional Operations' past use of Information Technology and Systems services. This information will enable us to project financial requirements under the agreement for the upcoming fiscal year.

Thank you for your co-operation.

c.c.: R. Faintly
ADM (Regional Operations)

C. Forties
ADM (Administrative Services)

Canadä

Electronic Mail

10.29 Introduction

With the widespread computerization of the workplace in the 1990s, more and more communications are being sent by electronic mail (often called e-mail). Given the advantages of this means of communication, its use is likely to increase, especially in administrative and business contexts.

In appearance an e-mail message is much like a memorandum, with a "From" field, a "To" field, and a "Subject" field, followed by the body of the message. Nevertheless, there are significant differences, which soon become evident when this form of sending messages is used.

10.30 Advantages

Speed
Communication by electronic mail takes much less time than writing and sending a letter or memorandum. E-mail can be delivered to all parts of the world in hours or even minutes. In addition, if you click on the "Receipt" or equivalent button, you will be automatically notified of the time your communication was read.

Versatility
Messages can be sent to specific individuals or to predefined lists of recipients within a local area network—all in the same amount of time. Moreover, it is possible to send attachments with your message, including files, programs, graphics, and audio and video material.

Efficiency
Not only can electronic letters or memorandums be delivered more quickly, but they can also be processed by the recipient in a fraction of the time required to receive, read, answer and send correspondence on paper. Even telephone and fax communication can involve more time and money.

10

Data sharing
With the spread of local area networks, employees can make use of shared storage locations. With this arrangement, it is possible to have access on your computer screen to a file for reviewing, editing or consulting purposes. Keep in mind that, when you have opened a document stored at a shared location, other users cannot work on it.

10.31 Disadvantages

- Electronic mail can be received only by those who are connected to the "electronic highway" through a local area network or an international network (such as the Internet).

- Despite advances in ensuring the privacy of electronic communications, e-mail is still easy to intercept and to forge, especially when coming across another network. Not all messages received can be assumed to be genuine. Do **not** send confidential or sensitive messages by e-mail.

- A basic level of computer literacy is required for people to take full advantage of the electronic medium.

- E-mail is more impersonal than traditional correspondence. In situations where an office memorandum would not be appropriate (for example, to congratulate an employee on 25 years' loyal service), do **not** use electronic communication.

Note

When including attachments with your message, you should ensure that the recipient will be able to understand the format. It is also helpful if you specify in your communication the software and version that you have used (Ami Pro, WordPerfect, MS Word, etc.). This will ensure that it can be readily accessed.

10.32 Presentation

Subject (title)

All communications should have a subject. In choosing a subject line (a short one is usually best), bear in mind that it summarizes what the text is about. It may also determine whether your message will be read immediately or not.

Message

Most e-mail programs impose certain standards for physical and data format. These govern, in particular, width (the number of characters per line) and the length of the document. If your lines are too long, there is a risk that they will be split into partial lines, which complicates reading of the message. Longer documents should be segmented into several shorter ones in a logical, topic-based manner to facilitate access to information.

Characters

Since documents may be viewed on a variety of systems, avoid using special characters and complex tables which cannot be viewed by all potential readers of your message. When in doubt, keep to ASCII characters. Be consistent in the use of fonts and typefaces. Do **not** send messages entirely in upper case.

10.33 Guidelines

Organizations usually have their own guidelines governing the sending of electronic mail. These concern such matters as the following:

- the purposes for which e-mail may be used (no commercial or social notices, for example);

- projection of the corporate image and logo;

- languages to be used in official documents;

- standard of language used (grammar and style);

- legislative requirements (such as those of the *Copyright Act*, the *Privacy Act* and the *Federal Identity Program*, in the case of federal government documents);

- obtaining the necessary approvals (in the case of widely distributed messages); and

- avoidance of links to potentially controversial or politically sensitive sites, in the case of the Internet.

10

Chapter Eleven

Reports and minutes

Reports

Minutes

11

Reports and Minutes

Reports

11.01 General

Almost everyone is called upon at some time to give a report, either oral or written, to a person or group. Minutes of meetings (see sections 11.22–11.27), the proceedings of conferences, seminars or colloquiums, and descriptions or reviews of books, concerts or motion pictures—these are all reports. Business reports are generated in ever-increasing numbers, in a variety of formats ranging from memorandums to formal reports. The same principle applies to reports as to all other communications: say or write it clearly and succinctly. In the case of a written report, the reader should be able to determine quickly who wrote it, for whom it was written, and why it was written.

11.02 Preparation

Before beginning to write a report or to collect the data for it, determine who is expected to read the report and what use the reader is likely to make of it. The content and format of a report will be significantly affected by whether it is written for specialists or non-specialists, and whether it is an internal document for a limited number of persons or a report for public distribution.

The purpose for which it is required is equally significant: it may be intended to note certain facts for information purposes, to make recommendations for action, to serve as a basis for discussion or debate, or to record the findings of an investigation or study.

Next, collect the data: documents, evidence, statistics and other potentially useful information. Then organize, analyse and evaluate the data collected, selecting what is essential. Finally, draw up a work plan in chronological order, order of importance, or a combination of the two. Now you should be ready to write the report.

11.03 Format

A report may consist of a single paragraph or several volumes. A short report can be put on a memo sheet; a long report may be published. In all cases the format should be appropriate to the nature and length of the report. The most common report formats include the memorandum or letter report, the semiformal report and the formal report.

(a) Memorandum or letter report

The memorandum format is used for short, informal reports directed by one person to another within the same organization, while the letter format is directed to a person in another organization. This type of report usually has no preliminary or supplementary matter. The subject line replaces the title. Headings and lists are sometimes used to focus attention on specific points. Figures and tables may be included as well.

(b) Formal report

The formal report will have a plan and consist of three parts: the introductory or preliminary matter; the body of the report; and the supplementary or back matter.

The composition of formal reports can vary considerably according to each organization's requirements. The following is a comprehensive list of the elements that may be included in a formal report and the order in which they are generally presented:

1. Preliminary matter

Covering letter
Fly page or cover page
Letter or memorandum of authorization
Letter of transmittal
Title page
Table of contents
List of tables
List of figures
List of abbreviations and symbols
Abstract or summary
Preface or foreword
Acknowledgments

2. Body of the report

Introduction
Background
Authorization information
Purpose
Scope and limitations
Materials and methods
Body of text
Findings or results
Discussion
Summary of findings
Conclusions
Recommendations

3. Supplementary matter

Appendixes
Glossary
Notes, references or bibliography
Index

A shorter version of the formal report, used for topics that are limited in scope, may include all or some of the following:

Title page
Summary
Authorization information
Statement outlining the purpose of the report, its scope and the methods used
Findings
Conclusions
Recommendations
Appendixes
List of endnotes
Bibliography

11.04 Letter of transmittal or preface

The letter of transmittal may be in letter or memorandum form, depending on whether the report is intended for external or internal distribution. Like the preface, used when the writer is aiming for a wider readership, the letter of transmittal may contain a brief description of the background, purpose, scope and content of the report. Acknowledgments may be made. The letter or memorandum is clipped to the report cover or inserted as its first page.

11.05 Title page

A title page will feature some of the following elements: the full title of the report; the name of the organization or person for whom the report was prepared; the name of the originating organization; the name(s) of the person(s) who wrote the report; the date the report was released; and a distribution list.

Although not all reports have a title page, a written report normally has a title. This title should convey accurately, clearly and concisely the subject of the report to the reader. The omission of verbs and articles, as is done in newspaper headlines, can condense the message. A title in two parts— the main title followed by a colon and subtitle—can make a long title seem shorter. The title must nevertheless contain all the key words needed for a proper description of the text.

11.06 Table of contents

A long or complex report requires a table of contents. The table should be accurate and detailed enough to tell the reader what each section is about. It should list all the main divisions of the report that come after the table of contents, including supplementary matter. Titles for the different parts, chapters and main chapter divisions need to be shown, preceded by chapter or division numbers where appropriate, and followed by page numbers. The wording, capitalization and order of the headings must be the same as in the report (see section 11.16, "Headings").

When a report contains numerous tables and illustrations, separate lists of tables and illustrations are included after the table of contents. The titles of the tables or illustrations are listed separately in numerical order and followed by the page number.

11.07 Abstract or summary

A report to be published as an article in a learned or scientific journal usually has an abstract, following the table of contents. It should be no more than 150–200 words long and be suitable for reprinting in a journal or collection of abstracts. An abstract is considered part of the preliminary matter. A summary, if needed, may run to several pages and is considered part of the body of the report. It may appear at the very beginning of the report proper or serve as a closing section at the end. Some reports may contain both an abstract and a summary.

The abstract or summary is prepared after the report is written and often by someone other than the author. It briefly indicates the purpose of the report, the method followed and observations made and, sometimes, the conclusions and recommendations. Its purpose is to enable a prospective reader to determine quickly whether the report contains useful information.

11.08 Introduction to report

The introduction describes the purpose and scope of the report, the sources and methods used to collect data, the terms of reference, and any pertinent background information. In long reports, the introduction may also include an outline of the organization of the report.

11.09 Findings and discussion

The report proper develops the theme, giving details of the methods used and the observations or findings, and commenting on their significance. The ideas should follow logically and smoothly from beginning to end. Any non-essential material that might interfere with the flow of ideas should be put in a footnote, endnote or appendix, with a reference number referring to it at an appropriate place in the text. A footnote should not extend over more than half a page. If it is too long, it belongs in an endnote or an appendix (see Chapter 9).

Arrange the body of the report in a logical manner, using headings and subheadings to separate the text into major divisions and the divisions into sections (see 11.16). To increase readability, break up solid text with graphic elements and lists. Use short, easily read lists to clarify information, and tables, graphs and illustrations to help readers understand it.

11.10 Ending

The body of the report ends with the results, conclusions and recommendations, if any. Some reports simply end in a summary of major findings. Others offer conclusions derived from the findings and discussion. The conclusions are enumerated or given in running text and may be combined with recommendations, if required. Conclusions and recommendations are sometimes placed at the beginning of the report and only summarized at the end.

11.11 Appendixes

The appendixes will contain notes and supplementary information such as copies of documents, formulas, statistical data, maps, charts, plans or drawings that the author believes will be useful to the reader.

All appendixes must be briefly mentioned in the report so that it is not necessary to refer to them to understand the report. Appendixes are numbered, generally with a capital letter, in the order that they are first mentioned.

11.12 Glossary

Special terms are defined when first used in the text. If they are numerous, an alphabetical list of terms with their definitions can be placed at the end of the report or immediately following the table of contents.

11.13 References

A report that is the culmination of a study will probably contain endnotes or footnotes and a bibliography. A serious yet common failing of writers of reports is inaccuracy, especially in quotations and references. A quotation should correspond exactly to the original. (For omissions and changes, see 8.09–10.) If a quotation is not exact or is attributed to the wrong author, or if the date, volume number or page number of the reference is wrong, a reader who needs to refer to the source will waste time and lose patience. It is therefore wise to check all references both before and after they are inserted into the report.

11

A bibliography lists the works most often consulted, as well as those likely to be of particular interest to the reader, even if not referred to in the text. See Chapter 9 for detailed information on footnotes, endnotes and the various ways of listing bibliographic entries.

11.14 Illustrations

A well-prepared illustration can take the place of several paragraphs or even pages of narration, and thus help the author make, explain or emphasize a point strongly and succinctly.

Although illustrations can be grouped together in an appendix, the best place for them is in the text, as close as possible to their first mention.

Each illustration should be identified by a figure or table number and a caption.

11.15 Tables and graphs

If you are conveying two or three short pieces of statistical information, incorporate them into a sentence in the text. Show more extensive information in the form of a table or, in order to highlight relationships and trends, in the form of a chart, graph or diagram. Significant aspects of the tables or charts should be interpreted in the text. Create tables and charts using the appropriate functions in your word-processing or spreadsheet program, and insert them as soon as possible after the paragraphs in which they are mentioned.

Follow these guidelines on form and content:

• Limit the amount of data in graphs and tables to essentials.

• Keep the display simple, with clear and concise headings (column heads) at the top of each column.

• If symbols are being used, place them at the head of each column.

• Singular forms are preferred in the column heads, e.g. *Country of origin, Currency.*

• Currency symbols can be placed before the first entry of each column, but do **not** repeat unit designations.

• With large sums, space can be saved by placing a notation such as

(in thousands)

or

($000)

directly beneath the column head.

• Explain abbreviations in the reference notes.

• Be consistent in the use of capitalization, fonts, italics and spacing in tables and charts.

• Make sure that bar and pie charts are visually accurate and that tables add up.

• Place footnotes for tables immediately below the graphic presentation and indicate them with a superscript number, letter or symbol (see 9.23).

• Give a source reference at the end of the table, where appropriate.

Consult *Scientific Style and Format: The CBE Manual for Authors, Editors, and Publishers*[1] for further information on tables, graphs and illustrations.

---

1. Council of Biology Editors, *Scientific Style and Format: The CBE Manual for Authors, Editors, and Publishers,* pp. 677–99.

The model table below illustrates many of the recommendations made in this section:

Table A
Foreign Currencies: Codes and Values

Country	*Currency*	*Code[1]*	*Value (C$)[2]*
Australia	dollar	AUD	$1.0774
Austria	schilling	ATS	0.1356
Belgium	franc	BEF	0.0464
Brazil	real[3]	BRC	1.4871
France	franc	FRF	0.2796
Germany	mark	DEM	0.9542
Greece	drachma	GRD	1.0060
Italy	lira	ITL	0.0009
Japan	yen	JPY	0.0134
Mexico	peso	MXP	0.2048
Netherlands	guilder	NLG	0.8537
Spain	peseta	ESP	0.0114
Switzerland	franc	CHF	1.1729
United Kingdom	pound	GBP	2.1356
United States	dollar	USD	1.3905

1. Source: International Standard ISO 4217.
2. Souroo: Bank of Montreal, March 0, 1990.
3. Official/restricted rate.

11.16 Headings

Headings (or heads) are used to introduce a change of subject in a report or other document and to indicate a hierarchy of topics. They are designed to guide readers and enable them to find the pages where a particular topic is discussed. The size and appearance of a heading should match its importance, and the same type of heading should be used consistently throughout a document to indicate subdivisions with the same degree of subordination. Headings that are of equal importance should have parallel grammatical structures.

You can set off the heading by various means depending, among other things, on how many levels of heading there are. These means include capitalization (full or initial letter only), underlining, centring, spacing, type size and the use of italic or boldface type. The specific means chosen to indicate the gradation of headings matter less than consistency in using them. The system adopted should be as simple as the nature of the text will allow.

Limit the number of levels of headings to three or four; otherwise the structure of your document will be cumbersome and complicated. If there are many headings or subheadings of equal importance, a numbering system, as used in this guide, can help to distinguish among them for reference purposes. Letters can be used for further subdivision of topics. This is less confusing than a system using several levels of numbers and

11

producing subdivisions such as 1.4.2.3. Another common method of numbering combines both Roman and Arabic numerals with letters and, if needed, parentheses:

I. Technical training needs
   A. First quarter objectives
      1. National Capital area
         a. Windows environment

Punctuation should be kept to a minimum in headings, and the wording should be as succinct as possible without being ambiguous. No periods are required, except in run-in heads.

Unless a heading is centred or full capitalization is used, only the first word and proper nouns are normally capitalized. In centred headings, capitalize the first letter of each word except the following (unless they are the initial word):

- articles

- short conjunctions (fewer than four letters)

- short prepositions (fewer than four letters)

Do **not** footnote a heading.

11.17 Margins

Make the top margin about 5 cm deep on the first page, so that the beginning is clearly marked, and 2.5 cm deep on the following pages. The bottom margin should be from 2.5 to 4 cm deep. The side margins should be at least 3 cm wide if room has to be allowed for stapling or binding; otherwise they can be narrower, but should be at least 2 cm wide in any case, to allow for reproduction and to ensure that the complete text on both pages can be seen when the document is opened flat.

11.18 Spacing

There are two important spacing requirements. First, determine the minimum amount of space needed for clear separation of paragraphs, headings, extracts and illustrations. Second, be consistent in the spacing.

11.19 Pagination

The preliminary matter is numbered with Roman or Arabic numerals in the bottom centre of the page. The title page is understood to be the first page, although no page number appears. The pages of the body of the text, beginning with the introduction, are numbered with Arabic numerals in the upper centre, lower centre or upper right corner of the page. A combination of chapter number and page number is sometimes used for long reports with several chapters written by different authors (i.e. 1-1, 1-2, 1-3, etc., for the first chapter). The pages of appendixes are numbered independently, often with a combination of the appendix letter and Arabic numerals (i.e. A-1, A-2, A-3, etc., for Appendix A). When supplementary matter is generated by the author, it can be paginated as a continuation of the report.

11.20 Underlining

Do **not** underline a heading in which all letters are capitalized.

Avoid underlining for emphasis. Attention can be focussed on a particular point with headings, indention, bullet lists, italics and other typefaces.

11.21 Mathematics in reports

Avoid using algebraic symbols and mathematical formulas in all but highly technical reports. Symbols should be defined at their first use. If they are numerous, include a separate list of symbols and definitions in the report.

Indent or centre an equation on the line immediately following that in which it is first referred to in the text. Break equations before an equal, plus or multiplication sign. Align a group of separate but related equations by the equal signs.

Keep in mind that equations ($a=b$) and inequalities ($a><b$) correspond to sentences in ordinary narrative and must therefore be grammatically correct. The expression $a=b$ is read "(The quantity) a is equal to (the quantity) b." The expression $a>b$ is read "(The quantity) a is greater than (the quantity) b."

When you write $E = mc^2$ you are writing an equation that is read "The amount of energy in a mass is equal to that mass multiplied by the square of the velocity of light." A formula, on the other hand, corresponds to a phrase and thus contains no equivalent of a verb. The formula for calculating E (the amount of energy in a given mass) is mc^2 (the mass multiplied by the square of the velocity of light).

11

Another principle to keep in mind is that equations and formulas can be written in more than one form. This is useful for fitting them on a page. For example,

$$\frac{a}{b}$$

can be shown as

a/b

and thus take up only one line.

Minutes

11.22 General

The minutes of a meeting are a record of the circumstances of the meeting, including the names of the participants, the topics discussed and the decisions reached. The minutes should include all essential information in as concise a form as possible. Special attention should be paid to the wording of resolutions, motions and other decisions, particularly if there is a chance that there will be differences of opinion on what was resolved, moved or decided. If it is a formal meeting, all motions must be written out verbatim.

11.23 Agenda

The agenda lists the order of business for a meeting and may include the items listed below, in the following order:

- call to order by presiding officer
- roll call
- welcoming of new members and guests
- reading and adoption of the agenda
- reading and adoption of the minutes of the previous meeting
- business arising out of the minutes
- other old business
- reading of correspondence
- reports of officers
- committee reports
- new business
- nominations and elections
- announcements (including date, time and place of next meeting)
- adjournment

If the agenda is short and few decisions are to be made, it can be incorporated into the minutes. If the agenda is long and many points are to be discussed and acted on, the agenda may be omitted and the following style adopted: a wide column at the left for the point discussed, and a narrower column at the right for the person or body responsible for carrying out any action decided on (see 11.27). The points are numbered and may be given subject headings.

11.24 Model agenda

Regional Development Branch

Meeting of Branch Executive Committee

Friday, January 19, 1996

9:00 a.m., Room 214

Agenda

1. Approval of BEC minutes of January 3, 1996
2. Senior Management Committee—debriefing
3. Assistant Deputy Minister—debriefing
4. Disk space allocation
5. Other business

11.25 Writing of minutes

An organization should use the format prescribed in its rules or regulations. If no restrictions exist, a standardized format should be adopted. Word processing simplifies the task greatly. Once a format suited to the needs of the organization has been developed, it can be used as a template and stored on disk.

The minutes should normally follow the order in which the business was conducted, even though this may differ from the agenda. They may include the items listed below:

- nature of the meeting (especially whether regular or special), date, time and place;
- identification of the person chairing the meeting;
- the names of participants and of the organizations represented, and of persons who should have attended but were absent;
- identification of the person taking the minutes;
- the agenda, if short and if not distributed beforehand;
- body of the minutes, following the order of business; the motions, their adoption or rejection, and the names of their originators; the names of persons responsible for taking action on the decisions reached may be given in a column at the right-hand margin;
- motion to adjourn or close the meeting;
- time of adjournment or closing of the meeting;
- signatures of the person who presided and of the person who took the notes;
- distribution list.

Reports from officers and committee chairpersons are sometimes appended to the minutes, as are motions.

11

11.26 Indirect speech

Bear in mind that minutes are a record of what was said at some point in the past. Therefore indirect (reported) speech is called for. This involves placing verbs in a past or conditional tense, if they express statements by persons at the meeting (e.g. *said*, **not** *says*; *had forecast*, **not** *has forecast*; *would decide*, **not** *will decide*).

However, the present or future forms of verbs may be used for general statements of fact not directly attributed to participants (e.g. *Alberta requires a finance officer*, in point 5 of the model minutes). In this example there is no specific source for the statement, other than the minute-writer. See 8.04 for more information on indirect speech.

11.27 Model minutes

Regional Development Branch
Minutes of Branch Executive Committee Meeting
Friday, January 19, 1996
9:00 a.m., Room 214

Present:	R. Burnett (Chair)	M. Benesh
	B. Parkins	B. Boucher
	S. Garnett	A. Farrell (Secretary)

1. *Approval of BEC minutes of January 5, 1996*   Action

The minutes were approved with the following
amendments:

Item 1—clarification

No decision had yet been made on what system would
be used for pay management as of April 1, 1996. Mrs.
Benesh requested that all branch heads be advised in
writing. This was approved.

R. Burnett

Item 2—clarification

The deadline could not be met because decisions on
some action items had yet to be made.

2. *SMC—debriefing*

The Operational Planning Framework was discussed,
but members did not get past the opening statement. It
was agreed that the statement was incomplete and
would be reviewed. A revised draft would be prepared.

B. Parkins

3. *ADD—debriefing*

The Cabinet Agenda was discussed. Items covered
included a paper on a water resources strategy for
Canada, the Alberta Memorandum to Cabinet, the
Dairy Program and the Livestock Pedigree Act.

The Deputy Minister and Mr. Burnett were to meet with
J. Faulds, the Regional Director for Nova Scotia, on
February 5.

The Manitoba Memorandum of Understanding had
been signed on January 8.

4. *Disk space allocation*

The message from Colin Jamieson was sent to 35 out of 48 accounts in the Branch. With over 45 percent of the Branch's disk allocation now in use, it was agreed that the Branch would not reduce its disk space allocation until the Information Systems Committee had met with Mr. Jamieson and obtained a clear definition of what the requirements were.

5. *Other business—assignment*

Alberta requires a finance officer for a short-term assignment. Finance and Administration would be approached.

S. Garnett

The meeting closed at 10:30 a.m.

_____   _____
R. Burnett   A Farrell

Distribution
ADM
Committee members

11

Chapter Twelve

Usage

12

Usage

12.01 Introduction

The purpose of this chapter is to give the correct usage of many terms
and expressions that are often misused because of inadequate knowledge
of or sensitivity to proper idiom, or because of confusion with a word
having a similar sound or meaning.

12.02 Prepositional usage

The list below contains nouns, verbs, adjectives and adverbs that are
often used with the wrong preposition or, in some cases, with some other,
inappropriate part of speech. The correct usage is given in each case:

abide *by* a decision

abstain *from* a thing **or** *from* doing

accede *to* a request

accord (*of* one's own)

accordance *with* (in)

accountable *for* something entrusted

accountable *to* one's employer

acquiesce *in*

act *on*

agree *on* terms

agree *to* a proposal

agree to do (**not** *accept* to do)

allow *for* (take into consideration)

answer *for* (assume responsibility for an action or a thing)

answer *to* (account to a person)

aspire *to* (a position, fame)

associate *with* (**not** associate *to*)

avenge oneself *on* someone *for* something

averse *to* violence

averse *to* doing something

aware *of*

bear a resemblance *to*

begin *by* doing

begin *to* do

begin *from* a point

begin *with* an act

benefits *of* the benefactor

benefits *to* the beneficiary

bring a charge *against*

capable *of*

capacity *for*

centre *on* (**not** *around*)

circumstances (*in* the)

commend a person *for* work well done

commensurate *with*

compare *with* (to note similarities and differences)

compare *to* (only when used in the sense of "liken to")

compliment *on*

comply *with*

concur *in* an opinion

concur *with* a person

conditions (live *in* squalid)

conditions (work *under* difficult)

conform *to*

conformity *with* (in)

consist *in* (definition: "Memory consists in a present imagination of past incidents.")

consist *of* (material: "The meal consisted of fish.")

consistent *with*

contend *with* a problem, a difficulty

contrast one thing *with* another

contrast *to* **or** *with* (in)

converge *on*

conversant *with*

correlate *with*

correspond *to* (resemble)

correspond *with* (communicate)

culminate *in* (**not** *with*)

default *on* a loan, a payment

defend *against* attack, accusation

defend *from* harm (ward off attack, keep safe)

delve *into* a question

depart *from* a practice, a procedure

deprive *of*

derive *from*

designate someone *as*

differ, -ent, *from* (**not** *to, than*)

differ *with* a person *on* a subject

disagree *with* a person

discourage *from* doing

dispense *with*

dissociate (**or** disassociate) oneself *from*

divest oneself *of*

effect (put *into*)

elaborate *on*

embark *on* a ship, a career

enamoured *of*

endowed *with*

excuse *from* doing

focus *on* (**not** *around*)

follow-up *to* (a)

forbid someone *to* do

free *from* **or** *of*

grasp *of* (have a good)

immune *from* an obligation, something unpleasant

immune *to* a disease

impinge *on/upon* (have an effect on, encroach upon)

Impressed *with* or *by*

incapable *of* doing

indifferent *to*

indispensable *to* a person

indispensable *for* a purpose

infested *with* insects, vermin

infringe the rules (*no preposition*)

initiative *in* (take the)

initiative (*on* one's own)

insight *into*

integrate *into* (incorporate)

integrate *with* (mix with)

intercede *for* someone *with* an authority

invest *in* stocks, shares, a business

invest *with* authority, an award, an office, an air of

join *with* a person or thing *in* something

keep abreast *of* the news, developments

labour *at/over* a task

labour *for* somebody, a purpose

12

labour *under* a disadvantage, a misapprehension

lay the blame *for* something *on* someone

levy *on* (impose a)

liable *to* dismissal, a fine

link *to* (in a physical sense)

link *with* (associate, connect with)

live *off* (the land, one's produce)

live *on* an income

lodge a complaint *with* an authority *against* someone

look *after* business

look *into* a matter

look *over* an account

made *of* (material or ingredients that go into making **something**)

made *from* (original material transformed into something else)

made *with* (specifies one or more of the constituent parts)

moment (*on* the spur of the)

moment's notice (*at* a)

oblivious *of* or *to*

opposite *of* (the)

opposition *to* (in)

order *of* (in the, of the)

originate *in* or *with* (**not** *from*)

parallel *with* **or** *to*

perpendicular *to*

persist *in*

perspective *of* (*from* the)

place to live *in* (**not** place *to live*)

point *at* a thing

point *to* a fact

prefer one *to* the other

preference *for*

preoccupied *with*

present someone or something *to* someone

present someone *with* something

preside *over/at*

prevent *from* doing

proceed *against* a person

proceed *to* (an act not previously started)

proceed *with* (an act already started)

prohibit *from* doing

provide *against* disaster

provide *for* an emergency

provide something *for* someone

provide someone *with* something

pursuance *of* (in)

pursuant *to*

put *in/into* place

reconcile *to* a thing, a state

reconcile *with* a person

reduction *in* pay

reference *to* (**preceded by** *with*, **not** *in*)

regard *for* a person (*with/in* regard *to* a subject)

regardless *of* whether something happens

register *with*

relieve one *of* a possession, a duty

remand *in* custody

remand (place *on*)

replace one person *with* another (**but** a person is replaced *by* another)

report *for* work

report *on/upon* (give information)

report *to* (complain about, inform of, answer to)

reproach someone/oneself *for* having failed to do

reproach someone/oneself *with* a shortcoming

research *in* a specialty

research *in/into* a question

responsibility (the) *of* deciding, *of* a position

responsibility *for* an action (assume)

responsible *to* a person *for* an action

result *from* an event

result *in* a failure

result (the) *of* an investigation

revolve *around*

right *of* way, *of* passage

satisfaction *in* something (find, take)

satisfaction *of* (have the)

satisfied *with* something

secure *against* attack

secure *from* harm

secure *in* a position

speculate *about*

substitute *for*

suggest *that* he do (**not** suggest *him to* do)

12

suited *to* a purpose, each other

suited *for* a job

sympathize *with*

sympathy *for* (have)

sympathetic *to/toward*

take account *of*

take *into* account

take exception *to*

tamper *with*

tend *toward* something (incline)

tend *to* do

unconscious *of*

variance *with* a person *on* something (be *at*)

versed *in*

virtue of (*by*) ("by means of")

virtue of (*in*) ("on account of")

view *of* the circumstances (*in*)

view *to* doing something (*with* a)

wary *of* a danger

withhold *from*

12.03 Words commonly misused or confused

accuracy, precision

Accuracy is a measure of how close a fact or value approaches the true value and the degree to which something is free of error. *Precision* is a measure of the fineness of a value. Thus 6.0201 is more precise than 6.02, but it may not be more accurate (if one of the last two digits is incorrect).

affect, effect

Affect, as a verb, usually means "influence":

Budgetary constraints have seriously affected our grants and contributions program.

As a verb, *effect* means "bring about"; as a noun, it means "result," "impact":

Her promotion effected a change in her treatment of her colleagues.

The Supreme Court ruling will have a lasting effect on official language services.

allusion, illusion, delusion

An *allusion* is an indirect reference; *illusion* applies to something appearing to be true or real, but actually not existing or being quite different from what it seems. *Delusion* applies to a persistent belief that is contrary to fact or reality:

> His allusion to the previous administration was out of place.

> Danby's paintings create a striking illusion of reality.

> The delusion that imports are always of superior quality must be dispelled.

alternate(ly), alternative(ly)

The primary meaning of *alternate* is "by turns," "first one then the other," or "every other one"; *alternative* refers to one of two or possibly more choices. The same distinction applies to the adverbial forms. Note, however, that *alternate* can also be used with the meaning of *alternative.*

amount, number

Use *amount* for something considered as a mass or total; use *number* with things that can be counted:

> A large amount of grain is handled at Thunder Bay.

> A number of employees fell sick.

See also *fewer, lesser, less* below.

anyone, any one

Anyone (everyone, someone) can be used only to refer to people. *Any one (every one, some one)* is the correct form when referring to things. However, *any one,* etc. must also be used with people when the meaning is "any single individual":

> Anyone can apply.

> We cannot rely on any one unit to handle the entire program.

appraise, apprise

Appraise means "set a value on"; *apprise* means "make aware of":

> I have had my house appraised by experts.

> All parties were fully apprised of the state of the negotiations.

12

approve, approve of

Approve means "to sanction" or "to ratify;" *approve of* means "to think well of":

> Treasury Board has approved the expenditure reduction plan.

> The Deputy Minister approved of Szabo's bold initiative.

apt, liable, likely

Apt means "having a tendency (to) because of the subject's character" or "fitting, suitable"; *liable* expresses legal responsibility or the probability that the subject will suffer or be exposed to something undesirable; *likely* simply means that something is "probable" or "likely to happen":

> We are apt to believe what we want to believe.

This student is apt for a career in journalism.

The company is liable to pay compensation in the event of work accidents.

Children are liable to measles.

The departmental reorganization is likely to occur before June.

as far as

This construction must be completed with a finite verb:

As far as education funding is concerned (goes), the Department is still reviewing its position.

assume, presume

The material following *assume* expresses a theory or even a hypothesis, whereas the words following *presume* express what the subject believes to be the case for want of proof to the contrary:

For the sake of argument, let us assume that our budget will be reduced by 10%.

I presume that our budget will be pared as a result of government spending cutbacks.

Presume can be replaced more readily by *assume* than the other way round.

assure, ensure, insure

To *assure* is to guarantee (a thing to a person) and to remove doubt, uncertainty or worry from a person's mind. The primary meaning of *ensure* is "to make sure or certain." *Insure* is related to insurance:

Thanks to the new regulations, the employees' job security was assured.

Register this letter to ensure that it reaches its destination.

attentiveness, attention

Attentiveness is the quality or state of being attentive or considerate. *Attention* refers to the action or faculty of attending to a matter or concentrating the mind on:

The innkeeper's attentiveness to his guests' comfort was much appreciated.

Thank you for your attention to this letter.

beside, besides

Beside is a preposition normally meaning "by the side of." *Besides* is an adverb meaning "moreover" or, occasionally, a preposition meaning "in addition to" or "except":

The clerk sat beside the machine.

That division does not have the financial resources to carry out the project. Besides, nobody there is competent enough to handle it.

biannual, biennial, semi-annual

Semi-annual means "occurring every six months or twice a year." *Biannual* means "occurring twice a year." *Biennial* means "occurring every two years or lasting for two years (plants)."

both . . . and

The material following *and* should correspond syntactically to the material following *both*:

Both *her* supervisor and *her* director were on the selection board.

not

Both her supervisor and director were on the selection board.

Do **not** write "Both . . . , as well as . . . ."

by (a specified time)

In expressions of time *by* means "not later than" or "at or before" a specified time. Thus "by June 25" means "on or before June 25," not just "before June 25."

characteristic, distinctive, typical

A *characteristic* quality is one that distinguishes and identifies. A *distinctive* feature denotes an attribute that sets a thing or person apart from a type or group. *Typical* relates to the characteristics peculiar to the type, class, species or group to which a thing or person belongs:

The Deputy Minister always included that characteristic flourish at the end of her memorandums.

The unit has a distinctive approach to training and development.

The reply was typical of a bureaucrat—long and rambling but short on content.

12

cite, quote

To *cite* something is to mention it or repeat it as proof of what is being said. To *cite* a person is to summon him or her before a court of law. To *quote* is to repeat something verbatim.

classic, classical

As adjectives, the words are partly interchangeable. Nevertheless, *classic* should be used when the meaning is "a famous or supreme example of its type," while *classical* is preferred in reference to ancient Greek and Roman culture or to any music composed in a traditional, serious style:

It was a classic case of mistaken identity.

He was an outstanding performer of classical Hindu music.

common, mutual

Common means "belonging to many or to all." *Mutual* means "reciprocal":

Misspelling is a common problem.

The couple's trust and respect were mutual.

Avoid using *mutual* redundantly as in "Canada and Mexico entered into a mutual agreement."

compare, contrast

Use *compare* when bringing out likenesses or similarities (with the preposition *to*) and when examining two or more objects to find likenesses or differences (with the preposition *with*). Use *contrast* to point out differences:

One could compare the leaderless team to a ship without a rudder.

Upon comparing her work plan with that of her colleague, she found that they bore a striking resemblance.

In contrast to my proposed budget, his is lavish.

compliment, complement

A *compliment* expresses praise, admiration or flattery. Things that are *complementary* may be different, but together they form a complete unit or supplement one other:

The director complimented his team on a job well done.

The information provided complements the data already on file.

comprise, constitute, compose

Comprise means "consist of." Avoid the expression *is comprised of. Constitute* and *compose* mean "make up, account for, form":

The opera comprises five acts.

The population of Ontario constitutes over 35% of the population of Canada.

Five small communities together compose (make up) the city of Kanata.

See also *include, comprise.*

concern, concerned

To concern can mean "relate to," " involve the interests of" and "make anxious." One can be *concerned for, about, over, at, by* and *with* something, or *concerned to* do something. One can also be *concerned that* something might happen:

The book is concerned with social issues.

The parents were concerned about their children's progress at school.

Care should be taken when using *concern* with the last-mentioned meaning of "to cause anxiety or uneasiness in." Often this usage can cause ambiguity, as in the following examples:

Not all employees were concerned by the cutbacks in positions.

The country's deficit concerns most Canadians.

continual, continuous

While the distinction between these words can sometimes become blurred, the rule is that *continual* implies a close recurrence in time, a rapid succession of events. *Continuous* means "uninterrupted in time or sequence":

The new chief's continual carping gradually alienated all his subordinates.

The continuous hissing of the white noise caused some office workers to become drowsy.

council, counsel

A *council* is a governing or consultative body (city council, council of grand chiefs, student council) made up of *councillors*. Sometimes *council* is used synonymously with "board" (e.g. Council of Egg Marketing Authorities). *Counsel* pertains to advice and guidance, especially in law (counsel for the defence). In a formal context, *counsel* is provided by *counsellors*.

decision (make/take a)

Although attempts are sometimes made to distinguish between *to make* and *to take a decision*, or to reject one in favour of the other, most modern dictionaries use them interchangeably in the sense of "to decide about something":

She has made a sound investment decision.

The decision to launch the attack was taken by the Cabinet.

but

decision making **not** decision taking

defective, deficient

Defective is that which is wanting in quality; *deficient* is that which is wanting in quantity:

Sixteen of the machines were found to be defective and were scrapped.

The test showed that the patients were deficient in vitamin C.

dependant, dependent

Dependant is the noun, *dependent* the adjective:

> A wage earner with dependants is fully entitled to this deduction.

> Many Third World countries are dependent on food aid.

different, various

The meanings of these words overlap to a large extent, but they cannot be used interchangeably in all contexts. As a general rule, *different* implies separateness or contrariness, while *various* stresses number and diversity of sorts or kinds:

> The various/different ingredients were all mixed together.

> Various people commented on his appearance.

disinterested, uninterested

Disinterested means "unbiassed," while *uninterested* means "not interested in":

> Legal Services were asked to give a disinterested opinion.

> The Director General was uninterested in the projects presented by her staff.

each

Grammatically, *each* must be treated as a singular and be used with a singular verb:

> Each of you now realizes the consequences.

> Each province administers its education system.

When the notion of plurality is pre-eminent, however, the plural is appropriate:

> Canada and the U.S.A. each have claims to a larger share of the salmon catch.

economic, economical

Economic relates to the economy, whereas *economical* refers to someone who is thrifty or to something that is efficient or avoids waste:

> Another economic crisis is looming in the West.

> He is economical of time and energy.

> Small cars are economical.

effective, efficient

Effective refers to producing the desired result ("effective ways of combatting pollution"). It can also have the meanings of "in force" (a law) and "actual" ("the effective leader was the commander of the armed forces"). *Efficient* refers to the skilful use of time and energy to produce desired results with little effort:

Despite no previous experience, the Minister proved highly effective in his new job.

Owing to increased energy costs and competition, car engines have become more efficient.

either . . . or, neither . . . nor

The constructions *either. . . or* and *neither . . . nor* should be used to co-ordinate two words, phrases or clauses. Note that the constructions following these correlatives should be parallel and that the verb agrees in number with the nearer subject:

Either they go or I go.

Either Mary or her brothers are to receive the prize.

Neither Nova Scotia nor New Brunswick is involved in the project.

I communicated with him neither by telephone nor by letter.

emigrate, immigrate, migrate

To *emigrate* is to leave a country or region to settle in another. To *immigrate* is to enter and settle in a country or region. To *migrate* means to move from one place to another (this can be seasonal and can apply to both people and animals). When deciding between *immigrate* and *emigrate*, the speaker's perspective determines the choice of word:

A large number of Italians emigrated after the Second World War.

The number of immigrants to Canada has remained constant in recent years.

Many Canadians have migrated from eastern Canada to British Columbia in recent years.

equally

This word should not be followed by *as*:

Her plan is equally (**or** just as) good.

12

fact

Exercise caution in using phrases such as *as a matter of fact, in fact, the fact is* and *actually*. They are often just an artificial means of assuring the reader that the writer is dealing with facts rather than theories and hypotheses, and may therefore be omitted in the interest of conciseness.

fewer, lesser, less

Fewer is used when referring to number; *lesser* and *less* are used for quantity, amount, size or number when the number is thought of as an amount:

We have bought fewer computers this year than last.

The lesser of two evils.

You will be assigned less work this week.

He had less than $100 in his pocket.

figuratively, literally, virtually

These words are often wrongly used to convey the exact opposite of their real meaning. *Figuratively* means "not literally, not really"; *literally* means "really, actually"; *virtually* means "almost entirely, for all practical purposes." Thus the statement "He was literally bowled over" is nonsensical. In the sentence "The sinking of the *Titanic* was a virtual disaster," the adjective is gratuitous and even detracts from the magnitude of the disaster.

financial, fiscal

Although to some extent synonymous, *financial* has a broader meaning and refers to money matters or transactions on a large scale. *Fiscal* applies usually to public revenues:

The company's financial outlook showed some improvement.

The government has implemented a program of fiscal restraint.

flaunt, flout

Flaunt means "display boastfully," whereas *flout* means "treat with contemptuous disregard":

He insisted on flaunting his expertise.

Employees should not flout the rules.

The error consists in using *flaunt* in place of *flout*.

flounder, founder

As a verb *flounder* means "struggle awkwardly without making progress." *Founder* means "fill with water and sink" (ship), "fail" (plans, etc.), or "break down/go lame" (horse):

The program was floundering and clearly needed strong direction.

The project foundered owing to lack of funds.

forego, forgo

Forego means "to go before or precede." It usually occurs in the forms *foregoing* and *foregone*. It also means "to abstain from, go without, relinquish," and in this sense has a variant spelling *forgo*:

The party's election was a foregone conclusion.

The board members were not prepared to forego (forgo) their privileges.

former, latter

Former and *latter* refer to only two items. For a group of more than two, use "first" (or "first-mentioned") and "last" (or "last-named") to indicate order.

gender, sex

In recent years the use of *gender* has been broadened from the designation of grammatical categories to cover uses formerly limited to the word *sex*. However, the two words are not interchangeable. *Sex* should be used in reference to biological categories and sexually motivated phenomena or behaviour, whereas *gender* should be used for social or cultural categories:

The effectiveness of the drug is partly dependent on the patient's sex.

The tests determined the baby's sex before birth.

In certain societies gender roles are more clearly defined.

The gender gap in remuneration is being steadily narrowed.

goods, good

Is the singular permissible in reference to products, wares and merchandise? In general contexts, the plural "goods" should be used or a singular noun such as "product" substituted. However, in specialized contexts the singular is sometimes used for convenience's sake, as in "the tax applies to any good or service purchased in Canada."

healthful, healthy

Healthful means "conducive to health"; *healthy* means "possessing health":

Healthy people have a healthful diet.

historical, historic

Historical is used in the general sense of "related to history" or "having existed." *Historic* is preferred for "something famous or important in history":

The discovery was of great historical interest.

Laura Secord was a historical character.

The historic victory by Donovan Bailey was the highlight of the 1996 season.

12

hung, hanged

When referring to capital punishment, use *hanged*. In all other contexts use *hung*.

i.e., e.g., etc.

The abbreviation i.e. means "that is" and introduces a definition; *e.g.* means "for example." Do not use *e.g.* (or *for example* or a synonym such as *including*) and *etc.* in the same sentence, since *etc.* would be redundant:

not

The Minister received the representatives of many African countries, *e.g.* Angola, Mali, Tanzania, Zaire, Zimbabwe, *etc.*

but

The Minister received the representatives of many African countries, *e.g.* Angola, Mali, Tanzania, Zaire and Zimbabwe.

or better still

The Minister received the representatives of many African countries, including Angola, Mali, Tanzania, Zaire and Zimbabwe.

imply, infer

Imply refers to meaning intended by the speaker, whereas *infer* refers to meaning understood by the receiver of a message:

What did the official imply by that statement?

What should we infer from her statement?

include, comprise

Include implies only part of a whole; *comprise* implies all:

The multilateral working group includes two Palestinian representatives.

Water comprises hydrogen and oxygen.

in regards to

The correct idiom is *in* or *with regard to* (singular). Note also *without regard to* and *as regards*.

inside of, off of, outside of

The *of* in each of these expressions is superfluous.

insure

See under **assure**.

intense, intensive

Intense means "existing in a high degree, strong, extreme"; *intensive* means "highly concentrated, thorough":

He experienced intense pain.

Intensive study of the problem should yield results.

irregardless

This is nonstandard usage. Write *regardless*.

its, it's

Its is the possessive form of *it*. *It's* is a contraction of *"it is"* or *"it has"*:

The committee amended its terms of reference.

It's an inappropriate term.

lay, lie

Lay (past tense "laid") always takes an object. *Lie* (past tense "lay") does not take an object:

The project leader will lay out the plans for you.

She laid the volume on its side.

Let us lie down with the lions.

The soldiers lay down in the shade.

lead, led

Lead is a present tense form of the verb *to lead*. *Led* is the past tense of the same verb, which is often misspelled with *ea*:

Lead the way, captain!

Surin led from start to finish to win the gold medal.

least, less

It is incorrect to use *least* when comparing only two persons or things:

He is the less (**not** least) effective of the two programmers.

Singh was the least nervous of the three candidates.

legible, readable

These terms can both mean "capable of being deciphered or read with ease." *Readable* also means "interesting to read":

The candidate's examination paper was barely legible.

I found Richler's latest book very readable.

loan, lend

The traditional distinction is that *loan* is used principally as a noun, whereas *lend* is invariably a verb. Although this distinction is being blurred in current Canadian usage, it should be observed in formal writing:

Could I have the loan of your car for the weekend?

I wonder if you could also lend me $200.

luxuriant, luxurious

Luxuriant refers to abundant growth; *luxurious* concerns luxury:

The camp was surrounded by luxuriant vegetation.

The president's room was full of luxurious furniture.

12

matériel, material

The term *matériel* (with or without the accent) is used for the equipment, apparatus and supplies of an organization (as distinct from personnel), especially in the military. In all other contexts, *material* is used.

media, medium

Although usage is evolving, in the context of modern communications use *media* as the plural and *medium* as the singular:

The story was given prominent coverage in the media.

I went to a school where English was the medium of instruction.

militate, mitigate

Militate means "act, work, operate (in favour of or against)"; *mitigate* means "reduce the severity of":

All these facts militate against renewal of the contract.

The government's policies are designed to mitigate the effects of unemployment.

Note that *mitigate* takes no preposition.

need, needs

Both *needs* and *need* are used as the third person singular of the verb *to need*, but in different contexts. *Needs* is the usual form in affirmative statements, either with noun objects or with *to* and an infinitive. *Need* is sometimes used as an auxiliary, followed by the infinitive without *to*, in negative statements and in questions. In formal English *need* may be used even when the negation is merely suggested by a word like *only*:

She needs more management experience.

He needs to practise.

The director need not be informed.

Need the director come?

The department need only identify itself in the letterhead.

non

Avoid using this prefix to create new words when a suitable opposite already exists:

inaudible **not** nonaudible

disagreement **not** nonconcurrence

temporary **not** nonpermanent

non-, un-

Un- has a negative connotation and means "the opposite of," whereas *non-* means "other than." Thus "non-scientific" means "not connected with science," while "unscientific" means "lacking scientific rigour."

Compare also "un-Christian conduct"" and "non-Christian religions"; "un-Canadian" and "non-Canadian"; "unserviceable" (so worn that it can no longer be brought back into service) and "non-serviceable" (not meant to be serviced).

one of those who

Use a plural verb after *who*:

> She is one of those (people) who always offer their assistance in a crisis.

on the part of

On the part of is often an awkward way of saying "by," "among," "for" or the like:

> A greater effort by (on the part of) your staff is required.

peculiar to, particular to

The phrase *peculiar to* means "characteristic of" and has nothing to do with being "peculiar" or "strange." *Particular to* is incorrect usage:

> Some plant species are peculiar to the Prairies.

practicable, practical

Practicable means "that which can be done, which is feasible"; *practical* means "having to do with action or practice, fit for actual practice," and is the opposite of "theoretical." Thus it may be practicable to come to work in a dogsled, but it is not practical.

preceding, previous, prior

Preceding refers to what comes immediately before. *Previous* and *prior*, which are synonymous, mean "existing or occurring (some time) before something else." *Prior* can also imply priority, as in "a prior engagement":

> The preceding clause spells out the conditions of the loan.

> She had a child from a previous marriage.

> Unfortunately, the President has a prior engagement.

12

preplanning

The prefix is redundant. *Planning* is the correct term.

principal, principle

Principal can be an adjective meaning "chief" or "leading"; it can also be a noun meaning "chief person" or "original sum of money" (as in a loan). *Principle* can be used only as a noun, meaning "universal law" or "rule of conduct":

> The freedom to choose is a principle of democracy.

> The principal element in the group's plan was surprise.

procedure, process

The words are not interchangeable. A *procedure* is a set way of doing something. It stresses the method or routine followed. A *process* is a series of progressive and interdependent steps carried out to achieve a particular result:

> A procedure exists for having complaints investigated.

> The article describes the process for producing methane from pig manure.

proportional(ly), proportionate(ly)

In current usage the two words mean the same thing and are largely interchangeable. *Proportional(ly)* is more common, especially in set phrases such as *proportional parts, proportional representation, proportional tax*.

raise, rise

As a verb, *raise* takes an object, whereas *rise* does not:

> They raise cattle for a living.

> It is expected that the temperature will rise to 33°C.

Note their principal parts: *raise–raised, has raised; rise–rose, has risen*.

reason is because

A sentence beginning "The reason . . . is (was)" should be followed by a noun, a noun phrase, or a noun clause usually introduced by *that*:

> The reason the trip was cancelled was a lack of funds.

> The reason for the failure of the project was that the financial requirements had been underestimated.

refer, refer back

The word *back* is superfluous:

> Refer to the note on page 1.

relation, relationship

Although largely synonymous, the two words are not interchangeable. Both express the idea of a connection between things or persons. *Relationship* tends to be preferred for human connections, *relation* for more abstract connections:

> She replied that the Minister's analysis bore no relation to reality.

> What is your relationship to the patient?

> The government's relations with the unions have stabilized.

> Sociologists believe there is a relation (**or** relationship) between unemployment and crime.

requisition

A *requisition* is a formal demand for the use of a vehicle, supplies or premises, especially in a military context. As a verb it is transitive and should not be followed by *for*:

> The clerk requisitioned supplies.

> **or**

> The clerk made a requisition for supplies.

reserve, reservation

"Indian *reserve*" in Canada; "Indian *reservation*" in the United States.

responsible

Use the adjective *responsible* only with persons or corporate entities, not with things:

> The company was not responsible for the explosion.

> The supervisors must assume responsibility for their units' performance.

> **but**

> A gas leak caused the explosion.

sanction

As a noun, *sanction* has two almost directly opposed meanings. It can mean "official approval or authority" as well as "penalty to enforce behaviour." As a verb, it can only mean "to authorize" or "to legitimize":

> The Minister sanctioned pay raises for senior officials.

> In some societies, social pressure operates as the principal sanction.

seasonal, seasonable

Seasonal means "of or occurring in a particular season"; *seasonable* means "normal for the time of year" or "timely." The corresponding adverbs are *seasonally* and *seasonably*:

12

> Unemployment figures are always seasonally adjusted.

> The weather is seasonable for this time of year.

sensual, sensuous

Sensual means "pertaining to the gratification of physical appetites as ends in themselves." *Sensuous* means "pertaining to the senses, involving aesthetic pleasure":

> Is modern society to blame for our preoccupation with sensual pleasures?

> A sensuous appreciation of Ontario's wilderness is evident in the work of the Group of Seven.

serve, service

Apart from specialized uses in finance and animal breeding, *service* is used mainly in the sense of "to repair or maintain." The more general term—especially when used in relation to people—is *serve*:

> This school board serves the Metropolitan Toronto area.

> We have our car serviced every six months.

set, sit

These two verbs are rarely interchangeable. *Set* usually requires an object, whereas *sit* does not:

> Please set the box on the table!

> Her coat sits well.

However, there are some exceptions: cement *sets* (no object) and one *sits* an exam (object).

stationary, stationery

If something is *stationary*, it is fixed or unmoving. *Stationery* is material used for writing, including paper, cards and envelopes:

> A cold front is stationary over Manitoba.

> The office keeps its stationery in a special cupboard.

subject to, subjected to

Subject to, an expression widely used in administrative writing, is an adjectival or adverbial phrase meaning "under the control of, bound by, likely to have, depending on." *Subjected to* is the past tense or past participle of the verb "to subject to," which means "to cause to undergo something, to bring under the control of":

> The new policy is subject to approval by the Deputy Minister.

> The conquered territories were subjected to ethnic cleansing.

tendency, trend

A *tendency* is a leaning or inclination to do something. *Trend* indicates the prevailing direction or course of something, or the current fashion:

> Politicians have a tendency to make promises before elections.

> There is a trend toward the basics in education.

these kind, those kind, these sort, those sort

Kind and *sort* are singular; *these* and *those* are plural. Write *this (that) kind, these (those) kinds, this (that) sort* and *these (those) sorts*. Another solution can be to rephrase your sentence.

till, until

Till and *until* are interchangeable as prepositions and as conjunctions, although the latter is somewhat more formal. Avoid *'til* and *up until*.

try and, try to

Although both expressions are idiomatic, they are not always interchangeable. *Try to* is more appropriate to formal writing.

un-, non-

See *non-, un-*.

unique

This is an absolute. Do **not** write "very unique" or "rather unique." Similarly, many other absolute adjectives (*perfect, empty, circular, perpendicular, right, eternal* and so on), when used in their strict sense, should not be modified by a comparative or superlative adverb. Note that *unique* is preceded by the indefinite article *a* (**not** *an*).

Unites States

The *United States* takes a singular verb, since the term designates a single country rather than a collection of states. "The Netherlands" and "the United Nations" are also treated as singular nouns:

> The United States is a signatory to the agreement.

> In what year was the Netherlands liberated?

up

Although many legitimate phrasal verbs include the adverb *up*, avoid the following, which are inappropriate in formal writing: *choose up, finish up, listen up, practise up* and *wait up*.

utilize, use

The proper meaning of *utilize* is "to put to (unexpected) practical use" or "to make use of in a profitable way." *Utilize* and *utilization* should **not** be used as pompous substitutes for *use*, as in "The incumbent will be expected to utilize a word processor":

> The reorganization enabled the company to utilize its resources more efficiently.

> I did not use all the supplies you left me.

12

was, were (if I, he, she, etc.)

When expressing hypothetical conditions or conditions contrary to fact, use *were*:

> He behaves as though he were a millionaire.

> If I were you, I would not go.

> **but**

> If she was there, I did not see her.

The last is a statement of a possible state of affairs relating to the past, and does not involve a hypothetical condition contrary to fact.

where . . . at

This phrase (as in *Where are we at?*) is colloquial and should **not** be used in writing.

who, whom

The former is the subject of a verb, the latter the object. Although this distinction is widely disregarded in spoken English and informal written English, it should be observed in formal writing:

> Who will be selected?
>
> Whom will she hire?
>
> It does not matter whom we select.
>
> Tell me who was hired.

who's, whose

The form *who's* is a contraction of *who is*. *Whose* is the possessive form of *who*.

would

This is widely misused in constructions such as "If I *would* earn an 'A' in the exam, I would be happy." The sentence expresses a hypothetical, though possible, condition and calls for the past tense, "should" or "were to," in place of the first *would*:

> If you were in trouble, I would (should) help you.

not

> If you would be in trouble, I would help you.

> If I had known, I would (should) have come.

not

> If I would have known, I would have come.

Chapter Thirteen

Plain language

13

Plain Language

13.01 Introduction

The purpose of a plain-language approach in written communication is to convey information easily and unambiguously. It should not be confused with an oversimplified, condescending style. Rather, by choosing straightforward vocabulary and sentence structures and by organizing and presenting your material clearly and logically, you can save the reader time and effort and ensure that your message will be clearly understood.

The Government of Canada calls for plain language to be used in its communications with the public:

> The obligation to inform the public includes the obligation to communicate effectively. Information about government policies, programs and services should be clear, objective and simple, and presented in a manner that is readily understandable. Messages should convey information relevant to public needs, use plain language and be expressed in a clear and consistent style.[1]

The need to provide relevant information in a clear and simple way also applies to communications within and between departments. Many types of documents are written by public servants for other public servants: memorandums, information on employee benefits, health and safety manuals, work plans, departmental policies, performance appraisals and so on. Use of plain language will help ensure that your message comes across clearly and that readers take appropriate action.

13.02 Focussing on the reader

The starting point of any writing project should be to identify the intended readership, the purpose of the material and the desired impact. Before you start writing, ask yourself the following questions:

Who are the intended readers?
Are you writing for specialists, young people, all taxpayers, or a group whose first language is not English?

What do the readers need to know?
Do they need the details or just an overview, the historical context and the reasons behind the decision or merely an explanation of the decision's impact on them? What needs to be emphasized?

---

1. Treasury Board, "Government Communications Policy," *Treasury Board Publications on CD-ROM*, p. 17.

How will the readers use the information?

Will they use it to make a decision, to determine whether they are eligible for something, to carry out a procedure? Will they need to read the entire document or concentrate on one or two sections?

Use a **personal tone** in your writing. Address your readers directly and include examples, where appropriate, to illustrate important points.

For example, write

> You must be a landed immigrant or permanent resident to apply. To find out how to become a landed immigrant or permanent resident, contact an Immigration Centre (the addresses are given on page 6).

not

> It is incumbent upon applicants who do not possess a status of landed immigrant or permanent resident prior to the submission of their application to communicate with the appropriate Immigration Centre in order to take the necessary steps to obtain such a status.

13.03 Text organization

Decide what information is most important to include and structure it in such a way that the document is logically presented and easily understood. Do this by putting yourself in the reader's place: What is the most important thing you would want to know if you were the reader? What would help you find the information needed?

- Divide your text into main points and secondary points.

- Decide on a structure. Is a brief summary of background information required? What are to be the main divisions of your document? How much detail is required? Is a question-and-answer approach appropriate?

- Put the most important ideas first—both in the document and in each paragraph.

- At the outset, tell your reader what your document is about and how it is organized. Use a table of contents and an introduction for longer documents.

See Chapter 11 for detailed information on the organization of reports.

13.04 Vocabulary

(a) **Use simple, familiar words and phrases** for clarity. In the list below, the column on the right gives a more straightforward and often shorter way to express the same idea:

advance planning	planning
After this is accomplished	Then
at an early date	soon
facilitate	help, make possible
five in number	five

in the absence of	without
It would be appropriate for me to begin by saying that	First,
owing to the fact that	because, since

(b) **Choose verbs over verb-noun phrases** to make your sentences clear and concise. For example, readers will understand your message more readily if you replace the phrase on the left with the word on the right:

carry out an examination of	examine
effect an improvement to	improve
ensure maintenance of	maintain
give consideration to	consider
make an enquiry	enquire

The following sentence becomes much more transparent if the two verb-noun phrases are replaced with verbs:

not

The recommendation of the committee favoured continuation of the applied research.

but

The committee recommended that the applied research continue.

(c) Concise writing is generally clearer. **Cut out unnecessary words** to shorten sentences.

For example, write

With fewer younger workers entering the job market, unemployment may drop over the next decade.

not

Slower labour force growth may attenuate somewhat the problem of unemployment over the next decade, since there will no longer be a need to absorb large numbers of new workers entering the labour market.

(d) **Avoid jargon** and unfamiliar acronyms or expressions, especially when writing for the public. Even for internal documents, consider using an alternative expression if some of your readers may not know the specialized term. Expressions such as *roll out, stakeholder* and *re-engineering* may be unclear except to a specialized audience and tend to be overused.

13

Sometimes an unfamiliar term is best omitted altogether. For example, the following sentence contains a Latin phrase—*ceteris paribus* (meaning "other things being equal")—which will confuse many readers and which adds little if any meaning:

From our perspective, Option 2 would seem to offer the most benefits and, *ceteris paribus*, would be more effective in ensuring the resolution of any problems.

The sentence could be written more clearly and concisely as follows:

> We feel that Option 2 would be the most effective way of solving any problems.

Administrative jargon and officialese can cloud the message and make it incomprehensible to many readers:

not

> The challenges of the position involve ensuring the provision of delivery of the program in the most efficient manner possible in light of an ever-changing client profile which is impacted on by the adjustments to the programs necessitated by changing federal legislation and by the incidence of federal cutbacks in resource allotments.

but

> The challenges of the position include delivering the program as efficiently as possible in light of an ever-changing client profile, changes in federal legislation and resource cutbacks.

(e) Explain complicated ideas. Make sure that complex notions or subtle distinctions are clarified. The following sentence requires specialized knowledge on the reader's part:

> Holders of locked-in RRSPs, currently limited to purchases of life annuities with those funds, will be allowed to purchase life income funds.

Is it clear to the reader how "locked-in RRSPs" differ from other RRSPs and what the distinction between "life annuities" and "life income funds" is? If not, explain these notions before going on.

(f) Avoid chains of nouns. Nouns can modify other nouns in English, but three or more nouns in a row can obscure the meaning: the reader has to differentiate between the concepts and decide how the nouns are interrelated. Examples of noun chains abound in administrative writing:

> departmental expenditure increase review
> investment income deferral advantage
> post-selection feedback session
> unemployment insurance premium rate increases

It is easier for the reader to understand the message if some of the nouns are linked by prepositions such as *of, for, to* and *in*. The first example could be reformulated as "a review of increases in departmental expenditures." Although the revised version uses more words, it is clearer and simpler to read.

13.05 Sentences

Sentences are the basic building blocks of any written material and must be designed to convey the message effectively. To achieve this objective, keep them relatively short, avoid verbiage, link your ideas logically and use the active voice. The same principles apply to paragraphs.

Keep sentences concise. Limit your sentences to one idea and avoid information overload. A sentence such as the one that follows is difficult to understand on first reading because it contains too much information:

> The amendment provides for pension benefits to be fully funded as they are earned by employees and for the basic pension accounts to be combined with the portion of the Supplementary Retirement Benefits Account that relates to each plan so that all future benefits, including all indexing payments, can be charged to the appropriate accounts.

The points could be more effectively expressed in two or three sentences:

> Under the amended policy, employees' pension benefits will be fully funded as they are earned. Moreover, the basic pension account for each plan will absorb the portion of the Supplementary Retirement Benefits Account that applies to that plan. In this way, all future benefits, including indexing payments, can be charged to the appropriate accounts.

In the sentence

> First of all, in a general sense, what is interesting is that in addition to the initial objective which was to restart the learning process, it was found that this literacy training would enable individuals, who are totally inhibited, to once again discover at least a minimum of self-confidence.

almost all of the first line is superfluous and there are no fewer than four subordinate clauses. Eliminate the filler material and recast the sentence to highlight the main idea:

> The literacy training met the initial objective of restarting the learning process. It also helped participants, who were very inhibited, to begin acquiring self-confidence.

13

Paragraphs, too, should be limited to one point, or to a series of related points if the information is not complicated.

Make your point clearly. Avoid empty introductory phrases and padding that obscure the meaning of a sentence. These include expressions such as "I would like to begin by indicating clearly to you that . . ." and "If this step, which may be necessary in some but not all cases, is deemed appropriate . . . ."

Say what you need to say concisely and clearly. Link ideas within sentences and paragraphs by giving your readers "signposts." Cohesion can be achieved in various ways, including the use of linking words (*moreover, however* and so on) and references to the topic at hand ("The new policy on . . . , " "This policy," "It").

Use the active voice. While the passive voice is useful in moderation and is common in administrative writing, it tends to be wordy and impersonal. Give preference to the active voice, in which the subject conveys the action and is generally near the beginning of the sentence, making it easier for the reader to understand the message:

not

It is requested that recommendations be submitted concerning ways and means whereby costs arising out of the use of the facsimile might conceivably be shared by both directorates.

but

Please recommend ways in which the two directorates could share the cost of the fax machine.

Convey your message positively. Where possible, use positive words to make your point. For example, write

Enter the information in one file only.

not

Enter the information in no more than one file.

Readers may miss or misinterpret short negatives such as *no, not, none* and *never* and negative words beginning with *in-, non-* and *un-,* particularly if several of them occur in the same paragraph. Such misreadings could have a serious effect on users' decisions and actions. So if you cannot reword positively, consider highlighting the negative by using boldface or italics.

13.06 Layout and design

Readers, especially members of the public, are more likely to read and use documents that are designed with plain language principles in mind. You can make your document more appealing visually and easier to read by removing obstacles to communication in various ways:

Choose appropriate type. Serif typefaces (such as Times Roman and Palatino), which have small lines at the ends of the letter strokes, are easier to read because they direct the reader's eye from letter to letter. Serif faces are therefore recommended for text, while sans-serif typefaces, such as Helvetica, provide contrast when used in headings.

The size of the type should generally be at least 10 points. Twelve-point type or larger may be required for readers with visual impairments.

Use open space. Provide extra white space around headings, lists, boxes and other visual elements to draw attention to the information in them.

Leave one extra line space between paragraphs if you are using the block format (see 10.02). If using the indent style (see 10.03), do **not** leave an extra line space, except in correspondence.

Break information down into lists, introduced by bullets or numbers. This opens up the document and guides your readers.

Words in lower case have distinctive shapes that are easy to recognize. Entire lines of capitalized text are difficult to read because the letters are all the same size. Similarly, left-justified text, with a ragged right edge, is more readable. In text with a justified right margin, the spacing between letters and words can be irregular and difficult to control, and the eye becomes tired from having to adjust constantly.

Create contrast. Use headings, subheadings and visual elements to produce contrast and lead your readers through the document. Colour and varied styles and sizes of type can also help create contrast. However, excessive use of lines, colours and visuals may distract readers' attention from your message.

13.07 Testing

It is important to test and revise a document before it is distributed or published.

Techniques for revision and proofreading are outlined in Chapter 16. However, it is also a good idea to check the readability and transparency of your document before it is released for distribution. A trial run with a potential reader or colleague who has knowledge of the target readership could be a useful test. Surveys, focus groups or field tests would provide an even more thorough indication as to whether your document will get the message across simply and clearly to the intended readership.

13

Chapter Fourteen

Elimination of stereotyping in written communications

Elimination of sexual stereotyping

Elimination of racial and ethnic stereotyping

Fair and representative depiction of people with disabilities

14

Elimination of Stereotyping in Written Communications

14.01 Introduction

A 1982 Government of Canada document entitled "Elimination of Sexual Stereotyping"[1] defines sexual stereotyping as "the use of words, actions, and graphic material that assigns roles or characteristics to people solely on the basis of gender, and without regard for the intrinsic potentials of women and men" and goes on to state that it is the policy of the Government to eliminate sexual stereotyping from all government communications.

Given that communications have a cumulative impact on people's perceptions, behaviour and aspirations, that most communications reach an audience composed equally of women and men, and that women are the prime target of sexual stereotyping, the document provides a number of guidelines for written communications.

In 1990, the Government of Canada issued "Fair Communication Practices,"[2] guidelines to eliminate sexual stereotyping and to ensure the fair and representative depiction of ethnic and visible minorities, Aboriginal peoples and people with disabilities. The guidelines are based on the principle that "all individuals, irrespective of gender, ancestry and ethnic origin or disability, are and must be portrayed as equally productive and contributing members of Canadian society." They are intended to help correct biases and stereotypes that constitute barriers to full participation in society. In practical terms, they require that material "be reviewed to eliminate words, images and situations that reinforce erroneous preconceptions or suggest that all or most members of a racial or ethnic group have the same stereotypical characteristics."

This chapter lists many of the stereotyping problems covered in the two federal government documents and in other pertinent material, and shows how those problems can be solved. The objective in each case is to ensure the equal treatment of men and women in written material, to depict all individuals as fully participating members of society, and to eliminate preconceived ideas about their functions and attributes.

Ultimately, the issue boils down to one of courtesy and respect for all, regardless of gender, origin or disability.

14

---

1. Treasury Board, *Administrative Policy Manual*, Chapter 484.
2. Treasury Board, *Treasury Board Manual, Information and Administrative Management, Appendix E.*

Elimination of Sexual Stereotyping

14.02 Correspondence; names and forms of address

The form preferred or used by the person being addressed or referred to should be retained if it is known. Otherwise, the following guidelines should be applied in order to ensure uniform and equal treatment of the sexes.

- In formal correspondence, use *Ms., Mrs., Miss* or *Mr.* When the addressee is a woman, and her preference cannot be ascertained, use *Ms.*:

  Dear Ms. Samuels:

- If the gender of the addressee is not known, begin your reply with "Dear" followed by the person's initials and surname:

  Dear J. D. Simmonds:

Where the name of the addressee is not known, use the form "Dear Sir/Madam" or "Dear Madam or Sir."

- When writing to an organization or to unspecified individuals, use an inclusive salutation:

  Dear Members of the Rotary Club:
  To the Consumer Relations Department:
  To whom it may concern:

An alternative is to use the memo format and omit the salutation.

See also 10.17

14.03 Parallel treatment

- When the names of a woman and man are mentioned together, use parallel language so that men and women are portrayed as equals:

  Alan Knight and Joyce Philips

  J. Philips and A. Knight

  Knight and Philips

  Joyce Philips, the engineer, and Alan Knight, the journalist

  not

  Mrs. J. Philips and Alan Knight

  or

  Alan Knight, the journalist, and Mrs. J. Philips

- Ensure parallel treatment of couples:

  Mr. and Mrs. James and Irene Luciano
  James and Irene
  Mr. and Mrs. Luciano
  James and Irene Luciano

not

Mr. and Mrs. James Luciano

or

James Luciano and his wife Irene

- Ensure parallel treatment of work associates:

    Raymond Kovacs and his assistant Karen White

    Margaret Thompson, Vice-President, and her executive secretary Bill White

    not

    Mr. Kovacs and his assistant Karen

    Margaret Thompson, Vice-President, and her executive secretary Bill

- Alternate order of reference so that one sex is not always given second place:

    Karen White and her immediate superior, Raymond Kovacs
    Joyce Philips and Alan Knight
    Mr. White and Ms. Thompson

- In distribution and other lists, use alphabetical order or list according to rank.

14.04 Pronouns

Because English lacks a singular pronoun that signifies the non-specific "he or she," customarily the masculine pronoun has been used. The following guidelines help to avoid this usage.

- Eliminate the pronoun completely:

    The section chief is responsible for maintaining good relations with clients *and ensuring* that deadlines are met.

    not

    The section chief is responsible for maintaining good relations with *his* clients. *He* ensures that deadlines are met.

- Repeat the noun:

    An employee must file a grievance within the prescribed time limit. *The employee's* union representative will usually be involved at this stage of the process.

    not

    An employee must file a grievance within the prescribed time limit. *His* union representative will usually be involved at this stage of the process.

- Use the plural:

  All responsibility centre manager*s* must prepare *their* own work plans.

  not

  Each responsibility centre manage*r* must prepare *his* own work plans.

- Use a neutral word such as "one", "individual" or "incumbent":

  the incumbent's duties **not** his duties

- Use both pronouns, but avoid using parentheses:

  his or her duties **not** his (or her) duties

- Address your reader directly. Substitute "you" or "yours" for "he" or "his," using the imperative mood where needed:

  Send two copies of *your* academic record to the Human Resources Officer.

  not

  The applicant must send two copies of *his* academic record to the Human Resources Officer.

- Use sentence fragments when writing job descriptions:

  Develops, implements and evaluates programs to improve information services; directs research in information resource management.

14.05 Personification

Avoid using feminine or masculine pronouns to personify animals, events, ships, etc.:

Once again the area was hit by hurricane Flora. *It* wrought havoc.

not

. . . *She* wrought havoc.

14.06 Titles of occupations

Eliminate titles and terms which suggest that a job is not typically performed by persons of either sex or that the task varies depending on whether the incumbent is a woman or a man. As far as possible, job titles should not imply that the job can be filled only by members of one sex.

- Do **not** feminize occupational titles by adding *ess*, as in "manageress," *ette* as in "usherette" and *ix* as in "executrix." Do **not** add gratuitous modifiers, as in "*lady* doctor" or "*male* nurse."

- Use feminine nouns when women are referred to, or gender-inclusive nouns when a man or woman is not specifically referred to:

  spokeswoman/spokesperson/representative **not** spokesman
  chairwoman/chairperson/chair **not** chairman[3]

---

3. In some cases, official names such as "chairman" and "alderman" cannot be changed without legal approval.

councillor **not** councilman **or** alderman
technician **not** repairman
trade worker **not** journeyman
cleaner **not** cleaning woman

- For non-discriminatory occupational titles, refer to the *Manual of Sex-Free Occupational Titles* and the *National Occupation Classification*.

14.07 Man, lady, girl, woman

- Avoid using the generic *man* to refer to people in general and, where possible, as part of a compound:

  anybody, anyone **not** a man
  nobody, no one **not** no man
  average person **not** common man
  ordinary people **not** the man in the street
  writer **not** man of letters
  staff/operate/run a booth **not** man a booth
  labour force, personnel, staff, work force **not** manpower
  synthetic **or** manufactured **not** man-made
  humanity, people **not** mankind
  compatriot **not** countryman

- Unless a minor is referred to or you wish to evoke refinement or high standing, use *woman*, **not** *girl* or *lady*:

  The men and women of the Administrative Support Division

  not

  The men and girls of the Administrative Support Division

  Seventy percent of the delegates were women.

  not

  Seventy percent of the delegates were ladies.

14.08 Full range of human characteristics and situations

All people, including women as individuals or as a group, should be treated with respect and dignity. To this end they should be depicted as living and working in a variety of circumstances and assuming a broad range of responsibilities.

14

- Avoid gratuitous reference to physical or other characteristics and undue emphasis on traditional roles:

  Dr. and Mrs. Rolfe

  or

  Dr. Erica and Mr. John Bruce

  not

  Dr. Rolfe and his charming blonde wife Dora

or

Mr. John Bruce and his doctor wife

- Do **not** suggest that men are the norm in certain situations and women in others. Show that members of each sex are now performing roles that were traditionally the preserve of the other sex:

Parent and child

not

Mother and child

People (**or** Families) are suffering increasingly from the burden of taxation.

not

Men and their families are suffering increasingly from the burden of taxation.

Professionals, their spouses and their children

not

Professionals, their wives and their children

the average worker

or

the average wage-earner

not

the average working man

- Ensure that women as a group are treated with respect, particularly in the role of homemaker. Refer to "women re-entering the work force," **not** to "women going back to work." Do **not** refer to "working women" or "working wives" in contrast to homemakers; use the expression "women working outside the home" or an equivalent.

Elimination of
Racial and Ethnic Stereotyping

14.09 Ethnic clichés

Eliminate and avoid expressions which cloud the fact that all attributes may be found in all groups: for example, "*inscrutable* Orientals," "*frugal* Scots" or "*lazy* Mexicans."

14.10 Gratuitous modifiers

Certain modifiers reinforce racial and ethnic stereotypes by giving information that suggests an exception to the rule. Avoid them:

not

The board interviewed a number of intelligent Black students.

but

. . . a number of Black students.

or

. . . a number of intelligent students.

14.11 Connotative modifiers

Be cautious in using adjectives that, in certain contexts, have questionable racial or ethnic connotations or insulting, often racist overtones, such as *primitive, conniving, savage, lazy, backward, culturally deprived, simple,* and *clannish.*

14.12 Identification of groups

Be aware of the current self-identification preferences of racial and cultural groups in Canada:

Black(s) **not** Negro(es)
ethnic (or cultural) minorities **not** ethnics
Aboriginal person **not** Aboriginal
Aboriginal people(s) in Canada **not** Aboriginal Canadians
Native people(s) **not** Natives
Inuk (*singular*), Inuit (*plural*) **not** Eskimo
Métis **not** Metis

Note that the term *African American* is gaining currency in the U.S.A.

Note also that the terms used to designate the Indigenous peoples of Canada have undergone considerable change in recent years. Although the Canadian *Constitution Act, 1982,* uses the term *aboriginal peoples* in the lower case, the words *Aboriginal, Indigenous and Native* have since come to be capitalized when used in the Canadian context. The terms currently preferred are the following:

Aboriginal people(s)
Native people(s)
Indigenous people(s)
First people(s)

Fair and Representative Depiction of People With Disabilities

14

14.13 Full range of human characteristics and situations

People with disabilities should be depicted as living and working in a variety of circumstances with a range of responsibilities, and as active participants in events. They should be identified by their achievements rather than their limitations.

The whole range of human characteristics and attributes applicable to non-disabled persons should be shown to apply to persons with disabilities.

14.14 Identification of groups

Do not define people by their disorders or use dehumanizing stereotypes, such as "the disabled," "the blind," "the retarded."

- Be aware of the self-identification preferences of individuals or groups:

  people/persons with disabilities **not** the handicapped
  Canadians with disabilities **not** disabled Canadians

- The generic term "people with disabilities" can be adapted to the purpose of the text:

  passengers requiring assistance to board the plane/train
  students who use wheelchairs
  clients with a hearing impairment

14.15 Neutral word descriptions

Avoid language that suggests characteristics of courage, suffering, pity or abnormality, such as *brave, inspirational, victim, special, incompetent* or *defective.* Use factual rather than emotional terms:

  person who has lupus **not** lupus sufferer
  wheelchair user **not** confined to a wheelchair
  congenital condition **not** birth defect
  person with cerebral palsy **not** spastic
  Down syndrome **not** mongolism
  hearing- and speech-impaired **not** deaf and dumb
  non-disabled students **not** normal students
  intellectually or developmentally impaired **not** retarded
  seizure **not** fit

- Avoid condescending euphemisms like "physically challenged" and "differently abled."

- Use precise words when describing disabilities. The degree of impairment must be taken into consideration:

  paraplegic **or** quadriplegic **not** crippled
  visually impaired **not** partially blind

Chapter Fifteen

Geographical names

Geographical names: types and composition

Translation of geographical feature names into English

Treatment of other types of toponym, provincial names and names of pan-Canadian significance

15

Geographical Names

15.01 Introduction

In a bilingual country such as Canada, questions arise as to the designations to be used in official documents for cities, towns, villages, lakes, rivers, mountains and other geographical entities and features that may have different but well-established designations in the two official languages or may be known by one name in one region and a different one elsewhere.

15.02 Background

On November 23, 1983, the Treasury Board issued its Circular No. 1983-58 to implement the policy adopted by the Canadian Permanent Committee on Geographical Names (CPCGN) regarding the linguistic treatment of geographical names on federal maps and in federal documents.

The principles enunciated in the policy are as follows:

- The official form of a geographical name is the one adopted by the provincial or federal authorities in whose jurisdiction an entity lies. This name can be found in the *Gazetteer of Canada*.

- Certain geographical names of pan-Canadian significance (see list at the end of this chapter) have well-known, official forms in both English and French. Both forms may be used on maps and in documents.

- All other geographical names have only one official form, which is the one to be used on federal maps in either official language.

- In documents, it is permissible to translate the generic portion of names of geographical features, that is, the portion that indicates the nature of the entity (*Lake* in "Arrow Lake"), but not the specific portion that names the entity (*Arrow* in "Arrow Lake").

- Names of inhabited places retain their official form in both English and French texts, e.g. *Montréal* (Que.), *Saint John* (N.B.), and *St. John's* (Nfld.)

The Treasury Board also designated the Translation Bureau as the organization responsible for determining what, in running text, should be the proper form of the names of geographical features in the other language.

In 1989 a committee made up of Translation Bureau and CPCGN representatives was assigned the task of examining the various problems encountered in translating official English names of Canadian geographical features into French and devising solutions. The committee produced the "General Rules for Translating and Writing the Names of Canadian Geographical Features,"[1] the purpose of which was to standardize the translation and writing of geographical feature names within a sentence (rather than on a map). Although the rules were written for the translation of English names into French, the committee did recommend that, where applicable, they also be followed for the translation of French names into English.

Geographical Names: Types and Composition

15.03 Official geographical names

Official geographical names (or toponyms) are those approved by a provincial, territorial or federal toponymic authority. They are generally listed in the *Gazetteer of Canada*, which is produced by the Canadian Permanent Committee on Geographical Names. Two kinds of geographical names are distinguished: names of inhabited places and names of geographical features.

15.04 Names of inhabited places

Only two municipalities in Canada have two official forms of their names, one in English and one in French: Grand Falls and Caissie Cape in New Brunswick, which are also known officially as Grand-Sault and Cap-des-Caissie. All other municipalities have only one authorized form: thus *Montréal* and *Québec* (the city) retain their accents in English.

15.05 Names of geographical features

In Canada most geographical features have only one official name, except for the 81 names of pan-Canadian significance that have official forms in both English and French. Some provinces (Manitoba, Ontario and New Brunswick) also recognize "alternate names" for well-known geographical features under their jurisdiction (see 15.15).

15.06 Generic and specific

As a general rule, the name of a geographical feature is composed of a generic and a specific. The **specific** is the part of the toponym that identifies the particular geographical feature in question. For example:

> In *Alexandria River*, the specific is *Alexandria*.
> In *Crown Prince Frederik Island*, the specific is *Crown Prince Frederik*.
> In *River of Ponds Lake*, the specific is *River of Ponds*.

The **generic** is the part of the toponym that identifies a general class to which a specific geographical feature belongs. For example:

---

1. Gélinas-Surprenant, Hélène, "Uniformisation de l'écriture des noms géographiques au Canada," *Terminology Update / L'Actualité terminologique*, 23, 3 (1990): 18–22.

In *Swampy Bay River*, the generic is *River*.

In *Bay d'Espoir*, the generic is *Bay*.

In *Little Francis Lake* the generic is *Lake*.

Translation of Geographical Feature Names into English

15.07 Reinstatement of official English toponyms

Where the generic of an English-language place name has been translated into French, it is essential to restore it to its original English form when translating the French document into English. In the following sentence, the toponyms have been translated into French but their official forms are English:

> Le relief du plateau est plus particulièrement remarquable dans le nord de l'**île Somerset**, sur la **presqu'île Brodeur**, ainsi que dans le centre et l'ouest de l'**île Prince of Wales**.

Since, in accordance with the rules, the specific parts of these toponyms (*Somerset, Brodeur, Prince of Wales*) have not been modified in any way, it becomes more a question of verifying the official English form in the appropriate gazetteer than a question of translation. The original names are *Somerset Island, Brodeur Peninsula* and *Prince of Wales Island*.

15.08 Translation of the generic

General rule

The generic of a geographical feature name may be translated:

> lac Beauchamp / Beauchamp Lake
> île Madame / Madame Island

French and English equivalents for generics have been established in the publication *Glossary of Generic Terms in Canada's Geographical Names*.[2]

Exceptions

The generic should not be translated in situations (a), (b), (c) and (d) below. The name is left in its official form and is followed, as needed, by a geographical term describing the nature of the entity, which will be indicated in the gazetteer of the province or territory concerned.

(a) The generic does not indicate the actual nature of the entity designated:

> île Cooks (*rock*) / Île Cooks rock
> lac Cochémère (*pond*) / Cochémère pond

(b) The generic is rare or borrowed from a language other than English or French:

15

> Hanbury Kopje hill
> Loch Erne lake

---

2. Canada, *Glossary of Generic Terms in Canada's Geographical Names: TB 176 / Glossaire des génériques en usage dans les noms géographiques du Canada : BT 176.*

(c) The generic is separated from the specific by one or more linking particles:

> lac aux Saumons / Lac aux Saumons
> baie de la Sorcière / Baie de la Sorcière
> anse de la Pointe / Anse de la Pointe

(d) The name is preceded by the article "Le (La, Les, L')," which is part of the toponym. The article is retained at the beginning of the toponym and the appropriate geographical term or a short description may be added for clarity:

> Les Chutes / Les Chutes **or** the falls known as Les Chutes
> La Grande Rivière / La Grande Rivière
> Le Petit Étang / Le Petit Étang **or** the pond known as Le Petit Étang

15.09 Non-translation of the specific

With the exception of names of pan-Canadian significance and some alternate forms approved by provincial authorities, the specific is not translated. It must be left in its official form (that is, the form in which it appears in the gazetteer of the relevant province or territory), with all hyphens, articles, accents, diacritical marks and capital letters. Nothing is added and nothing omitted:

> pointe Enragée / Enragée Point
> rivière Saint-Augustin / Saint-Augustin River

15.10 Adjectives and points of the compass

Adjectives such as *grand, petit, supérieur, inférieur,* as well as points of the compass, are translated when they qualify the generic:

> ruisseau Saint-Jean Nord / North Saint-Jean Creek
> Petit lac Saint-Amour / Little Saint-Amour Lake
> Petite rivière Grand / Little Grand River

They are not translated if they qualify the specific or replace it, or if they precede a generic not followed by a specific:

> lac Grande Gueule / Grande Gueule Lake
> rivière Ouest / Ouest River
> Petit Ruisseau / Petit Creek

Treatment of Other Types of Toponym, Provincial Names and Names of Pan-Canadian Significance

15.11 Scientific and geological names

Certain scientific names, and in particular names of geological features such as eskers, moraines, potholes, sandbanks, slides and spurs, seldom have official status. Only by consulting a gazetteer can you determine if the name used is an official geographical name.

15.12 Names of national parks

Names of national parks, national historic parks and canals, and historic sites are established by Parks Canada. The publication *Toponymy and Terminology Used by Parks Canada* contains a list of all such names and their equivalents.

15.13 Names of undersea features

Several names of undersea features have official forms in both English and French that have been approved by the Advisory Committee on Names for Undersea and Maritime Features. Consult the most recent edition of the *Gazetteer of Undersea Feature Names*.

15.14 Names of Indian reserves

All Indian reserves have an official name in both English and French. See the CPCGN gazetteers of provinces and territories for the appropriate equivalents.

15.15 Alternate names and provincial translations

Although the official names of toponyms should always be given preference, provincial and territorial authorities allow, in certain circumstances, the use of geographical names that are not official. New Brunswick has official names in both English and French for certain features and places.

Manitoba

Official name / Equivalent name approved for use

Plum River / Rivière aux Prunes

Rat River / Rivière aux Rats

Equivalent name / Official name

Marais River / Rivière aux Marais

New Brunswick

English official name / French official name

Caissie Cape (*rural community*) / Cap-des-Caissie

Second Falls (*falls*) / Deuxième Sault

Grand Falls (*town*) / Grand-Sault

St. Francis River / Rivière Saint-François

Green River / Rivière Verte

15

Ontario

Official name / Recommended official alternate name

Detroit River / Rivière Détroit

French River / Rivière des Français

St. Clair River / Rivière Sainte-Claire

15.16 Names of pan-Canadian significance

The 81 names of pan-Canadian significance established by the Treasury Board of Canada (Circular 1983-58) have well-known forms in both English and French. For the purposes of federal government publications, both forms are considered official.

A

Abitibi, Lake / Lac Abitibi
Anticosti Island / Île d'Anticosti
Appalachian Mountains / Les Appalaches
Arctic Ocean / Océan Arctique
Athabasca Lake / Lac Athabasca
Athabasca River / Rivière Athabasca
Atlantic Ocean / Océan Atlantique

B

Baffin Bay / Baie de Baffin
Baffin Island / Île de Baffin
Beaufort Sea / Mer de Beaufort
Belle Isle, Strait of / Détroit de Belle-Isle
British Columbia / Colombie-Britannique

C

Cabot Strait / Détroit de Cabot
Cape Breton Island / Île du Cap-Breton
Chaleur Bay / Baie des Chaleurs
Champlain, Lake / Lac Champlain
Churchill River (Man.) / Rivière Churchill
Churchill River (Nfld.) / Fleuve Churchill
Coast Mountains / Chaîne Côtière
Columbia River / Fleuve Columbia

D

Davis Strait / Détroit de Davis

E

Ellesmere Island / Île d'Ellesmere
Erie, Lake / Lac Érié

F

Franklin, District of / District de Franklin
Fraser River / Fleuve Fraser
Fundy, Baie of / Baie de Fundy

G
Georgian Bay / Baie Georgienne
Great Bear Lake / Grand lac de l'Ours
Great Slave Lake / Grand lac des Esclaves

H
Hudson Bay / Baie d'Hudson
Hudson Strait / Détroit d'Hudson
Huron, Lake / Lac Huron

I
Prince Edward Island / Île-du-Prince-Édouard

J
James Bay / Baie James

K
Keewatin, District of / District de Keewatin

L
Labrador Sea / Mer du Labrador
Laurentian Mountains / Les Laurentides

M
Mackenzie, District of / District de Mackenzie
Mackenzie River / Fleuve Mackenzie
Manitoba, Lake / Lac Manitoba
Michigan, Lake / Lac Michigan (*not actually in Canada*)

N
Nelson River / Fleuve Nelson
New Brunswick / Nouveau-Brunswick
Newfoundland / Terre-Neuve
Niagara Falls / Chutes Niagara
Nipigon, Lake / Lac Nipigon
Nipissing, Lake / Lac Nipissing
North Saskatchewan River / Rivière Saskatchewan Nord
Northumberland Strait / Détroit de Northumberland
Northwest Territories / Territoires du Nord-Ouest
Nova Scotia / Nouvelle-Écosse

O
Ontario, Lake / Lac Ontario
Ottawa River / Rivière des Outaouais

P
Pacific Ocean / Océan Pacifique
Peace River / Rivière de la Paix

Q
Quebec (province) / Québec (province)
Queen Charlotte Islands / Îles de la Reine-Charlotte
Queen Elizabeth Islands / Îles de la Reine-Élisabeth

15

R

Rainy Lake / Lac à la Pluie
Rainy River / Rivière à la Pluie
Red River / Rivière Rouge
Restigouche River / Rivière Restigouche
Rocky Mountains / Montagnes Rocheuses

S

Sable Island / Île de Sable
Saguenay River / Rivière Saguenay
St. Clair, Lake / Lac Sainte-Claire
Saint John River / Rivière Saint-Jean
St. Lawrence River / Fleuve Saint-Laurent
St. Lawrence, Gulf of / Golfe du Saint-Laurent
Saskatchewan River / Rivière Saskatchewan
South Saskatchewan River / Rivière Saskatchewan Sud
Superior, Lake / Lac Supérieur

T

Timiskaming, Lake / Lac Témiscamingue

U

Ungava Bay / Baie d'Ungava

V

Vancouver Island / Île de Vancouver

W

Winnipeg, Lake / Lac Winnipeg
Winnipegosis, Lake / Lac Winnipegosis
Winnipeg River / Rivière Winnipeg
Woods, Lake of the / Lac des Bois

Y

Yukon River / Fleuve Yukon
Yukon Territory / Territoire du Yukon

Chapter Sixteen

Revision and proofreading

16

Revision and Proofreading

16.01 Introduction

The purpose of this chapter is to give the writer or editor guidance on how to check, correct and improve texts.

Many labels have been attached to the rereading process—revising, editing, reviewing, quality control, quality assurance, checking, post-editing, technical accuracy and conformity test, and so on. In this chapter, we will use the term "revision" to cover the full range of improvements that can be made to the form of a document, including organization of the content.

Revision and proofreading overlap, but proofreading is generally restricted to detecting and correcting omissions, grammar mistakes, and errors in typography, numerical expressions, names and titles, geographical names and addresses, and format. Proofreading for such errors is essential as a final check before distribution; it may also be a cost-effective alternative to extensive revision if time is of the essence.

16.02 Extent of revision

In establishing a revision method, you should keep in mind the time available, the cost of revision, the sensitivities of the person or persons whose work you are about to revise, and above all the end use of the document at hand. A report to be read by a small group of experts for information purposes may require proofreading, not revision, and attention to style and usage will be cursory. In revising a draft of your organization's annual report, however, you will have to detect, and correct, errors of many different types. Revision in this context may entail making improvements to or even recasting portions of a document which contains few, if any, errors of typography, grammar or usage but which requires changes in style and a reorganization of ideas.

For most purposes, you will deliver a satisfactory product if you eliminate, in accordance with the recommendations in the relevant chapters of this guide, errors of the types listed in 16.05. The guidelines presented below are based on the premise that the goal of revision is generally not to rewrite a text or make it conform to the reviser's personal preferences, but to identify errors and correct them. They may be adapted to fit the specific conditions under which the work is being performed and the end use of the document.

16.03 Preparation

Keep a copy of the unrevised draft. You may decide to reinstate a part of it at a later stage.

If you are revising a print copy of the document, use double or triple spacing, so that your changes are distinct and legible.

Make sure that the required reference tools—dictionaries, style guides, works on usage and grammar, and language databanks—are within easy reach so that you do not waste time looking for them.

If your client has in-house style guidelines or certain spelling, terminology or other preferences, respect them.

Use a checklist, such as the one presented in 16.08, to organize the revision process efficiently, to ensure that all problems are covered, and to help you meet your deadlines.

16.04 Timing

If time constraints permit, do not start revising your own text immediately after completing the first draft. Following a "cooling-off" period of at least several hours, you will be able to take a fresh look at your material.

Take the time to revise the whole draft; if you adopt a piecemeal approach, it will be difficult to ensure uniformity of style and vocabulary throughout the text, particularly if the draft is the result of a joint effort by several writers.

16.05 Sequence

The steps involved in revision will vary according to individual preference and working conditions. If time is limited, it is important to decide which features of the text should be given priority—style, usage and overall format, or just spelling and grammar. The following sequence is designed to ensure that the process is carried out in a logical, thorough manner. One or more steps may be combined in order to expedite matters, and you may want to take a second look at certain problems or pages requiring further revision or research (see checklist in 16.08). But keep in mind that the most effective approach is to check for one broad category of error at a time.

(a) Content check

Reread the whole draft for omissions, obvious factual errors, and lack of clarity or illogicality in the flow of ideas. Although not a problem of form, failure to situate each sentence in the context of the whole argument and to ensure that each idea flows logically from the previous sentences and paragraphs is a common shortcoming, which a reviser should detect and, if not correct, at least bring to the attention of the writer.

Rectify any problems, after speaking with the author if necessary. You may have to compare the current draft with an earlier one in order to ensure that no paragraphs, illustrations or tables have been dropped.

(b) Style and usage; plain language

Correct any weaknesses of the types listed below early in the revision process. As in step (a), they may require recasting of parts or all of a sentence or paragraph, as well as significant deletions.

- Unnecessarily long, complex sentences
- Unacceptable neologisms or jargon:

   People who are within five years of retirement will be *attritted.*

- Long multiple-noun phrases
- Verbiage and redundancy (*"excessive* verbiage"; "countries *such as* Japan, Indonesia, Malaysia, Singapore, *etc.*")
- Excessive repetition:

   While most *job* seekers spend fewer than five hours a week looking for a *job, job* seeking is considered a full-time *job* in the *Job* Finding Club.

- Ambiguity
- Improper prepositional usage
- Misuse of a word (see 12.03 for *affect/effect, amount/number* and other problems)
- Gallicisms in vocabulary and syntax ("*realize* a project," "training program *of* nurses")
- Wrong level of language or style, given end use of document
- Mixed metaphors ("We must put our shoulders to the wheel and take the bull by the horns.")
- Uneuphonic effects:

   Presentation of the new *provincial prison program* will be *postponed pending* further *planning.*

(c) Uniform vocabulary

Ensure that only one term is used for the same concept (*"eligibility for/admissibility to/right to* benefits").

(d) Elimination of stereotyping

Correct any parts of the text that fail to give a fair and representative picture of women, ethnic and visible minorities, Aboriginal people and people with disabilities. Here, too, corrections may necessitate structural change.

16

At this stage the paragraph and sentence structure of the text is to all intents and purposes final. You can begin to check the more technical features.

(e) Names and titles; geographical names; addresses

- Misspelling of a person's name or failure to adopt preferred spelling

- Failure to use appropriate form of address (*The Right Honourable, The Honourable,* etc.)

- Erroneous official title (*Commission* instead of *Board, President* instead of *Chairman)*

- Inconsistent presentation of a person's title

- Wrong English version of a place name

- Use of commas and parentheses in a street address:

    168 Radcliffe Crescent
    Regina, Saskatchewan

    not

    168, Radcliffe Crescent
    Regina (Saskatchewan)

(f) Spelling; punctuation; hyphenation and compounding; abbreviations; numerical expressions; grammar

Because of deletions and recasting of phrases and sentences, pay particular attention to punctuation, capitalization and grammar. For instance, sentences may lack a verb, an initial capital letter, a co-ordinating conjunction, or an essential punctuation mark. Redundancy may also have been introduced.

The following types of error are commonplace.

- Misspelling

- Misprints

- Punctuation errors, including the overuse of quotations marks

- Incorrect capitalization

- Erroneous compounding or word division

- Failure to ensure that, when first used, an abbreviation follows the full name of the entity it represents, unless the abbreviation is well known

- Incorrect form of an abbreviation

- Inconsistency in presenting numbers (as numerals or words)

- Erroneous or inconsistent use of decimal point

- Inconsistency in presenting SI/metric symbols, including spacing between symbols and figures

- Inaccurate transcription of numbers from one draft to the next

- Arabic in place of Roman numerals, and vice versa
- Non-agreement of subject and verb and use of singular noun where plural is required:

  The customer service *thrust* of this and other department*s* *have* been poorly communicated to the general public.

  The Tab and Caps Lock *key is* found on the left-hand side of the keyboard.

- No finite verb:

  not

  What to do about it?

  but

  What should we do about it?

- Comma splice:

  Cod stocks were dropping at an alarming rate, swift action had to be taken.
  (co-ordinating conjunction *and* required after *rate*)

- Dangling participle:

  Omitting the overture, *the music* began.

  Arising out of a conflict of personalities, *the Director General, Finance and Administration*, felt compelled to resign and move on.

- Faulty or imprecise antecedents for pronouns:

  Employees in management positions or positions of confidentiality *who* are acting on behalf of an excluded manager may be excluded.

  Sam visited his brother every day while *he* was unemployed.

- Faulty parallelism:

  The new sales program was stimulating and *a challenge.*
  (. . . *challenging.*)

  The solution lies not in prohibition or censorship but in *developing* self-control.

  (. . . *the development of* . . .)

  This type of product has three advantages:

  –It is strong.

  –It is inexpensive.

  –Long life. (*It has a long life.* **or** *It is durable.*)

- Misuse of restrictive and non-restrictive constructions (see 7.14)

16

- Incomplete constructions (faulty ellipsis):

    Aircraft *land* and take off *from* Winnipeg airport at very short intervals. (. . . *land at* . . .)

    The building is as *old, if not older than*, the Library of Parliament. (. . . *as old as* . . .)

(g) Reference notes

- Incomplete references to cited works
- Failure to give a reference for a work cited in the text
- Cross-references leading nowhere
- Erroneous numbering of references
- Too many footnotes per page

(h) Format

- Inconsistent indention of paragraphs or quotations
- Inconsistent line length
- Inconsistent presentation of headings

    –fluctuations between italics, boldface and underlining
    –headings randomly centred and placed at left margin
    –failure to number sections of document in a logical order
    –variable spacing after headings

- Inconsistent use of different type sizes, fonts and typefaces
- Confusion between the letter "l" and the numeral "1" and between the letter "O" and the numeral "0"
- Widows and orphans (see 16.07 (c))
- Non-alignment of columns, particularly in tables
- Too much white space within the body of the text
- Faulty presentation of quotations

(i) Research

If solutions are not readily available, make a note of problems to be resolved and conduct the required research after steps (a) to (h) have been completed. You can thus avoid frequent interruptions to your work.

(j) Final check

Reread the revised text for uniformity and completeness.

See 16.08 for revision checklist.

16.06 Interrevision

In order to ensure that all drafts undergo quality assurance, while at the same time circumventing the constraints and potential conflicts inherent in reviser-writer relations, many professionals exchange texts, alternately drafting their own material and revising that of others. Interrevision makes for variety in activities and provides a fresh look at each document.

16.07 Proofreader's marks

If you are not responsible for producing final copy and have to indicate your revisions on the draft, you must use proofreader's marks to help the typesetter or other specialist understand and make the changes required.

If you are proofreading typeset material, you must distinguish between typesetting errors and changes you or the author have decided to make. The mark "AA" (author's/editor's alterations) indicates such alterations.

Copy should be at least double-spaced within a 4-cm margin around the text. Proofreader's marks can be made in red ink in the right-hand space; editing notes can be made in another colour in the left-hand space.

(a) Common proofreader's marks and their use

Marginal marks are on the left; where required, in-line marks are on the right within the explanatory text.

Style of type

wf	Wrong font (size **or** style of type)
lc	Set in LOWER CASE or LOWER CASE
caps	SET IN capitals
lc & uc	Lower Case with Initial Caps
sc	Set in small capitals
rom	Set in roman (or regular) type
ital	Set in italic (*or oblique*) type
lf	Set in lightface type
bf	Set in boldface type
⌄ᵛ/	Set superscript character
ᵥ/	Set subscript character

279

Positioning

⅂   Move to right⏌

⊏   ⎡Move to left

‖   Align vertically

=   Align horizontally

⊔   ⎣Move down⌟

⊓   ⎡Move up⟍

tr   Transpose letters in a word

tr   Transpose enclosed in ring matter

][   ]Set in centre[

⌠   Break line or word

Delete or insert

℮   Delete one character

℮   Delete two or more characters characters and close up

stet   Let it stand—(all matter above dots)

osc   Set missing material, including *out see copy page 10* in the revised draft.

        If possible, make photocopy and staple to page with OSC marked.

sp   Spell out (21 gr.)

Paragraphing

¶   Begin a paragraph

no ¶   No paragraph

run on   Run on

flush ¶   ⎡No paragraph indention

Spacing

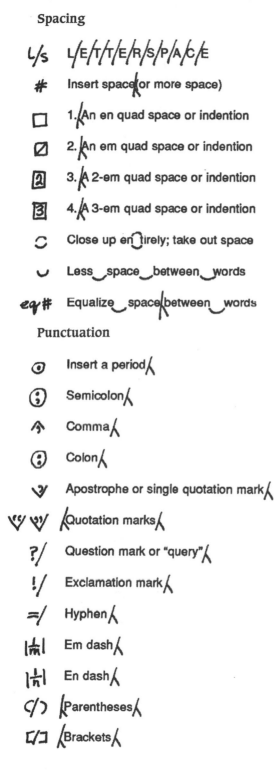

L/s	L/E/T/T/E/R/S/P/A/C/E
#	Insert space (or more space)
□	1. An en quad space or indention
⊘	2. An em quad space or indention
2	3. A 2-em quad space or indention
3	4. A 3-em quad space or indention
⌒	Close up entirely; take out space
⌣	Less space between words
eq#	Equalize space between words

Punctuation

⊙	Insert a period
⨀	Semicolon
∧	Comma
⨀	Colon
⩗	Apostrophe or single quotation mark
⩗ ⩗	Quotation marks
?/	Question mark or "query"
!/	Exclamation mark
=/	Hyphen
|m|	Em dash
|n|	En dash
(/)	Parentheses
[/]	Brackets

16

(b) Example of proofread page

]Emphasis on back injury reduction[— 1 line ⚟   ⊐⊏ / bf /

During recent years work injury rates for the Public service   uc

of Canada have shown a consistant decline. In 1994-95,   e /

this trend towards improved health and safety has been

maintained, with the overall (PS) injury frequency rate   (sp)

assessed at 4.5 injuries per 100 full-time equivalents

(F I Es), representing an 8 per cent decrease over than of   c / t /

the previous year. Similarly, the severity injury rate also   tr

decreased by 8 per cent, to 29.1 days lost per   ‿

100 FTEs.   *run on*

These injury and severity rates, compiled from work injury

reports submitted under the Government Employees   *ital*

Compensation Act, are the accepted performance indicators

for reporting and comparing work injury experience, for the   *stet*

fiscal year during which the work injuries are incurred. In   ⁋

comparing the performances of individual departments

during 1994-95 with the previous year, 12 departments had   tr

fewer injuries, 10 reported no injuries and the remainder   ⌃ ⌃

experienced little or no change in their rates. This overall

improvement in the work injury and severity rates suggest   #

that the Public Services Occupational Health and Safety

Program is having a positive impact. A variety of new health

and safety program initiatives are under way or in the   lc / that /

planing stage will, with the cooperation and participation or   n / = /

operating departments, help to maintain these positive

results. See list attached.   c / ɔ

(c) Glossary of terms

Alterations	Changes made in the copy after it has been set in type.
Bullets	Large dots indicating items in a series.
Composition	General term for typesetting material.
Folio	The page number.
Font	A complete set of type of one size and face.
Italic	The style of letters that slope forward, in contrast to upright or roman letters.
Justify	To adjust spacing in a line so that all lines are of equal length, start at the same point on the left-hand side of the page, or end at the same point on the right-hand side.
Leaders	Dots or dashes.
Letterspace	The space between letters—usually in display type, headlines, etc.
Measure	Width of line of type, always indicated in picas.
Orphan	A word or short line standing alone at the bottom of a page.
Pica	Unit of measure with 72.27 points to the inch.[1]
Point	There are 12 points to a pica.
Roman	A standard or upright typeface.
Sans-serif	A typeface without serifs.
Serif	The short cross-lines at the ends of the main strokes of many letters in some typefaces.
Small caps	An alphabet of small capital letters.
Stet	A proofreader's mark signifying that copy marked should remain as it was.
Widow	A word or short line standing alone at the top of a page.
Wrong font	The mark "WF" indicates a letter or numeral of the wrong size or face.

16.08 Revision checklist

Use a checklist to organize your work, particularly when revising or evaluating long, complex documents. It will help you to cover all pertinent facets of the writing process and to meet your deadlines. The checklist below may serve as a guide; adapt it to fit your specific requirements. When you find problems warranting additional revision or research, indicate the relevant page numbers in the appropriate column (see second column below) for easy reference later on.

16

---

1. Errors in pica measurement are made when computer manufacturers round off the pica points to 72 or 6 picas to the inch. Clarification of measurements for team members and production staff will minimize errors.

Checklist

Content		
Start date/time: _____	Target date/time: _____	Date/time completed: _____
Review item	**Page(s) requiring further attention**	**Comments**
Factual accuracy		
Logical flow of ideas		

Style and usage; Plain language; Uniform vocabulary; Elimination of stereotyping; Names; Titles; Addresses		
Start date/time: _____	Target date/time: _____	Date/time completed: _____
Review item	**Page(s) requiring further attention**	**Comments**
Sentence structure		
Neologisms/jargon		
Multiple-noun phrases		
Redundancy/repetition		
Clarity (ambiguity)		
Usage/Gallicisms		
Level of language		
Metaphors		
Euphony		
Uniform vocabulary		
Stereotyping		
Personal names		
Official titles		
Place names/addresses		

Spelling; Punctuation; Capitalization; Grammar; Etc.		
Start date/time: _____	**Target date/time:** _____	**Date/time completed:** _____
Review item	**Page(s) requiring further attention**	**Comments**
Comments		
Spelling		
Punctuation		
Capitalization		
Compounding/word division		
Abbreviations		
SI/metric symbols		
Grammar and syntax		

16

Reference Notes

Start date/time: _____	Target date/time: _____	Date/time completed: _____
	Page(s) requiring further attention	Comments

Format

Start date/time: _____	Target date/time: _____	Date/time completed: _____
	Page(s) requiring further attention	Comments
Indention of paragraphs/		
Quotations		
Line length		
Headings		
Typeface, font, size		
Widows/orphans		
Columns/tables		
Quotations		

Final Check

Start date/time: _____	Target date/time: _____	Date/time completed: _____
	Page(s) requiring further attention	Comments

Appendix

French typographical rules

Appendix

French typographical rules

A.01 Introduction

In Canada, English documents often contain French-language words, phrases, names, titles, quotations, abstracts and bibliographic references. This appendix gives the basic rules of French typography. If you follow them when writing or revising, you will ensure that French-language material is correctly presented.

For further information, see *Le guide du rédacteur de l'administration fédérale.*[1]

A.02 Acronyms, initialisms and abbreviations

(a) Use upper-case letters; do **not** use periods:

OTAN	Organisation du Traité de l'Atlantique du Nord (*NATO*)
SEE	Société pour l'expansion des exportations (*Export Development Corporation*)

(b) Do **not** retain the accent on initial letters:

CEE	Communauté économique européenne

(c) The gender of an acronym is normally that of the initial noun:

le BIT	Bureau international du travail

But acronyms from another language take the gender of the French equivalent of the generic noun:

le GATT	General Agreement (*accord*) on Tariffs and Trade
la BBC	British Broadcasting Corporation (*société*)

(d) Use a period with the abbreviations for *Monsieur* and *Messieurs*, but **not** with those for *Madame* and *Mesdames*:

M. Ladouceur   MM. Jalbert et Roussel

but

Mme Fortier   Mmes Joanisse et René

Note 1

When inserting any of these abbreviations into English text, add a period:

Mmes. Sauvé and Legros have yet to express their opinion.

---

1. The second edition of this guide is scheduled for publication in 1997.

A

Note 2

Messrs. is the English equivalent of *MM*.

Note 3

The French title *Madame* may refer to unmarried as well as married women.

A.03 Word division

Divide a word at the end of a line as follows:

- between two consonants (*car-gaison, ex-caver, dic-taphone*);
- before a consonant separating two vowels (*cargai-son, poly-culture*);
- between the two parts of a compound (*bloc-moteur, coûts-bénéfices*);
- between recognizable logical components of a word (*électro-statique; trans-action*);
- between two vowels in compounds, unless the second vowel belongs to the first part of the compound (*extra-ordinaire, réunir* **but** *oléo-duc*).

See 2.04(j) for information on the hyphenation of French words used as compound adjectives.

A.04 Capitalization

(a) Capitalize *nord, sud, est* and *ouest* when included in the name of a building, geographical feature, address, region, state, territory, continent or part of a continent:

la rive Sud	la Caroline du Nord
le Grand Nord	l'Amérique du Sud
la tour Est	le cap Nord
la rivière Nicolet	rue Sainte-Catherine
Sud-Ouest	Ouest

For further information on the treatment of French-language place names, see Chapter 15.

Do **not** capitalize these words when they represent a point of the compass, a direction or a part of a building or other entity:

le nord géographique
30 kilomètres à l'est de Gatineau
le côté ouest de l'étage

(b) Capitalize the definite article when it is part of a person's name:

Michel Le Cavalier
Jean de La Vérendrye

See also 4.03(d).

(c) Capitalize nouns designating peoples, races and inhabitants of a particular country or region, and capitalize both parts of a compound noun used for this purpose:

les Autochtones un Noir
les Canadiens une Ontarienne
les Anglo-Saxons un Néo-Zélandais

Do **not** capitalize such words when they are used adjectivally or to refer to a language:

les citoyens canadiens les femmes noires
le pétrole albertain un Canadien français
une Basque espagnole apprendre l'arabe

(d) Capitalize the following nouns when they are part of the official name of a government body, a sector of a government department, an institution, or an international organization: *Administration, Agence, Association, Banque, Bureau, Caisse, Chambre, Comité, Commission, Conseil, Cour, Direction générale, Division, Fédération, Office, Organisation, Parlement, Régie, Secrétariat, Sénat, Service, Société, Syndicat, Tribunal, Université,* etc.:

la Banque mondiale
la Commission de la fonction publique
la Cour fédérale du Canada
la Direction générale des finances
la Division de la formation
l'Office du crédit agricole
la Régie des rentes du Québec
le Tribunal du commerce extérieur

Exception

Do **not** capitalize the word *ministère* in a French text, but capitalize it in an English text:

le ministère de l'Industrie
le ministère des Affaires indiennes et du Nord

but

An agreement has been reached with the Government of Quebec—specifically with the Ministère des Ressources naturelles.

Note

If you are including the French name of an institution in an English text, do **not** use the French definite article (*le, la, l'*) unless it is part of the official name and must be retained for legal purposes:

Queen's University will co-operate with *the*
Université Laval on this federally funded project.

(e) Do **not** capitalize position titles unless they are being used to address a specific person:

A

le directeur des Ventes
le ministre des Finances

but

Monsieur le Recteur et cher ami
Monsieur le Directeur

(f) In general, capitalize the first word and any proper noun in the title of a book, periodical, newspaper, report or article:

Artisanat et création au Québec
Le nouvel ordre économique international
Rapport du vérificateur général du Canada

Exceptions

Le Devoir
Le Droit

A.05 Numerical expressions

Present the time of day and dates as follows:

23 décembre 1995 **or** 95-12-23
Heures de travail : de 9 h à 17 h 30
l'année financière 1995–1996 **not** 1995–96

Use the comma as the decimal marker in French texts and place the dollar sign after the numerals:

2,3 millions de dollars **or** 2 300 000 $

Note the space between the numerals and the dollar sign.

See also 5.09 and 5.26.

A.06 Italics

In general, use italics for the same purposes as in English writing: titles, emphasis, etc.

See 6.03 for the italicization of French words and phrases in English text.

A.07 Punctuation

Adopt the following rules for spacing with punctuation marks.

Mark	Before	After
Asterisk before word	1 space	No space
Asterisk after word	No space	1 space
Colon	1 space	1 space
Comma	No space	1 space
Decimal comma	No space	No space
Dash (em)	1 space	1 space
Ellipsis points at beginning of sentence	No space	1 space
Ellipsis points in middle or at end of sentence	No space	1 space
Exclamation mark	No space	1 space
Oblique	No space	No space
Parenthesis/bracket (opening)	1 space	No space
Parenthesis/bracket (closing)	No space	1 space
Period	No space	1 space
Question mark	No space	1 space
Quotation mark (opening)	1 space	1 space
Quotation mark	1 space	1 space
Semicolon	No space	1 space

See 8.14 for information on the presentation of French quotations and translations.

See 9.06 for the presentation of bibliographic entries.

See 9.45 for the presentation of French names in indexes.

A

Selected Bibliography

1 Dictionaries

Acronyms, Initialisms & Abbreviations Dictionary 1985–86. 3 vols. Edited by Jennifer Mossman, 19th ed. Detroit: Gale Research Co., 1994.

The BBI Combinatory Dictionary of English: A Guide to Word Combinations. Compiled by Morton Benson, Evelyn Benson and Robert Ilson. Philadelphia: John Benjamins Publishing Company, 1986.

Canadian Dictionary of the English Language, Toronto: ITP Nelson, 1997.

The Concise Oxford Dictionary of Current English. 9th ed. Oxford: Clarendon Press, 1995.

The Dictionary of Canadian Biography. 13 vols. to date. Toronto: University of Toronto Press, 1966–.

A Dictionary of Canadianisms on Historical Principles, Toronto: W. J. Gage Ltd., 1991.

Funk & Wagnalls Canadian College Dictionary. Rev. Markham, Ont.: Fitzhenry & Whiteside, 1989.

The Gage Canadian Dictionary. Revised and expanded. Toronto: Gage Educational Publishing , 1997.

The Houghton Mifflin Canadian Dictionary of the English Language. Edited by William Morris. Markham, Ont.: Houghton Mifflin Canada Ltd., 1982.

The New Shorter Oxford English Dictionary. 2 vols. 4th ed. Oxford: Clarendon Press, 1993.

The Penguin Canadian Dictionary. Edited by Thomas M. Paikeday. Markham, Ont.: Penguin Books Canada Ltd., 1990.

The Random House Dictionary of the English Language. New York: Random House, 1987.

Webster's Ninth New Collegiate Dictionary. Markham, Ont.: Thomas Allen & Son Limited, 1991.

Webster's Third New International Dictionary of the English Language, Unabridged. Springfield, Mass.: G. & C. Merriam Co., 1993.

The Winston Dictionary of Canadian English. Toronto: Holt, Rinehart and Winston of Canada Ltd., 1975.

2 National and International Standards

Anglo-American Cataloguing Rules. 2nd ed. Edited by Michael Gorman and Paul W. Winckler. Ottawa: Canadian Library Association. 1988.

Canada. Canada Post Corporation. *The Canadian Addressing Standard Handbook,* Ottawa, 1995.

Canada. Treasury Board. Office of the Comptroller General of Canada. Circular No. 1979-7, "Writing Dollar Amounts on Payment Instruments and Other Documents." Ottawa, 1979.

———. Treasury Board. Office of the Comptroller General. Circular No. 1984-64, "Standard for Writing Dollar Amounts on Payment Instruments and Certain Other Documents." Ottawa, 1984.

———. Treasury Board. *Federal Identity Program Manual,* Ottawa, 1987–1990.

———. Treasury Board. *Treasury Board Publications on CD-ROM* [CD-ROM]. Ottawa, 1995.

Canadian Standards Association. *ABBR: Abbreviations for Scientific and Engineering Terms.* Rexdale (Toronto), Ont., 1983.

Canadian Standards Association. *Canadian Metric Practice Guide.* Rexdale (Toronto), Ont., 1989. (CAN3Z234.1-89)

International Organization for Standardization. International Standard ISO 999. *Documentation— Index of a Publication.* 1st ed. Geneva, 1975.

———. International Standard ISO 2384. *Documentation—Presentation of Translations.* 1st ed. Geneva, 1977.

———. International Standard ISO 4. *Documentation—Rules for the Abbreviation of Title Words and Titles of Publications.* 2nd ed. Geneva, 1984.

———. International Standard ISO 5963. *Documentation—Methods for Examining Documents, Determining Their Subjects, and Selecting Indexing Terms.* 1st ed. Geneva, 1985.

———. International Standard ISO 690. *Documentation—Bibliographic References—Content, Form and Structure.* 2nd ed. Geneva, 1987.

———. International Standard ISO 8601. *Data Elements and Interchange Formats—Information Interchange—Representation of Dates and Times.* 1st ed. Geneva, 1988.

———. International Standard ISO 31/0. *General Principles Concerning Quantities, Units and Symbols.* 3rd ed. Geneva, 1992.

———. International Standard ISO 832. *Information and Documentation—Bibliographic Description and Reference—Rules for the Abbreviation of Bibliographic Terms.* 2nd ed. Geneva, 1994.

National Information Standards Organization. American National Standard ANSI/NISO Z39.22-1989. *Proof Corrections.* New Brunswick, N.J.: Transaction Publishers, 1991.

3 General Reference Works

Buttress, F. A. *World Guide to Abbreviations of Organizations.* 10th ed. London: Blackie Academic & Professional, 1993.

———. Department of Canadian Heritage. *Precedence of Canadian Dignitaries and Officials.* Ottawa, 1993.

———. Department of National Defence, *Manual of Abbreviations,* Ottawa, 1985. (A-AD-12-1-FOl/JX000)

Canada Year Book 1994. A Review of Economic, Social and Political Developments in Canada. Ottawa: Statistics Canada, 1994.

Canadian Almanac and Directory 1995. Edited by Ann Marie Aldighieri. Toronto: Copp Clark, 1995.

The Canadian Encyclopedia. 4 vols. Edited by James H. Marsh. 2nd ed. Edmonton: Hurtig Publishers, 1988.

Canadian Who's Who. Edited by Kieran Simpson. Toronto: University of Toronto Press, 1995.

1995 Canadian Trade Index. 2 vols. Toronto: Canadian Manufacturers' Association, 1995.

Colombo, John Robert. *Colombo's Canadian References.* Toronto: Oxford University Press, 1976.

1995 Corpus Almanac & Canadian Sourcebook. 1 vol. 30th annual ed. Edited by Barbara Law. Don Mills, Ont.: Southam Inc., 1995.

Dictionary of Canadian Quotations. Edited by John Robert Colombo. Toronto: Stoddart, 1991.

Directory of Associations in Canada / Répertoire des associations du Canada. Edited by Brian Land. 16th ed. Toronto: Micromedia Ltd., 1995.

Encyclopedia Canadiana. 10 vols. Toronto: Grolier of Canada Ltd., 1977.

Lowe, D. Armstrong. *A Guide to International Recommendations on Names and Symbols for Quantities and on Units of Measurement.* Geneva: World Health Organization, 1975.

Measures, Howard. *Styles of Address. A Manual of Usage in Writing and in Speech.* 3rd ed. Toronto: Macmillan, 1974.

Unesco. *World List of Social Science Periodicals.* Paris: Unesco, 1991.

4 Manuals of Style and Usage

American Institute of Physics, *Editorial Handbook,* 2nd ed. New York, 1989.

American Institute of Physics, *AIP Style Manual,* 4th rev. ed. New York, 1990.

Angell, David, and Brent Heslop. *The Elements of E-Mail Style: Communicate Effectively via Electronic Mail.* Don Mills, Ont.: Addison-Wesley Publishing Company, 1994.

Baker, Sheridan. *The Practical Stylist.* 3rd ed. New York: Harper Collins, 1995.

Blackburn, Bob. *Words Fail Us: Good English and Other Lost Causes.* Toronto: McClelland & Stewart, 1993.

Buckley, Peter. *CP Stylebook: A Guide for Writers and Editors.* Rev. ed. Toronto: Canadian Press, 1992.

Canada. Department of Multiculturalism and Citizenship. *Plain Language Clear and Simple.* Ottawa: Canada Communication Group, 1991.

———. Department of National Defence. *DND Administrative and Staff Procedures Manual: Administrative Procedure for NDHQ.* Ottawa, 1993.

———. Department of the Secretary of State. *Le guide du rédacteur de l'administration fédérale.* Ottawa, 1983.

Canadian Press. *Caps and Spelling.* Rev. Toronto, 1992.

The Chicago Manual of Style. 14th ed. rev. and expanded. Chicago: University of Chicago Press, 1993.

Council of Biology Editors. *Scientific Style and Format: The CBE Manual for Authors, Editors, and Publishers.* 6th ed. Cambridge, U.K.: Cambridge University Press, 1994.

Cutts, Martin. *The Plain English Guide: How to Write Clearly and Communicate Better.* Oxford: Oxford University Press, 1995.

De Vries, Mary Ann. *Prentice Hall Style Manual.* Englewood Hills, N.J.: Prentice Hall, 1993.

Flick, Jane, and Celia Millward. *Handbook for Writers.* 2nd Canadian ed. Toronto: Harcourt Brace Jovanovich, 1993.

Freelance Editors' Association of Canada. *Editing Canadian English.* Edited by L. Burton et al. Toronto: Douglas and McIntyre, 1987.

Fowler, H. W. *A Dictionary of Modern English Usage.* 2nd ed. Revised by Sir Ernest Gowers. Oxford: Oxford University Press, 1965; rpt. 1991.

Fowler, H. W., and F. G. Fowler. *The King's English.* 3rd ed. London: Oxford University Press, 1931; rpt. 1974.

The Gazette Style. Montréal: The Gazette, 1995.

Giraldi, Joseph. *MLA Handbook for Writers of Research Papers.* 4th ed. New York: Modern Language Association, 1995.

Gowers, Sir Ernest. *The Complete Plain Words*. Boston: David R. Godine Publisher, 1988.

Greenbaum, Sidney. *The Oxford English Grammar.* Toronto: Oxford University Press, 1996.

Hacker, Diana. *A Canadian Writer's Reference.* 2nd ed. Toronto: Nelson Canada, 1996.

Hodges, John C., Mary E. Whitten, Judy Brown, and Jane Flick. *Harbrace College Handbook for Canadian Writers.* 3rd ed. Toronto: Harcourt Brace Jovanovich, 1990.

Mager, N. H., and S. K. Mager. *Encyclopedic Dictionary of English Usage.* 2nd ed. revised by John Domini. Englewood Cliffs, N.J.: Prentice Hall, 1993.

McFarlane, J. A., and W. Clements. *The Globe and Mail Style Book: A Guide to Language and Usage.* Toronto, 1994.

Messenger, William E., and Jan de Bruyn. *The Canadian Writer's Handbook.* 2nd ed. Scarborough, Ont.: Prentice Hall, 1986.

Moore, M. D. *A Writer's Handbook of Current English.* 3rd ed. Toronto: Gage Publishing Ltd., 1988.

Mullins, Carolyn J. *A Guide to Writing and Publishing in the Social and Behavioral Sciences.* New York: John Wiley and Sons, 1977; rpt. 1983.

Pearsall, Thomas E., and Douglas H. Cunningham. *How to Write for the World of Work.* 5th ed. Toronto: Harcourt Brace College Publishers, 1994.

Sabin, William A., and Sheila O'Neill. *Reference Manual for Secretaries and Typists.* 3rd Canadian ed. Toronto: McGraw-Hill Ryerson, 1986.

Shaw, Harry. *Handbook of English.* Revised by Dave Carley. 4th Canadian ed. Toronto: McGraw-Hill Ryerson, 1985.

United States Government Printing Office. *Style Manual.* Rev. ed. Washington, D.C., 1984.

Wilcock, Anne E., and Brian P. Wilcock. *"Some Assembly Required": A CSA Guide to Writing Instruction Manuals.* Rexdale, Ont.: Canadian Standards Association, 1995.

Wood, Frederick T. *Current English Usage: A Concise Dictionary.* Rev. ed. London: Macmillan and Co., 1981.

5 Other works on language and related subjects

Kirby, Patricia. "English Word Division." *Termiglobe*, VII, 4 (Nov. 1984): 24–25.

Lauriston, Andy. "Hyphenation" (Part One). *Termiglobe*, VI, 4 (Nov. 1983): 22–23.

———. "Hyphenation" (Part Two). *Termiglobe*, VI, 5 (Jan 1984): 29–30.

6 Works relating specifically to reference matter

American National Standards Institute. ANSI Standard Z39.4-1984. *Basic Criteria for Indexes.* New York, 1984.

Books in Print. New Providence, N.J.: R. R. Bowker, 1992–1993.

Bonura, Larry. *The Art of Indexing.* New York, John Wiley and Sons, 1994.

Borko, Harold, and Charles L. Bernier. *Indexing Concepts and Methods.* New York: Academic Press, 1978.

British Union—Catalogue of Periodicals Incorporating World List of Scientific Periodicals / New Periodical Titles 1980. Toronto: Butterworths, 1981.

Canadian Books in Print: Author and Title Index. Edited by Mariam Butler. Toronto: University of Toronto Press, 1993.

The Canadian Guide to Uniform Legal Citation. 3rd ed. Scarborough, Ont.: Carswell, 1992.

Cleveland, Donald B., and Ana D. Cleveland. *Introduction to Indexing and Abstracting.* 2nd ed. Englewood, Colo.: Libraries Unlimited, 1990.

Knight, G. Norman. *Indexing, The Art of,* London: Allen Unwin, 1979.

MacEllven, Douglass T. *Legal Research Handbook.* 3rd ed. Toronto and Vancouver: Butterworths, 1993.

Mulvany, Nancy C. *Indexing Books.* Chicago: University of Chicago Press, 1994.

7 Works relating to the elimination of stereotyping

Canada. Correctional Service. *On Equal Terms: How to Eliminate Sexism in Communications.* Ottawa, 1984.

———. Department of Employment and Immigration. *Manual of Sex-Free Occupational Titles.* Ottawa, 1977.

———. Department of Employment and Immigration. *National Occupation Classification.* Ottawa, 1983.

———. Department of Public Works and Government Services. Terminology and Linguistic Services. Recommendation Notice No. 2, "Aboriginal Peoples in Canada." Ottawa, 1994.

———. Department of the Secretary of State. Multiculturalism. *A Matter of Balance.* Ottawa, 1988.

———. Department of the Secretary of State. Status of Disabled Persons Secretariat. *A Way With Words: Guidelines and Appropriate Terminology for the Portrayal of Persons With Disabilities.* Ottawa, 1991.

———. Public Service Commission. *Guidelines on the Elimination of Sexual Stereotyping, and Representative Depiction of Ethnic and Visible Minorities, Aboriginal Peoples and People With Disabilities.* Ottawa, 1992.

———. Treasury Board. *Administrative Policy Manual,* Chapter 484, "Elimination of Sexual Stereotyping." Ottawa, 1982.

———. Treasury Board. Circular No. 1984-4, "Guidelines for the Representative Depiction of Visible and Ethnic Minorities and Aboriginal Peoples in Government Communications." Ottawa, 1984.

———. Treasury Board. *Information and Administrative Management Manual.* Ottawa, 1994.

Dumond, Val. *The Elements of Nonsexist Usage: A Guide to Inclusive Spoken and Written English.* New York: Prentice Hall, 1990.

King, Ruth. *Talking Gender: A Guide to Nonsexist Communication.* Mississauga, Ont.: Copp Clark Pitman, 1991.

Maggio, Rosalie. *Non-Sexist Word Finder: A Dictionary of Gender-Free Usage.* Boston: Beacon Press, 1991.

———. *The Dictionary of Bias-Free Usage: A Guide to Nondiscriminatory Language.* Phoenix: Oryx Press, 1991.

Ontario. Ministry of Citizenship. Office for Disability Issues. *Word Choices: A Lexicon of Preferred Terms for Disability Issues.* Toronto, 1992.

———. Ontario Women's Directorate. *Words That Count Women Out/In.* 2nd ed. Toronto, 1993.

8 Works relating to geographical names

Canada. Department of Canadian Heritage. Parks Canada. *Toponymy and Terminology Used by Parks Canada.* Ottawa, 1995.

———. Department of Energy, Mines and Resources. Canadian Permanent Committee on Geographical Names. *Gazetteer of Canada.* 12 vols. Ottawa, 1983–94.

———. Department of Energy, Mines and Resources. Canadian Permanent Committee on Geographical Names. *Gazetteer of Canada. Ontario.* 4th ed. Ottawa, 1988.

———. Department of Energy, Mines and Resources. Canadian Permanent Committee on Geographical Names. *Principles and Procedures for Geographical Naming.* Ottawa, 1990.

———. Department of Energy Mines and Resources. Canadian Permanent Committee on Geographical Names. *Gazetteer of Canada. New Brunswick.* 3rd ed. Ottawa, 1993.

———. Department of Energy, Mines and Resources. Canadian Permanent Committee on Geographical Names. *Gazetteer of Canada. Nova Scotia.* 3rd ed. Ottawa, 1993.

———. Department of Energy, Mines and Resources. Canadian Permanent Committee on Geographical Names. *Gazetteer of Canada. Manitoba.* 4th ed. Ottawa, 1994.

———. Department of Fisheries and Oceans. Canadian Permanent Committee on Geographical Names. *Gazetteer of Undersea Feature Names.* Ottawa, 1987.

———. Department of the Secretary of State. Canadian Permanent Committee on Geographical Names. *Glossary of Generic Terms in Canada's Geographical Names: TB 176 / Glossaire des génériques en usage dans les noms géographiques du Canada : BT 176.* Ottawa: Canadian Government Publishing Centre, 1987.

Dugas, Jean-Yves. "Terminologie et toponymie : un mariage de raison." *L'Actualité terminologique / Terminology Update,* 15, 3 (March 1982): 1–6.

Fillion, Laurent. "Pour une politique fédérale du traitement linguistique des noms géographiques." *L'Actualité terminologique / Terminology Update,* 15, 7 (Aug.–Sept. 1982): 1–6.

Gélinas-Surprenant, Hélène. "Uniformisation de l'écriture des noms géographiques au Canada." *L'Actualité terminologique / Terminology Update,* 23, 3 (1990): 18–22.

Québec. Commission de Toponymie. *Répertoire toponymique du Québec.* 3e éd. Québec: Éditeur officiel, 1987.

Index

Note

References beginning with the letter A refer to sections of the Appendix.

Words with their correct prepositions are listed alphabetically in 12.02; words often misused are listed alphabetically in 12.03.

The definitive writing and editing tool!

TERMIUM®, *the Government of Canada linguistic data bank*
- **THE** English-French, French-English electronic dictionary!
- The most up-to-date terminology in all subject fields!
- Three million terms and names at your fingertips!
- Contextual information: definitions, contexts, examples of usage, observations.
- A large number of official titles of national and international organizations, acts and programs, abbreviations, geographical names, etc.
- The equivalent of 400 diskettes or 200,000 pages of text!

TERMIUM® enables you to
- communicate precisely and effectively
- save on research time
- find expressions easily by key words

TERMIUM® is a user-friendly interface running under Windows • DOS • Macintosh in standalone and network versions.
- Cut and paste terms from *TERMIUM®* into your text, as easy as 1-2-3.

Check out our other publications!
Over 80 terminology vocabularies and glossaries in a wide variety of subject areas: administration – agriculture – law – economy – environment – informatics – health – sciences – transport – public works – finance. These publications contain English and French terminology. A few also include Spanish.

Free on Internet!
A glossary of 350 Internet terms available on the *TERMIUM®* site — http://www.pwgsc.gc.ca/termium

Get your free TERMIUM® demonstration diskette!
Telephone: (819) 997-9727   1-800-TERMIUM (Canada and U.S.)

Fax: (819) 997-1993   E-mail: termium@piper.pwgsc.gc.ca